Gold: The Monetary Polaris

by Nathan Lewis

Published by Canyon Maple Publishing
PO Box 98
New Berlin, NY 13411
nathan@newworldeconomics.com
newworldeconomics.com

Fourth edition October 2019

If you think in terms of a year, plant a seed; if in terms of ten years, plant trees; if in terms of 100 years, teach the people.

–Confucius

[I]n all cases human society chooses for that basis-article we call "money" that which fluctuates least in price, is the most generally used or desired, is in the greatest, most general, and most constant demand, and has value in itself. "Money" is only a word meaning the article used as the basis-article for exchanging all other articles. An article is not first made valuable by law and then elected to be "money." The article first proves itself valuable and best suited for the purpose, and so becomes of itself and in itself the basis-article – money. It elects itself. ...

[The precious] metals proved their superiority. These do not decay, do not change in value so rapidly ... [T]hese metals are less liable to fluctuate in value than any article previously used as "money." This is of vital importance, for the one essential quality that is needed in the article which we use as a basis for exchanging all other articles is fixity of value. The race has instinctively always sought for the one article in the world which most resembles the North Star among the other stars in the heavens, and used it as "money "– the article that changes least in value, as the North Star is the star which changes its position least in the heavens; and what the North Star is among stars the article people elect as "money" is among articles. All other articles revolve around it, as all other stars revolve around the North Star.

We ... have now dropped all perishable articles and elected metals as our "money"; or, rather, metals have proved themselves better than anything else for the standard of value, "money."

–Andrew Carnegie, "The A B C of Money," *The North American Review*, 1891

Introduction

by Steve Forbes

No subject intimidates people, including smart people, more than monetary policy. Sadly, and dangerously, we know less about this critical subject than we did a century ago. The result is subpar economic performances around the world that will have increasingly ugly political side effects.

Getting money right is the most important thing in economics, and if anyone can dispel the anxiety and mystery surrounding this crucial subject it's Nathan Lewis. He knows economics and money inside out. More importantly, he writes about the subject lucidly and insightfully in a soothing and reassuring way. Readers will come away from reading this, scratching their heads and saying, "My goodness, this really isn't that complicated. I understand it now."

Most investors, for example, know the basic way exchange-traded funds work. Using that knowledge as a springboard, Lewis felicitously explains how a gold standard works. Notice that article "a." One of the myths Lewis wonderfully demolishes is that there is a one-and-only gold standard. Actually, there are countless varieties, but the real ones all share a common characteristic: They use gold as a measuring rod to keep the value of money stable. Why? Because the yellow metal keeps its intrinsic value better than anything else on the planet.

And that leads us to another myth Lewis debunks: that there must be 100% gold-backing for paper money. Theoretically (although Lewis doesn't advocate this), you don't need an ounce of the yellow metal to operate a gold standard; all you need is to refer to the price in the open market.

While we're on the subject of myths, Lewis performs here – just as he did in his previous masterpiece, *Gold: The Once and Future Money* – a vital historic service. With real facts and figures on industrial output and crop harvests he points out just what a mighty boom – and one without historic precedent – the U.S. underwent between 1879 (when we returned to the gold standard after suspending it during the Civil War) and the First World War. It's amazing that ignorant historians and ideologically blinded economists still try to trash the economic performance of countries when they were on gold standards. Most economists today sound like intellectual luddites when discussing gold.

Another service Lewis performs is setting forth the idea that you don't need big economic summits of central bankers, global leaders and economic experts to create a gold-based monetary system. What is known as the classic gold standard, and which was in place during the decades immediately prior to World War I, came about in an evolutionary way. And the specifics of how each country operated it were different. Lewis suggests ways that a gold standard could be reintroduced and includes a fascinating discussion on bringing in a parallel currency, that is, for a while a country would have a gold-based money operating alongside its current fiat money.

Lewis rightly gives the International Monetary Fund a bashing. Few institutions in history have been as guilty of economic malpractice as this one.

As this book gains attention, as it surely will, a lot of "experts" will try to trip up Lewis with technicalities. Thankfully, he can play that game, too. He won't be caught looking like a deer in the headlights if someone brings up stuff like "bullion points."

There are plenty of historic interpretations readers can take issue with, as well as with some of Lewis' musings on how 21st century capitalism will evolve. But these are sideshows to the main event. Gold is indeed the monetary Polaris, and this book is the best one yet in explaining why.

Steve Forbes
June, 2013

Preface

After the publication of *Gold: The Once and Future Money*, several people told me that their favorite part of the book was the section describing the technical details of how to operate a gold standard system. I thought this would be too arcane for most readers, and that they would skim it to get to the historical drama. Only a few serious economic students, I thought, would delve into these detailed discussions of operational mechanisms. Those serious economic students will be the ones to actually create, manage and operate the gold standard systems of the future, so that section was for them.

Instead, a broad range of readers seemed to enjoy being taken into the inner workings of how monetary systems operate. They sensed that it is, actually, not as complicated as the economic high priesthood implies. Also, they sensed that the economic high priesthood doesn't actually know what it is talking about; and now they could understand that this is indeed correct. I often say that a typical lay reader, with no background in economics, can, in the space of a year, learn how to do this better than the great majority of economic professionals, including those who have unfortunately been given the responsibility of managing our monetary affairs. This is no exaggeration or rhetorical flourish. It is the actual truth.

This book consists mostly of an expanded discussion of monetary operating mechanisms, covering all the likely variations for any future gold standard systems. This serves a number of purposes. First, obviously you cannot have a gold standard system in the future if nobody knows how to do it. Second, the political process towards a new world monetary system is presently blocked by the strong sense that those who would charged with the particularities of establishing and operating such a system (including many of today's gold standard advocates) don't actually know what they are doing. This impression is correct, and the likely result would be disaster rather than success. Lastly, most economic history by academics today is grotesquely malformed due to the fact that these academics have no real idea how the systems in place at the time worked. The result is much like what one would get if you asked a primitive tribesman of New Guinea to describe the workings of an airplane.

When people – mostly those without formal training in economics – grasp how easy and robust this system actually is, and the results it has produced and can produce again, they see our present arrangement as the monstrosity that it is. This change of outlook can happen quite quickly. They never look back again.

Nathan Lewis
July, 2013

TABLE OF CONTENTS

Chapter 1:
The Classicals and the Mercantilists

*Some men hold that any king or prince may, of his own authority,
by right or prerogative, freely alter the money current in his
realm, regulate it as he will, and take whatever gain or profit may
result: but other men are of the contrary opinion. ... Perhaps my
words will rouse them finally to settle the truth of this matter, so
that the experts may all be of one mind, and come to a conclusion
which shall be profitable both to princes and subjects, and indeed
to the state as a whole.*
    –Nicholas Oresme, introduction to *De Moneta*,
      circa 1375 A.D.

For the first 182 years of United States history, from 1789 to 1971, the
U.S. followed the principle of stable money – in practice, a currency
whose value was linked to gold bullion at a specified and unchanging
ratio. Since 1971, the U.S. has had a policy of a floating currency,
whose value varies minute-by-minute, in an unpredictable and
chaotic fashion. We now have ample experience with both options.

Which is better?

Better for what?

Some people want a currency that is stable in value, neutral,
predictable, unchanging, free of human influence, a universal constant
of commerce – the monetary equivalent of other constants of measure
such as the kilogram or meter. They search for a way to achieve this

goal, and, throughout history, have found that the best way to do so is to adopt a gold standard system. For them, a currency that changes value constantly is as abhorrent as a "kilogram" or "meter" whose weight or length changes chaotically from day to day.

Others want a currency that can be managed or manipulated to serve a variety of policy goals, such as reducing unemployment, spurring economic activity, managing interest rates, adjusting the terms of trade (relative exchange rates), relieving debtors' burdens, financing the government, or many other such objectives. For them, a currency that is stable, neutral, unchanging and free of human influence is wholly contrary to their aspirations. They want a floating currency, which can be adjusted as needed to help achieve their various policy ambitions. If a gold standard system is being used at the time, they complain about the "golden fetters" that are keeping them from – they promise – fixing the pressing economic problems of the day with some form of currency distortion.

The first strategy can be called the Classical paradigm. It has been around in some form wherever money is used, from antiquity to the present. The Classical paradigm was espoused by those great economists of the 18th and 19th centuries that we now call the Classical economists.

The second strategy can be called the Mercantilist paradigm. It has also been around in some form wherever money is used. The Mercantilist paradigm was promoted by those economists of the 17th and early 18th centuries known as the Mercantilist economists.

Let's see how economic thinkers throughout history have described the Classical monetary paradigm:

A currency, to be perfect, should be absolutely invariable in value.
    –David Ricardo, "Proposals for an Economical and Sound Currency," 1816

There must, then, be a unit, and that fixed by agreement (for which reason it is called money); for it is this that makes all things commensurate, since all things are measured by money.
    –Aristotle, Nichomachean Ethics, circa 350 B.C.

The most important thing about money is to maintain its stability ... You have to choose between trusting the natural stability of gold and the honesty and intelligence of members of government.

With due respect for these gentlemen, I advise you, as long as the capitalist system lasts, to vote for gold.
—George Bernard Shaw, The Intelligent Woman's Guide to Socialism and Capitalism, 1928

In order that the value of the currency may be secure from being altered by design, and may be as little as possible liable to fluctuation from accident, the articles least liable of all known commodities to vary in their value, the precious metals, have been made in all civilized countries the standard of value for the circulating medium; and no paper currency ought to exist of which the value cannot be made to conform to theirs.
—John Stuart Mill, Principles of Political Economy, 1848.

Among the Mercantilists we find one William Potter who, in 1650, presented *The Key of Wealth: or, a new Way, for Improving of Trade*[A]: *Lawful, Easy, Safe and Effectual*. This "new Way" was simply an increase in the circulating currency. Among the twenty-four claimed advantages of this scheme were to:

Enrich the people of the land
Settle a secure and known credit
Extend such credit to any degree needful
Quicken the revolution of money and credit
Diminish the interest for moneys
Fill the land with commodity
Abate the price of commodity
Relieve and employ the poor
Augment custom and excise [tax revenue]

Another seventeenth-century Mercantilist, Gerard de Malynes, found one factor behind all of England's economic difficulties:

For a Conclusion therefore let us note, That all the said causes of the decay of Trade in England, are almost all of them comprised in one, which is the want of money; ... which maketh us to find out so easie a Remedie, whereby the Kingdome shall enjoy all the

---

[A] "Trade" here means economic activity in general.

three essentiall parts of Traffique under good and Politike Government.
—Gerard de Malynes, *The Maintenance of Free Trade*, 1622.

In 1705, John Law produced *Money and Trade Considered; with a Proposal for Supplying the Nation with Money*, which stated:

But as this addition to the money, will employ the people are now idle, and these now employed to more advantage: so the product will be increased, and manufacture advanced.

Law also wanted to lower the rate of interest, by supplying more currency:

Some think if Interest were lowered by Law, Trade would increase, Merchants being able to Employ more Money and Trade Cheaper. Such a Law would have many Inconveniences, and it is much to be doubted, whether it would have any good Effect; Indeed, if lowness of Interest were the Consequence of a greater Quantity of Money, the Stock applied to Trade would be greater, and Merchants would Trade Cheaper, from the easiness of borrowing and the lower Interest of Money, without any Inconveniences attending it.

James Denham Steuart, known as the "last of the Mercantilists," culminated two centuries of Mercantilist thought with poise and sophistication.

If money can be made of paper, ... a statesman has it in his power to increase or diminish the extent of credit and paper money in circulation, by various expedients, which greatly influence the rate of interest. ...

From these principles, and others which naturally flow from them, may a statesman steer a very certain course, towards bringing the rate of interest as low as the prosperity of trade requires.
—James Denham Steuart, *An Inquiry Into the Principles of Political Economy*, 1767.

Centuries passed, but the arguments of the Mercantilists did not change much. Ludwig von Mises summed up the Mercantilism of the mid-twentieth century, then generally known as "Keynesianism":

> *The most fanatical attacks against gold are made by those intent upon credit expansion. With them credit expansion is the panacea for all economic ills. It could lower or even entirely abolish interest rates, raise wages and prices for the benefit of all except the parasitic capitalists and the exploiting employers, free the state from the necessity of balancing its budget – in short, make all decent people prosperous and happy. Only the gold standard, that devilish contrivance of the wicked and stupid "orthodox" economists, prevents mankind from attaining everlasting prosperity.*
> –Ludwig von Mises, *Human Action*, 1949.

The Keynesian variety of modern Mercantilism tended to be somewhat left-leaning and socialist in its political orientation. The mid-twentieth century also saw another variety of Mercantilism, this one rather more right-leaning and libertarian in its overall flavor. This was known as Monetarism, and its leader was Milton Friedman.

Monetarism focused on quantity-based measures of money and credit, while the Keynesians focused on interest rates. These were simply two approaches to the same goal: managing the economy via currency distortion. Friedman was a rabid critic of the gold standard, and a tireless advocate of floating currencies. Federal Reserve Chairman Ben Bernanke, an arch-Mercantilist, cited Friedman as a central influence.

The Classical and Mercantilist paradigms are contradictory and mutually exclusive (Table 1.1).

A gold standard system has a specific purpose: to achieve, as closely as is possible in an imperfect world, the Classical ideal of a currency that is stable in value, neutral, free of government manipulation, precise in its definition, and which can serve as a universal standard of value, in much the manner in which kilograms or meters serve as standards of weights and measures. One might argue that a gold standard system does not quite achieve this perfect ideal. However, after many centuries of trying, nobody has found a better way to do so. In practice, the results enjoyed by those countries that used gold standard systems for extended periods were excellent, and the imperfections of the gold standard systems in use were small enough that they could be ignored. A gold standard system is not perfect – nothing in human affairs has ever been – but it has been the most perfect way of achieving the goal of stable monetary value.

Classical Paradigm	Mercantilist Paradigm
"Rule of Law"	"Rule of Man"
Stable currency value is the goal	"Full employment" via monetary distortion is the goal
Avoid government manipulation of the currency	Constant government "management" of the currency.
Gold standard achieves stable money goal	Gold standard prevents economic management via monetary distortion
Unstable money causes problems	Money manipulation solves problems
Leave credit up to the free market	Manipulate credit for macro effect
Interest rates left to free market	Manage interest rates for macro effect
Fixed exchange rates are good	Floating currencies allow "adjustment"
"You can't devalue yourself to prosperity"	"In the long run, we are all dead."

Table 1.1: The Classical and Mercantilist Paradigms

The United States adhered to the Classical principle of a stable currency, and in practice a gold standard system, for nearly two centuries until 1971. During that time, it became the most successful, most economically vibrant, wealthiest, most innovative, best-governed, most militarily powerful country in the world. The U.S. dollar became the premier international currency, and New York eclipsed London as the world's premier center of finance. The last two decades of the gold standard era – the 1950s and 1960s – were among the most prosperous of U.S. history. The U.S. middle class attained a level of affluence and comfort that had never before been seen, and perhaps has not been seen since 1971.

The gold standard period didn't end because the gold standard didn't work. It wasn't broken and it didn't have to be replaced. The broad results were splendid, and the gold standard era ended on a high note. Rather, the gold standard era ended because governments had migrated towards the Mercantilist paradigm, and consequently, found the gold standard system to be directly contrary to their ambitions. This began in the late 19th century, a reflection of a broader trend of increasing government involvement and statism that expressed itself in Karl Marx's *Communist Manifesto* of 1848, the spread of government welfare policies in the late 19th century, and then in Russia's communist revolution in 1917. Government intervention and management of monetary affairs was part of a series of experiments in government influence in all areas of life. During the difficulties of the 1930s, Mercantilist arguments became more fashionable among the intelligentsia, notably their chief proponent John Maynard Keynes. However, the world still adhered, for the most part, to the Classical principles of stable money that had served so well in the pre-1914 era.

Virtually all governments experimented with devaluation and floating currencies during the 1930s. Although some positive effects were attained, governments concluded that the experience was generally problematic. In the Bretton Woods agreement of 1944, forty-four of the world's major governments agreed to re-establish a world gold standard system.

Despite this renewed commitment to a worldwide gold standard system in 1944, the years that followed saw a gradual deterioration in understanding of the Classical economic principles that formed its foundation, and the specific operating mechanisms necessary for its practical maintenance. Mercantilist theories, regarding economic management via currency distortion, had become dominant in academia. The gold standard system began to be regarded as a useless relic of an unsophisticated age, barely more than a superstition. Its purpose was forgotten. The Mercantilists chafed at the "golden fetters" that prevented them from fully realizing their dreams of all-encompassing economic management – the apparent end of the business cycle and unemployment.

The rupture took place in 1971, in response to the relatively minor recession of 1970. President Richard Nixon's advisors suggested that the unemployment problem could be resolved with a dose of monetary expansion – William Potter's "New Way" – in time for the presidential election of 1972. Nixon acquiesced, famously declaring: "I am now a Keynesian in economics."[1] (In fact, Nixon's exact strategy was of the Monetarist variety of modern Mercantilism, which aimed for a certain nominal GDP level by way of a certain calculated increase in money supply.)

Since then, the United States has had a Mercantilist monetary system, in which a chaotic floating fiat currency enables ad-hoc, day-to-day monetary management in response to economic conditions and political expediency. Despite the hopes of the Mercantilists, recessions still occur regularly, with intensity at least comparable to the downturns of the gold standard era of the 1950s and 1960s. The first effect of the introduction of Mercantilist monetary policy was a worldwide economic disaster. Currencies around the world plummeted in value, with the U.S. dollar falling eventually to about a tenth of the value it had during the Bretton Woods period. Inflation raged worldwide. This was tamed temporarily during the 1980s and 1990s, but especially since 2001, the notion of trying to solve nonmonetary economic problems with Mercantilist easy-money solutions remains ascendant.

In British history, the Mercantilist thinkers were eventually replaced by the Classical thinkers such as David Hume, Adam Smith and David Ricardo. The reason for this is simple: The Classical paradigm produces better results. The success of the Classical ideas was reflected in Britain's own success. Britain, an economic backwater in the 17th century compared to flourishing Holland, during the 18th century became the birthplace of the Industrial Revolution, and in the 19th century, the most successful, most economically dynamic, wealthiest, most innovative, most militarily powerful country in the world, presiding over a global empire of unprecedented extent, until it was eventually challenged and eclipsed by the United States.

* * *

Mercantilist monetary approaches tend to amount to forms of currency devaluation, even if that is not their overt goal. Usually, they are focused on some other factor, such as interest rates, unemployment, economic growth statistics, and so forth. The words "currency devaluation" remain distasteful in public discourse. Mercantilists usually promote "more money" to deal with economic difficulties; perhaps not a single Mercantilist, up through to the present day, has ever advocated "less money." The result of this oversupply of currency tends to be a decline in its value over time.

By 2012, the value of the U.S. dollar had fallen to less than a thirtieth of its value in 1970, compared to gold. During this time, "devaluation," "depreciation" or "inflation" was rarely an overt policy goal. Usually, the opposite was the case. Nevertheless, that's what happened.

A currency can only do three things: go up in value, go down in value, or remain the same value. If the goal is for the currency to remain the same in value, then a Mercantilist monetary approach is hardly necessary – that is the goal of the Classical paradigm, and, in more practical terms, a gold standard system. There is no particular reason to wish for a rise in currency value, except perhaps to remedy some prior decline. This, too, was normally the purvey of the Classical economists, as they sometimes wished to repair wartime devaluations. Thus, the option of declining currency value is the Mercantilists' specialty.

"You can't devalue yourself to prosperity" is one of the Classical economists' most enduring aphorisms. The briefest investigation shows that the wealth of a nation is not the amount of paper chits it has, but rather the real goods and services of value it produces. The potential output of real goods and services cannot be increased by jiggering the currency. If that was all there was to it, everyone in the world would be wealthy by now.

It is possible that a decline in currency value could lead to greater production of goods and services for some period of time, particularly if there are a lot of unused resources such as unemployed workers and idle factories available. Rampant currency devaluation in Germany in the 1919-1923 period led to a very low unemployment rate often below 3%. Observers were amazed at the tempo of commerce and activity. However, this was mostly due to "money illusion." The additional activity does not lead to greater wealth. Rather, it is ultimately wasted effort. In the German case, the low unemployment and buzz of industrial activity were related to the fact that, due to the collapse of the German mark, German products could be sold internationally for very low prices. These very low prices translated into very low real wages for German people, and consequently, very low living standards. German workers, laboring from dawn to dusk every day, could barely feed themselves. The daily caloric intake of the average German fell by about 30% during that time. It wasn't because they all decided to go on a diet together.

This is the opposite of wealth. The world is full of places where people work hard all day, but barely get enough to survive. The great success of the developed countries is to allow people to work less, yet enjoy material comforts of a level unprecedented in world history.

It is not all that hard to simply increase production of some item. It is conceivable, for example, that U.S. steel production could double if the steel industry were nationalized, and the government agency now in charge of the industry decided that production should double. The problem is, there is no need for so much steel. If there were, the capitalist system would already provide it. The extra steel production is essentially a waste of time, effort and resources. If private industry attempted to produce this much steel, the industry would be unprofitable. This is the capitalist system's way of indicating that the value of the resources used in the production of the excess steel are greater than the value of the steel itself. In other words, wealth was destroyed. Greater production does not lead to greater productivity. The more excess steel that is produced, the poorer the overall society becomes, as it consumes valuable resources – labor, capital, and materials – in the production of valueless products. If the capitalist system's delicate internal communications are mangled in such a way, due to Mercantilist currency distortion, that these signals of value are confused, then such wealth-destruction becomes commonplace. Wealth-destroying activities that should be prevented by their unprofitability, become unnaturally profitable, and thus continue and even expand. Other activities, which genuinely create wealth, become unnaturally unprofitable, and thus are abandoned. The resources of the society are directed towards waste.

In more practical terms, a decline in currency value leads to a decline in the real value of wages paid in that currency. Rising real wages – and the goods and services they can buy – are the whole purpose of economic development. Higher incomes are, for the great majority of people, the meaning of a "wealthy country." Although nominal wages will adjust higher to reflect the decline in currency value, they generally do not adjust fully, and thus the real value of wages declines. This reflects the diminished productivity and chronic wealth-destruction of the economy. As the capitalist system is distorted due to currency distortion, capital investment goes into unproductive activities, and productive activities are starved of capital.

Ultimately, the productivity of the capitalist economy is closely related to specialization and trade. People's economic roles become more and more specialized, and consequently their trade with each other becomes greater and greater. The outcome of this is that many, many people must cooperate to produce things, which might have been done in the past by a single person. The advantage is that these many people, working together, can produce much more than the same number of people working independently. This cooperation is organized, for the most part, by way of money; in other words, trade within the market-based economy. The most basic form of cooperation and trade is the production of food itself, which every

10

person needs. In the past, people themselves created the food they eat, either by hunting and gathering, or by agricultural activities within the household. They did not have to cooperate with others to obtain the food they need every day. The consequence is that every person must be a hunter-gatherer or farmer, leaving no-one to specialize in some other product or service. The economy as a whole produces food and nothing else (except a few other handcrafts also produced within the household), a state of very low material productivity.

Today, only about 2% of the population of the United States is involved in farming. The rest of the population must obtain its food in trade. Food production itself requires vast quantities of products and services from others, such as fertilizer, machinery, fuel, and electricity. The agricultural products themselves are often nearly inedible in their natural state, but must then be processed by others, typically large corporations also with extensive machinery and other inputs obtained in trade. The food is transported across continents and oceans, by other companies, using more machinery obtained from still more companies, and eventually sold in a supermarket, which itself requires a vast number of inputs from a vast number of suppliers, all obtained in trade. Somehow – nobody knows exactly how – this inconceivably complex network of cooperation manages to feed everyone. Not only that, but it provides a stupendous variety of ways to eat, including ripe pineapples in the middle of the Boston winter, and seventy-nine varieties of ice cream continuously available, from a dozen producers with factories scattered throughout the continent, with not even a single day of empty shelves.

This astonishingly complex, near-miraculous system is organized through the use of money, and the system of prices within the marketplace. Its efficiency is maximized when money is stable in value. The market's signals, the information transmitted in prices or profit and loss, are then least distorted, and people can cooperate in the fashion that results in the greatest efficiency and thus greatest production. For this reason, humans have always sought the most stable, definite and predictable forms of money that they could possibly attain. When left to their own devices, humans will always tend to do business in the most stable, definite and predictable terms possible. Often, people are coerced into using whatever junk fiat currency is provided by the local government. However, they can use whatever foreign currency they prefer. In practice, they always prefer the one that is perceived to be the most stable and reliable. Historically, the premier international currencies have always been gold standard currencies, from a politically stable government that is not seen at risk of military invasion. Since 1971, no major country has provided a gold-based currency. The U.S. dollar has retained its leading role as an international currency because it has been the most stable and reliable, among dozens of inferior options. When a more stable and reliable alternative appears, people will migrate toward it, slowly at first, and then more quickly.

* * *

Nevertheless, recessions and periods of economic distress happen, even when a country uses a gold standard system. Some of these may be due to natural events within the capitalist system. At times, certain investment ideas or business practices become widely followed and imitated, leading to a period of excess. This might be a wave of bank lending for property purchases, or overinvestment in some particular industry like hotels, telecommunications or pharmaceuticals. Stock and bond markets regularly and predictably sway between periods of unusually high valuation, and periods of unusually low valuation. These events are inevitably followed by a period of losses and reorganization. Capitalism does not prevent stupidity and error. However, it does punish and correct this behavior eventually, thus making it less common and less long-lived than it would otherwise be.

These kinds of natural capitalist events may happen even if a government was a paragon of superlative economic policy. However, it is often the case that the government itself is pursing some policy that is highly damaging to the capitalist economy – the delicate network of investment, specialization and trade – even while it maintains a gold standard system. Most commonly, this would be some increase in taxation, including tariffs. Governments may also damage the private economy by some form of regulation, such as nationalization of industry, price controls and regulations on labor. The government may threaten to default on its debt, throwing the economy into turmoil. The political system may be unstable, for example if the country has been led for a long time by a strongman who is close to death, with no clear plan for succession. A communist party may win a majority in an election, or some region may threaten to secede.

In the capitalist system, a major problem is not that productivity and general wealth is higher or lower, but rather that some people, even in the best of times, have no productivity at all. They are unemployed. When the numbers of unemployed swell, the political consensus may migrate to a stance that some broad sacrifices could be made in order that the unemployed could have some minimal means of sustenance. The government soon feels its support waning, and the calls go forth to "do something" about the problem. This is reasonable: the government should do something about its problems.

At this point, the Mercantilist economist steps forward, with his various plans and promises, which haven't changed much since William Potter listed them in 1650. The list of claimed advantages is impressive; better yet, the plan doesn't seem to have any cost. Typically, it can be achieved by some sort of executive order, or even an informal agreement with the currency manager, without having to go through the difficult and time-consuming process of parliamentary legislation. Sometimes, it even works; for the reasons described, and depending on the particular state of the economy at the time, unemployment may indeed decline and the economy may seem to become more active, over a period of eighteen months or so. If no particular beneficial effects are seen, and perhaps things get even worse, the Mercantilist advisor can always claim that the remedy was insufficiently aggressive in its application.

One thing about the Mercantilist "easy money" remedy is that it doesn't require any actual understanding of the fundamental cause of the economic problems. Whatever the problem is, the remedy is the same: "easy money." It is thus a popular solution among simpletons, including the majority of people calling themselves "economists," such as academics and government advisors. The simpleton economists, perhaps as a way to hide their ignorance, or perhaps just because they are simpletons, often mislabel symptoms as causes. They say that a recession is caused by an "insufficiency in aggregate demand." This doesn't mean anything more than: "there's a recession."

Debates ensue, and the Classical economist argues that: "In the long run, this 'easy money' policy will lead to economic decline and impoverishment." This is correct, but not quite relevant. It is certainly not a solution to the pressing problems of the day. The Mercantilist argues that: "In the long run, we are all dead." The most important thing is the next twenty-four months. Politicians side with the Mercantilist.

Unfortunately, the "laissez-faire" principles of the Classical economists have too easily become "do nothing" recommendations in times of economic difficulty. There are as many simpletons among the Classical economists as there are among the Mercantilists.

Thus, the difficulty of the Classical approach is: what to do during an economic downturn. Simply pointing to a chart that suggests things will be looking up forty years later is not enough.

Economists set themselves too easy, too useless a task if in tempestuous seasons they can only tell us that when the storm is past the ocean is flat again.
– John Maynard Keynes, *A Tract on Monetary Reform*, 1924

The best approach is to begin by identifying the problem, which is often a problem of government economic policy. Typically, if the currency is securely linked to gold, this is some major deterioration in tax policy, in the form of rising tax rates. When government policy itself is a major cause of the difficulties, the solution is to simply reverse or amend those policies. Herbert Hoover allowed an explosion of tariffs in 1930, followed by an explosion of domestic taxes in 1932. The results were predictably disastrous. One solution would have been to simply eliminate these novelties, and go back to the successful policy of 1928. Alas, government leaders are often incapable of reversing their decisions, even the worst of them. They typically have to be replaced, which is one advantage of the democratic system. However, even the replacement leaders seem to feel some obligation to persist in the worst of the preceding government's errors. This is unfortunate, but the proper remedy is still to reverse and amend the government's economic policy problems.

All things in nature have an ebb and flow. Even healthy and well-cared-for children have times of rapid advancement and growth, and times of assimilation and latency. Typically, busts that follow some unsustainable boom, the natural ups-and-downs of a well-managed capitalist economy, have relatively minor effects upon the economy as a whole. The resources that were misapplied in the boom become redirected in some better fashion, where employment swells to absorb the unemployed resulting from the bust. The economy returns to a productive path in a relatively short time. Today, we hardly remember the recessions of the 1950s and 1960s, which were minor perturbances during a period of extraordinary advancement.

However, even these events that seem relatively minor, with the hindsight of history, can seem very important at the time. Some form of welfare should be provided, because no government, no matter what its economic policies are, can claim moral superiority when many are destitute. Today, this has been institutionalized as unemployment insurance, food assistance, medical assistance and so forth, whose rosters swell during difficult times. If a government's economic policies are already exemplary – as has been the case in Hong Kong or Singapore for many years – then little need be done there. If a government's economic policies could be improved, then the crisis atmosphere would be a fine time to introduce long-awaited reforms, even if government policy was not the actual cause of the crisis. The improved policy would help with the recovery process, and improve the general conditions for business in the long term afterwards. In the United States, for example, conservatives have long argued that governments would gain great advantage from extensive tax reform. Even if government tax policy was not the cause of the downturn, a major tax reform would provide a huge boost for the economy as a whole, thus accelerating the recovery. For another country, perhaps a reform of labor laws would remove a major impediment to increasing employment.

Possibly, a reform of regulation may be called for, to prevent the sort of excess that caused the boom and bust. In the United States, one example was the Glass-Steagall Act, which separated the commercial banking and brokerage industries in 1933, and regulation regarding use of margin for stock trading. The United States economy and financial system prospered for many years afterwards, with no particular ill effects.

The Classical economist, of sufficient insight and ability, has a broad range of solutions for economic difficulties that do not involve "easy money" – or "do nothing." These solutions are fundamental reforms to deal with fundamental problems, and produce fundamental improvements – increasing wealth and employment – in the long term, and in the medium and short term as well. Often, an economy will begin to pick up even while economy-positive legislation is still being debated in parliament, as businessmen conclude that they should be prepared and positioned for the good times soon to come. The Mercantilist strategy of applying monetary solutions to nonmonetary problems obviously leaves the original problem unfixed. If the problem was caused by an explosion of tariffs or domestic taxes, then no amount of currency fiddling will remedy the changes in the tax code. Unfortunately, by trying to fix a tax policy problem with a currency-fiddling solution, the Mercantilists introduce a new element – unstable money – which can quickly become quite problematic itself.

* * *

Richard Nixon's gambit worked. The recession of 1969-70 – caused in part by his increase in the capital gains tax rate to near 50% – was apparently resolved by a powerful application of monetary expansion. This was overseen by Arthur Burns, handpicked by Nixon for the job and installed as the Chairman of the Federal Reserve in February 1970. The year 1972 was, by popular appearances, a marvelous year. The official "real" economic growth rate was a whopping 5.3%, following 3.4% in 1971. At the end of 1972, one Wall Street observer asserted that: "there is no reason to be anything but bullish."[2] Nixon won a second term as president in November of that year.

During the Bretton Woods gold standard period, the dollar's value was supposed to be held at $35 per ounce of gold – in other words, the dollar was to be worth the same as 1/35th of a troy ounce of gold, or 13.714 troy grains. When Burns entered office, the market value was $35.20/oz. At the end of 1972, the dollar had fallen to $65.20 per ounce of gold. Nixon's achievement was accomplished at the cost of cutting the dollar's value nearly in half. In March of 1973, the other governments participating in the Bretton Woods system decided they had had enough. They weren't going to follow the U.S. down the devaluation path. They delinked their currencies from the dollar, and allowed them to float freely. However, those governments couldn't find a political path to re-establish a gold standard system, while the world's dominant international currency itself was depreciating fiat junk. In practice, all countries indeed followed the United States down the devaluation path in the 1970s, with several, including once-respected Britain, actually out-devaluing the Americans.

That is how today's floating fiat system began, a reflection of the Mercantilist principles that had saturated Nixon's administration, and the administration of most governments around the world. There was no great international conference, such as the one the marked the start of the Bretton Woods system. There was no actual plan to create a floating fiat currency system. The Bretton Woods system was the result of an agreement; the floating fiat system was the result of a disagreement. Nixon himself said that the end of the dollar's link to gold on August 15, 1971 was a temporary measure. In December 1971, only a few months later, he attempted to fix his error with the

Smithsonian Agreement, which committed the United States to maintaining the dollar's value at $38.02/oz. The European and Japanese governments that delinked from the dollar in the spring of 1973 had no interest in creating a floating fiat currency system. They were happy with the Bretton Woods gold standard system, and begged the U.S. government to stop undermining it with Burns' "easy money" strategy.

It was an accident.

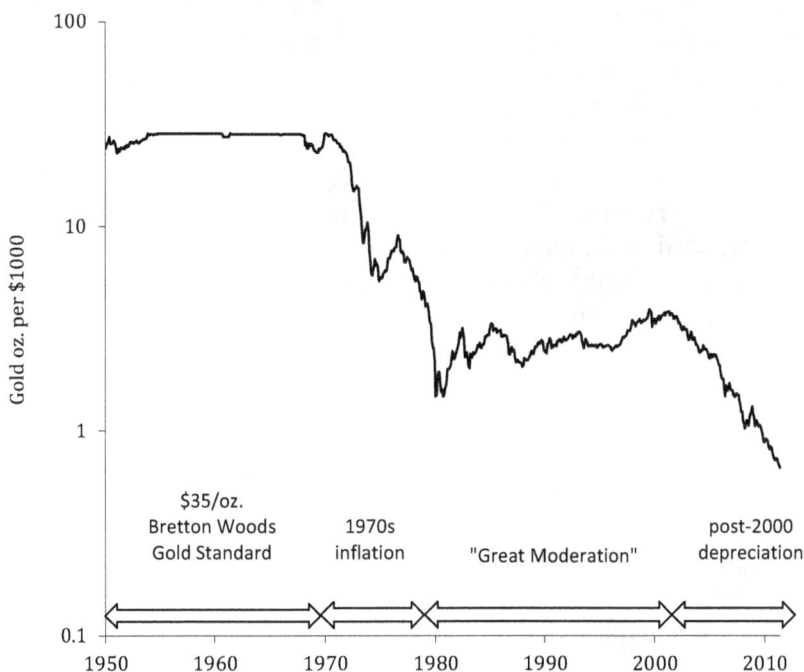

Figure 1.1: U.S.: Value of $1000 in Gold oz., 1950-2011
logarithmic scale

Four decades on, we can review some of the results of this accident. The United States managed to get the inflationary impulses of its political system under control at the end of 1979, when Paul Volcker became the Chairman of the Federal Reserve and immediately embarked on a crusade to end the disastrous devaluation trend of the 1970s. During the 1980s and 1990s, the value of the dollar floated around $350/oz., having fallen to one-tenth of its value during the Bretton Woods years. This period of crude dollar stability, combined with Ronald Reagan's tax reforms, allowed the economy to recover from the inflationary disaster of the 1970s. Some economists call it the "Great Moderation," typically with no understanding of what made it possible. Mercantilists might point to this "Great Moderation" as evidence that their Mercantilist policies can indeed lead to periods of substantial progress. The Classicals say: see, a stable currency works. If the dollar began and ended that two-decade period around $350/oz. of gold, wouldn't it have been simpler and better just to maintain the dollar's value at exactly $350/oz. with a gold standard system? Was there anything gained by producing a gold standard-like result with crude Mercantilist tools? Although Federal Reserve Chairman Alan Greenspan was later hailed as "the Maestro" for overseeing this prosperous time, in fact the performance of the economy during those years fell far short of what had been accomplished during the Bretton Woods years.

William McChesney Martin presided as the Chairman of the Federal Reserve from 1951 to 1970, the bulk of the Bretton Woods gold standard era. Greenspan was the Chairman from 1987 to 2005. Let's look at Greenspan's record, compared to Martin's, based on the official U.S. government statistics:

Statistic (average during tenure)	Greenspan 1987-2005	Martin 1951-1969
CPI-U all items	3.09%	2.26%
Industrial Production	3.00%	5.07%
Nonfarm real compensation per hour	1.28%	2.66%
Nonfarm business output per hour (productivity)	2.24%	2.52%
10-year Treasury bond yield	6.30%	4.09%
Unemployment rate	5.5%	4.6%

Martin wins in all categories – this despite the fact that the methods of compiling the statistics themselves changed considerably by Greenspan's time, always in favor of making them look better. If the statistics were compiled in the same fashion in both eras, Martin's advantage would have been greater.

The Mercantilist solution had brought a decade of inflationary disaster in the 1970s. However, the Mercantilists' promises of "ending the business cycle" proved false. Recessions still happened, many of them worse than the recessions of the Bretton Woods period or, for that matter, the recessions of the decades prior to 1914.

Beginning in 2001, "easy money" again became the favorite option for dealing with economic difficulty. At first, Greenspan himself was responsible for this, cutting the Fed's policy target rate to 1% in 2003. This was in part due to the fact that the dollar had risen well above its long-term plateau around $350/oz., to as far as $260/oz. in 2001. As the economy recovered and the dollar fell in value, Greenspan steadily raised the Fed's policy target rate until he left office in January 2006. The value of the dollar was $569 per ounce of gold when his term ended, with the market anticipating the introduction of a new Fed Chairman.

Greenspan, who had been an outspoken gold standard advocate in his youth and never subscribed to the Mercantilists' "easy money" dreams, was replaced by a career Mercantilist: Benjamin Bernanke. Bernanke's academic work – his own youthful advocacy – amounted to the claim that the Great Depression could have been prevented with an "easy money" solution. In response to economic crises having mostly to due with the bursting of a property bubble, and consequently, widespread default on properly-related lending, Bernanke cut the Fed's interest rate target to an unprecedented zero percent in 2008. He later followed this with still further measures in the form of "quantitative easing," or direct purchases of government and agency debt using the Fed's money-creation function. By the end of 2012, four successive rounds of quantitative easing had been introduced, and the Fed's target rate remained at zero percent. This was a degree of Monetarist "easy money" unprecedented in United States history.

The Great Moderation of the 1980s and 1990s was over. The value of the dollar had fallen far from its plateau around $350/oz. At the end of 2012, it was at $1,650 per ounce, only 21% of its Great Moderation-era value, and only 2.1% of the value it had during the 1960s. The floating fiat dollar was sinking. Again.

* * *

We can now look back upon these four decades of Mercantilist monetary policy. We know that, if the dollar had not been devalued, and the Bretton Woods gold standard arrangement persisted, the dollar would still be worth 1/35th of an ounce of gold as it was in 1970 – or, that $35 would be worth the same as an ounce of gold. A troy ounce of gold today can be considered equivalent to $35 Bretton Woods dollars, if those dollars had not been devalued.

Gross Domestic Product, as we know it, has only been compiled since 1947. During the 1930s, it was assembled on a more provisional basis by academics – obviously, without the resources of the Bureau of Economic Analysis. Estimates of GDP from before 1914 should be considered crude guesses at best, compiled from a skimpy historical dataset.

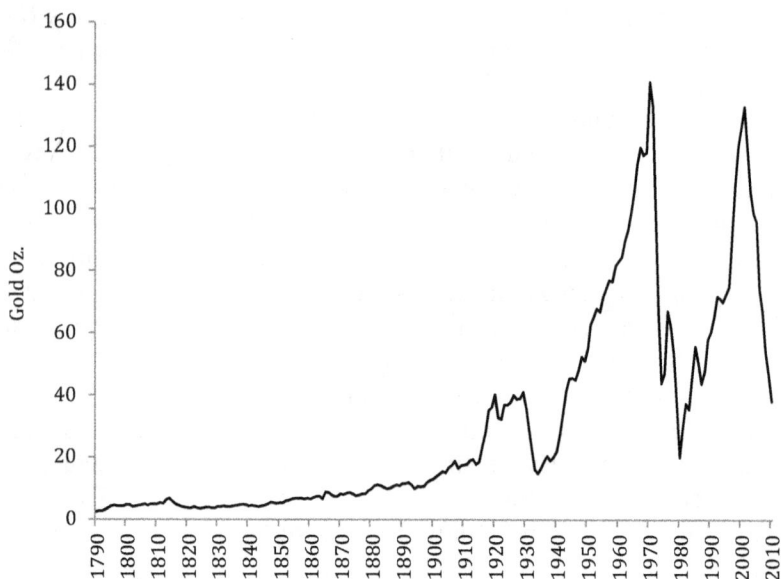

Figure 1.2: U.S. Per Capita GDP in Gold Oz., 1790-2010

Nevertheless, using what sketchy data we have, we can estimate the per-capita GDP of U.S. citizens from 1790 to the present (Figure 1.2).

Per-capita GDP, as measured in gold dollars, increased throughout U.S. history, until 1971. The Great Depression was a major setback, but even in that case, per-capita GDP recovered within a couple decades and made dramatic new highs.

One way to look at this data is in terms of average growth over a forty-year period (Figure 1.3). Was the average American better off after forty years? To put it more simply, were children more prosperous than their parents? Although there were major difficulties along the way, the Civil War and Great Depression especially, per-capita GDP eventually recovered and continued its nearly two-century-long path higher.

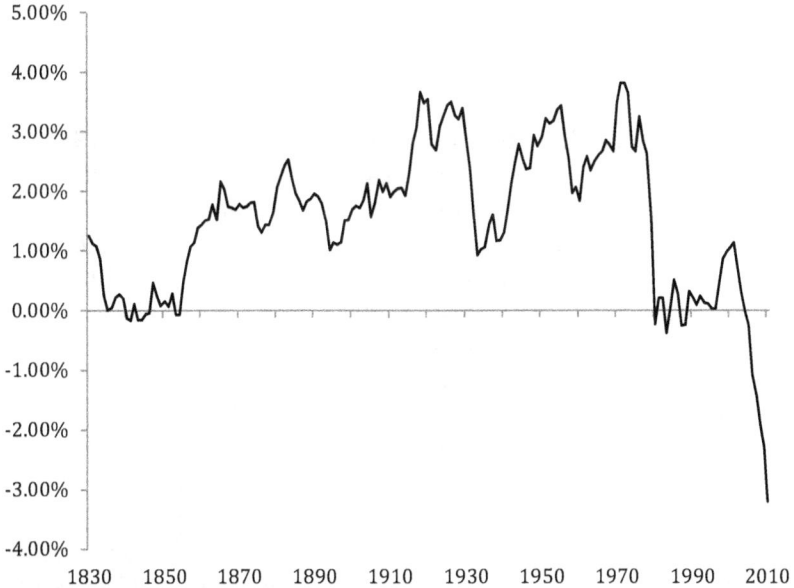

Figure 1.3: U.S.: Per Capita GDP in Gold Oz., 1790-2010, Annualized Rate of Change Over Previous Forty Years

Per-capita GDP, as measured in ounces of gold – a measure independent of any manipulated government statistics, and the traditional way value was measured in the United States – made a peak in 1971, which it has never again attained.

A major recovery took place during the Great Moderation period, when Volcker and Greenspan's efforts managed to keep the dollar's value in a broad band around $350/oz. This amounted to a crude approximation of the Classical principle of stable currency value. However, as another episode of declining dollar value began around 2001, wages and GDP naturally declined along with the nominal unit of measure. At the end of 2010, per-capita GDP, as measured in ounces of gold, had fallen to early-1950s levels.

This was despite a dramatic increase in working women since 1960. Due to the way GDP statistics are calculated, women's work is counted as a GDP addition when it is done for a salary, while work done within the household, although it certainly contributes to the actual production, wealth and well-being of the family and country, is not recorded. The decline in per-capita GDP (measured in gold) has taken place despite these factors, which would tend to increase the measure.

Gold: The Monetary Polaris

For the first time in U.S. history, Americans were not better off than those of forty years previous – their parents – by this measure. It is true that technology improved during that time, which led to many improvements in lifestyle. However, it was also true that many things that the median single-earner family could enjoy in the late 1960s – a house, a car or two, decent healthcare, a college education for the children, and a 10% savings rate – became strangely unobtainable, even with two working parents. Technology improved throughout the United States' two-century-plus history. The advances of recent decades were not particularly superior to the introduction of electricity, automobiles, trains, paved roads, air travel, refrigeration, synthetic fabrics or antibiotics in the past. Along with these advancements, per-capita GDP in terms of gold also improved.

Even by the U.S. government's own statistics, the "real" median full-time male income has been stagnant for four decades (Figure 1.4). This measure increased by leaps and bounds during the 1950s and 1960s, despite numerous official recessions during those years. The time series makes a clear inflection point; it peaks in 1972, when the Nixon's funny-money boom went bust.

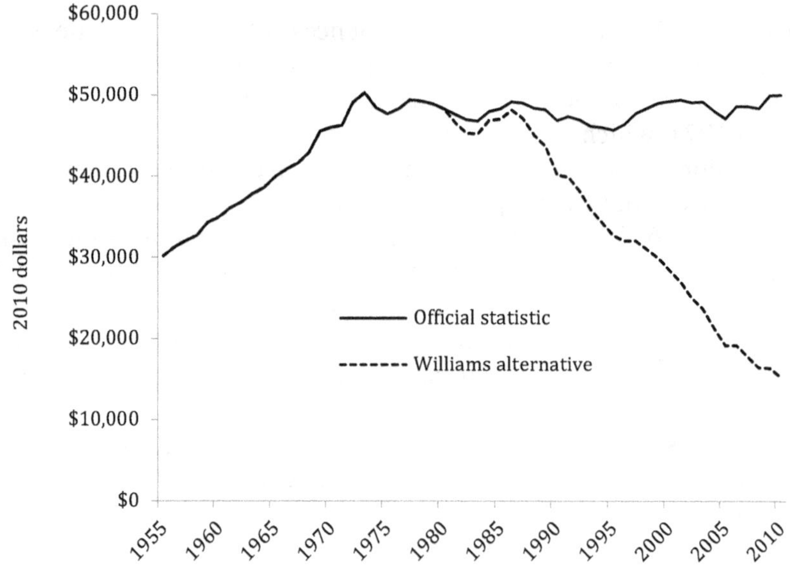

Figure 1.4: U.S.: "Real" Median Full-Time Male Income, 1955-2010
Williams alternative statistics normalized at 1980

The government statistics have been heavily altered, making them look better than they would have without changes to the way they are compiled. The economist John Williams adjusted the official statistics to show what they would have reported, if not for a series of methodological changes since 1980.[3] In other words, Williams attempted to create an apples-to-apples comparison. The results of this straightforward methodology are rather dramatic, and show a steady deterioration in effective incomes.

The same statistics, expressed in terms of ounces of gold (Figure 1.5), also show a more difficult picture. The equivalent gold value of the income of the full-time working male in the United States has fallen drastically since the beginning of the Mercantilist monetary era. The decline in dollar value since 2001 has of course accelerated this trend downwards; as the dollar's value declines, the value of wages paid in dollars declines also.

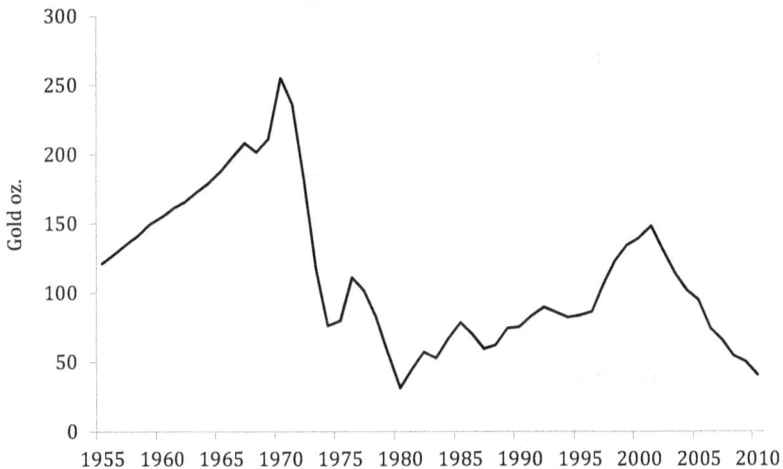

Figure 1.5: U.S. Median Male Full-Time Income in Gold Oz., 1955-2010

The Classical economists' warnings proved true. We didn't devalue ourselves to prosperity. Even the Great Moderation period was merely a passing episode of recovery in a longer tale of self-impoverishment that began in 1971.

The Mercantilists' claims of "solving the business cycle" didn't work out very well. Recessions and unemployment remained. Indeed, recessions and unemployment were worst during the times when "easy money" was most aggressive – during the 1970s, and also the 2001-2011 period.

One reason for this is unstable money's effect upon the business cycle itself. The whole purpose of Mercantilist monetary techniques is to introduce monetary distortions into the normal workings of the capitalist economy – distortions that the Mercantilist money-tweakers believe they can manage to their benefit. These monetary distortions, the confusion of the price signals of the market, cause errors in commerce, capital allocation and investment activity. The process by which Mercantilist funny money reduces unemployment is to distort the capitalist system's signals of reward and failure to induce business owners to make investments and hire employees that, in the absence of monetary distortion, they would not.

In other words, the Mercantilists want to create an artificial boom. Although booms and busts appear in any capitalist economy even with a gold standard system, we could reasonably expect more and bigger booms in an environment of Mercantilist money distortion. These booms are founded on an even flimsier basis, and thus turn to bust, accompanied by rising unemployment. Usually, a nation is so chastened by the bursting of a major asset bubble (defined as a two-standard-deviation peak in valuation) that it becomes wary for a generation. However, the United States had two full-scale asset bubbles, in equities and then property, within a mere decade, 1997-2007. This was followed by perhaps another bubble, in bonds, which reached their highest prices in U.S. history in 2012.

* * *

After 182 years of experience with gold standard systems, and over forty years of experience with various forms of a Mercantilist floating currency, we can make some clear conclusions. American families have, for the first time in U.S. history, failed to make significant progress over a period of decades. By many measures, they are worse off. Unemployment was never particularly low during the post-1971 Mercantilist era, not even during the "Great Moderation" years. Recessions were not particularly rare, or mild in their incidence. There does not seem to be any great reason at all to adopt a Mercantilist strategy. The British came to the same conclusion in the 18th and 19th centuries, when the first body of Mercantilist thought was eventually discarded as fallacious rubbish.

Keynes is dead. We are living in his "long run."

The Classical economists must accept some blame. They tend to be rather bad at dealing with times of economic difficulty, and often make the situation worse. The Classical economists – the advocates of a stable money policy – have often been the same ones to also advocate a destructive "austerity" strategy during downturns. "Austerity" commonly amounts to a combination of much higher tax rates, and often a reduction in spending focused on welfare-type programs and other public services, at the time when they are needed most. Typically, the higher tax rates cause greater tax avoidance and a slumping economy, and produce no additional revenue. The crumbling economy increases the need for welfare assistance, and makes existing spending impossible to reduce. Budget deficits increase. The additional economic problems imposed create even more motivation to "do something" via Mercantilist money manipulation. The Classicals are not very popular due to their failed "austerity" strategy, and many conclude that they should be expelled from positions of influence. In the vacuum, the Mercantilists have unrestrained influence over the government's policy.

The Mercantilists often have some sort of "stimulus" approach. Welfare assistance can be highly appreciated during a downturn, but simply spending money is not – in itself – an economic plan. Deficits soar, and the government's debt burden becomes an issue. Taxes often head higher to pay for new welfare programs, and to address budget deficits, once again creating new economic problems. The "easy money" option is embraced wholeheartedly.

The Mercantilists typically make such a mess of things that people conclude that it is their turn to be expelled from positions of influence. In this way, governments have cycled between Classical and Mercantilist paradigms. The United States is a young country. There has been only one change thus far, in 1971, with a precursor in 1933. In Britain, France or China, we can trace back many such changes, over a period of centuries. The United States will again turn back to the Classical principles that once made it great. At least, the political impetus will build among the people; whether a successful adoption of Classical principles into concrete policy takes place depends on the responsiveness of the political system. It may not happen, in which case the torch of economic leadership will pass to another region, perhaps for many centuries.

In the 15th and 16th centuries, Spain was the world's economic and military powerhouse. Spanish adventurers discovered the New World, and, in amazingly short time, ruled over its inhabitants. In Europe, under Charles V (reigned 1519-1556), the Spanish Empire eventually included much of today's southern Italy, and stretched from today's eastern France to western Poland and Hungary. Overseas, the Spanish Empire stretched from California to the Philippines. California was named by Spanish explorers in the 16th century, the name apparently derived from the Latin *calida* and *fornax*, meaning "hot oven"; the Philippines were named in the 16th century after King Philip II of Spain. The Greatness of Spain seemed wondrous, incredible, untouchable.

Spain's government eventually entered a spiral of decline, punctuated by ever-increasing taxes, regular currency devaluations, and increasing payoffs to political cronies and welfare handouts to maintain support for the unpopular government. Spain never recovered. It has been a laggard of Europe up to the present day. Nor did Argentina, in 1900 one of the world's wealthiest countries. Today, Argentina is not even considered an "emerging market," instead relegated to that sad disposal bin of chronic failures known as "frontier economies."

In the midst of economic difficulties, the U.S.A. may cease to exist. It may dissolve into a number of smaller republics, in a manner similar to the way that other acronymic, continent-spanning empire, without ethnic or geographic continuity – the U.S.S.R. – dissolved during the 1990s. Texas was once a separate country; it may become one again. The individual States may even decide that they are no longer served by the Union they agreed to in 1789, desperate to escape the continuing tragedy of government policy failure emanating from Washington, DC. If the North American continent should become home to fifty separate countries, that would not be much different than the situation in Europe or Africa.

That need not happen. The Classical principle of stable, gold-based money once made Americans wealthy. It could do so again.

Chapter 2:
How a Gold Standard System Works

The term "gold standard system" is used here to mean a currency system with a precise policy goal – to maintain the value of a currency at a specified ratio with gold, also known as a gold "parity." From 1789 to 1834, the United States had a policy of maintaining the value of the dollar at 24.75 troy grains of pure gold, or 1/19.39th of a troy ounce of gold – also notated as "$19.39 per ounce of gold." From 1834 to 1933, the U.S. gold parity was 23.2 troy grains of pure gold, or $20.67/oz. From 1933 to 1971, the official gold parity was 13.714 troy grains of gold, or 1/35th of an ounce, or $35/oz.

FIRST, a gold standard is a fixed-value policy. The value of the currency remains fixed compared to some benchmark, in this case gold. Thus, a gold standard system is a subcategory of a broader class of fixed-value policies. You could have a policy of fixing a currency's value to another currency, as the East Caribbean dollar (used by six Caribbean countries) is maintained at a fixed ratio with the U.S. dollar today, and the Central African CFA franc (used by six African countries) is maintained at a fixed ratio with the euro. You could have a policy of maintaining a currency at a fixed ratio compared to some commodity basket, or a basket of currencies (as Singapore does today), or a lot of other things.

SECOND, it has to work. There must be an operating mechanism that can actually accomplish the goal of maintaining a currency's value at the specified ratio with gold, reliably and indefinitely. A proposal that doesn't have a proper operating mechanism that will actually produce

27

the intended results is merely wishful thinking. It is like an automobile without an engine. It looks like an automobile, but it is useless.

All functional operating mechanisms have some way of managing the value of paper banknotes (and other forms of base money) that we use as currency. Banknotes have no intrinsic value. They are made of paper. But, by making them artificially scarce, they have a much higher value, in trade, than the value of their paper content or cost of production. By managing the supply of paper banknotes – adjusting the degree of artificial scarcity – we can make these worthless paper chits have a specific value, namely that of a certain quantity of gold bullion.

A lot of different, specific proposals could be created that meet our two basic requirements above, and thus could be called a "gold standard system." For example, you could have a system that only used gold coins. This is impractical for a lot of reasons, but we can see that, if you actually make the currency out of gold, its value should be the same as gold. This is approximately the system that the United States began with in the 1790s. A gold coin, made by anyone anywhere, was acceptable according to the weight of contained bullion. In those days silver coins were used too, so it was a "bimetallic" system rather than a "monometallic" gold-only system. Also, private commercial banks in the U.S. issued gold-based paper currencies, even then.

You could have a system with no gold coins at all, only paper banknotes. If the banknotes' value was maintained at a gold parity, with a viable operating mechanism of some sort, then that would work too. This was roughly the way things were done in the United States between 1934 and 1971. During those years, it was illegal for U.S. citizens to own gold coins or bullion, but the government nevertheless had a policy of maintaining the value of the dollar at a 35:1 ratio with gold. Somewhere in the middle, you can have a system with both gold coins and banknotes, which was the normal state of affairs for most of United States history until 1933. You could have a system with gold coins and electronic fractional ownership of gold bullion, similar to the services offered by companies like Gold Money or Bullionvault, but no paper banknotes. You could even have a system without either gold coins or paper banknotes, only a form of "electronic money" such as debit cards. (Technically, this would mean that the bank reserves held at the central bank would have a value linked to gold.)

The term "gold standard system" encompasses a lot of specific systems that could be created, each with their idiosyncrasies but which all share the same goal of maintaining the currency's value at a certain gold parity. Historically, every country had a system that was a little different. The Bank of England, for example, had a monopoly on currency issuance during the 19th century. However, in the United States, hundreds and eventually thousands of small commercial banks issued their own currency, all of which was linked to gold. Later, the Federal Reserve assumed an effective monopoly on banknote issuance in the United States, mirroring that of the Bank of England. Sometimes, these banknotes were "redeemable in gold" by the currency issuer, whether a small commercial bank or the Federal Reserve. At other times, during the 1950s and 1960s, they weren't redeemable, unless you were a foreign central bank. Some countries, like Russia and France, had very large gold reserve holdings, while others, like Germany and Italy, had rather small holdings, relative to the size of their economies and currency in circulation. Some countries, like the Philippines and Japan, had a policy of maintaining a stable value not with gold directly, but with a major international currency linked to gold such as the British Pound or U.S. dollar. If your currency has a fixed exchange rate with the British pound, and the British pound has a fixed exchange rate with gold, then in effect your currency has a fixed exchange rate with gold. Thus, this is also a form of gold standard system.

To use another automobile analogy: every specific model of automobile is different. Often, between two automobiles, not a single part is the same. There is no "one true automobile." There is no ideal automobile, as each specific model has strengths and weaknesses, to match different needs and desires. However, they all use the same operating principles, of an internal combustion engine driving a transmission and wheels, with all of the specific engineering details that entails. They all work.

In the late 19th century, virtually every country in the world used some kind of gold standard system. Probably none of these systems were exactly alike. Each one was probably a bit different, in response to the needs and interests of that particular country. They changed, over time, as those needs and interests also changed. They all worked.

The term "gold-based currency" will be used to describe a currency that is operated under some form of a gold standard system – in other words, a currency whose value is linked to the value of gold bullion.

Just as those systems were appropriate for their time and place, we can design a system that is appropriate to our situation today. We can change it as our needs change. But, like all gold standard systems in the past, it will be a fixed-value system with gold as the policy target, or, as it is known, the "standard of value."

And, it has to work.

* * *

We are talking here about creating and managing monetary systems. We better have a good idea of what a "currency" or "money" is.

This is a lot easier than you think.

We will use the term "money" to mean: the thing commonly acceptable as payment in transactions.

Of course we mean "monetary" transactions, not barter. We all have a pretty good idea of what barter is: one cow for twelve woolen blankets. This is cumbersome. Before too long, an item becomes mutually acceptable in trade, not because of its utilitarian usefulness, but because it can be reliably traded again for something else. It becomes a medium for transactions. This quickly resolves down to a few or, ideally, one item, because a medium for trade is most useful when everyone uses it. When one item becomes generally accepted as a medium for trade, we call that item "money."

Today, the thing we use as "money," in the United States, is "dollars."

These dollars take two forms. One is the paper banknotes and coins that we are familiar with, and carry with us in our wallets and purses. A hundred and fifty years ago, this was the only form of money there was – physical coins and banknotes. To make large transactions, banks often used very large denomination paper banknotes, of $1,000, $10,0000 or more (and the dollar was worth a lot more then too).

This was rather cumbersome, so the banks got together and created a "clearinghouse" for interbank payments -- basically, a bank for banks. These did not issue currency, but as note-issuing "central banks" were established, in the form of the Federal Reserve and similar sorts of institutions worldwide, they adopted the role of a clearinghouse for interbank payments. Banks kept their "reserves" at the central bank. In the past, these "reserves" were literal bundles of paper banknotes, a "reserve of cash." The Fed recorded their "reserves" as a deposit at the Federal Reserve. Now, if a bank wanted to pay another bank, it didn't have to deliver physical bundles of banknotes. It would just ask the Fed to reduce the "bank reserves" recorded at the Fed from one account, and add it to another account. (Note that transferring "bank reserves" from one account to another does not change the total amount of "bank reserves" in existence.)

If a bank wanted to convert its bank reserves into paper banknotes, it would simply ask the Fed to do so, and the Fed would deliver paper banknotes. You can think of these bank reserves as something like another denomination of banknotes. Our dollars can take the form of $1 bills, $5 bills, $20 bills and so forth, and, if you are a commercial bank, it can take the form of these bank reserves recorded as deposits at the Fed.

You can think of "bank reserves" as a vault full of banknotes – which is what it actually was in the past. Today, this metaphoric "vault" is at the Federal Reserve, which makes it easy for banks to pay each other because the money is "all in one place." The idea of "bank reserves" can be confusing because it is new for most people, but in fact it is very simple.

The currency manager (typically a central bank today) may also hold deposits from the government or other government institutions. These are functionally equivalent to banks' deposits at the currency manager.

Money today is known as "base money," and consists of banknotes and coins outstanding, and these bank reserves and other deposits recorded at the currency manager (central bank), such as the Federal Reserve. All "base money" is recorded as a liability on the balance sheet of the Federal Reserve.

The official balance sheet of the Federal Reserve at the end of 2007 (before complications arising from the financial crisis of 2008) appears in Table 2.1. Table 2.2 shows a simplified version.

All monetary transactions today are performed with base money – either paper banknotes ("currency in circulation") or deposits at the Federal Reserve, also known as "bank reserves." This is the only thing acceptable in monetary payment.

This might be confusing, because it seems like we can pay for things with "money in our bank account," or "money in our money market account," or with credit cards, debit cards, Paypal, store gift cards, bank checks, money orders, wire transfers, traveler's checks, and so forth. These are all mechanisms by which one bank eventually pays another bank, using bank reserves – in other words, base money. Let's look at what actually happens.

Assets	$millions
Reserve Bank Credit	873,512
Securities held outright	754,605
U.S. Treasury securities	754,605
Bills	241,856
Notes and bonds, nominal	470,984
Notes and bonds, inflation-indexed	36,911
Inflation compensation	4,855
Federal Agency debt securities	0
Repurchase agreements	39,536
Term auction credit	20,000
Other loans to depository institutions	4,828
Primary credit	4,802
Secondary credit	0
Seasonal credit	26
Float	-902
Other Federal Reserve Assets	55,445
Gold stock	11,041
Special drawing rights certificate account	2,200
Treasury currency outstanding	38,807

Liabilities	
Currency in circulation	825,624
Reverse repurchase agreements	39,120
Foreign official and international accounts	39,120
Dealers	0
Treasury cash holdings	246
Deposits with F.R. Banks, other than reserve balances	11,906
U.S. Treasury, general account	4,910
Foreign official	97
Service-related	6,615
Requiring clearing balances	6,615
Adjustments to compensate for float	0
Other	283
Reserve balances with F.R. Banks	5,865
Other liabilities and capital	42,799

Table 2.1: U.S.: Federal Reserve Balance Sheet, 2007-end

We are all familiar with buying something and making payment in paper banknotes and coins. But what happens when we use some sort of bank intermediary?

Let's say you have "$1,000 in your bank account." There is no $1,000 – banknotes and coins – in a bank vault somewhere, corresponding to your account balance. Actually, what you have is a demand deposit, which is a loan to the bank that can be repaid on demand. This deposit is recorded on banks' balance sheet as a loan to the bank – in other words, a form of credit, not "money." It's the same as if you loan your next-door neighbor $1,000, with repayment on demand. You go there the next day, and ask him to repay $50. He pays you $50 in banknotes. You agree that he now owes you $950. Your neighbor does not have your $950 in the form of banknotes in a drawer, but he is nevertheless required – as part of the debt agreement – to deliver any amount, on demand, up to the remaining balance of the loan.

Assets	$millions
U.S. government and agency bonds	754,605
Loans	63,462
Other Federal Reserve assets	96,452
Gold stock (valued at $42.22/oz.)	11,041

Liabilities	
Currency in circulation	825,624
Borrowings	39,120
Deposits	17,487
U.S. Treasury, general account	4,910
Foreign official	97
Banks	12,480
Other liabilities and capital	42,799

Table 2.2: U.S.: Federal Reserve Balance Sheet, 2007-end, Simplified

When you use a check, electronic check, debit card or wire transfer, what actually happens is that, upon your request, your bank pays the payee (probably another bank) the amount requested. Your deposit – the amount the bank owes you – is correspondingly reduced. When your bank pays the payee's bank, this payment is done with base money, possibly in the form of banknotes but probably in the form of bank reserves recorded at the Federal Reserve. Thus, these transactions are also made with base money. The same thing happens when you use a credit card, but, instead of the bank adjusting how much the bank owes you (a bank deposit account), the bank adjusts how much you owe them (a credit balance).

For example, let's say you purchase $57.63 of clothing in a store and use a debit card from Bank A in payment. The clothing store's bank is Bank B. What then happens (in principle) is that Bank A pays Bank B the $57.63 in the form of "bank reserve" deposits held at the Federal Reserve. The Federal Reserve, acting as interbank payments clearinghouse, reduces Bank A's "bank reserves" by $57.63 and increases Bank B's "bank reserves" by $57.63.

In practice, banks add up all the payments they are supposed to make to each other, and net them out at the end of the day. If Bank A is supposed to make 32,447 payments totaling $45,442,674.60 to Bank B, and Bank B is supposed to make 75,220 payments totaling $57,405,398.02 to Bank A, then the banks net out their payments such that Bank B pays $11,962,723.42 to Bank A, using base money in the form of Bank B's deposits at the Fed. Bank B's deposit account at the Fed is debited by this amount, and Bank A's account is credited.

Sometimes both the payer and payee have accounts at the same bank, in which case the bank simply nets the transaction internally. Bank A "pays itself." This is a special case of the general principle.

All forms of "electronic money" are actually just different means of communication by which you ask your bank to pay another person or bank some amount of money. The bank does this with base money – bank reserves, banknotes and coins. Thus, all monetary transactions are done with base money. It is the only actual means of monetary payment. That is why base money – and base money alone – is actual money. Everything else is credit.

Credit is merely an agreement denominated in money. When you loan your next-door neighbor $1000, with the agreement that he will repay the loan on demand, you have a credit agreement denominated in dollars. A ten-year bond is merely an agreement to make certain monetary payments (using base money) on certain dates. You can also have a credit agreement denominated in some other thing, like cat-sitting. If you agree to watch your neighbor's cats for ten days while she is away, then she now has a "debt" or obligation to "repay" you by watching your cat for ten days while you are away. This credit agreement, denominated in cat-sitting, is not money. Nor is a credit agreement denominated in dollars.

U.S. banks today don't actually "create money" or "reduce money." They cannot change the amount of base money in existence. They create and reduce credit. "Credit" just means a loan of some sort. We all know that banks make loans, and borrow money. There is nothing mysterious about it. You can read a full description of their operations in their public quarterly and annual financial reports. We also know that, in the United States, banks do not create paper money. Have you ever seen a dollar bill issued by Bank of America or Wells Fargo Bank?

Figure 2.1: Banknote issued by the
Consolidated National Bank of Tucson, 1902

In the past, regular commercial banks in the U.S. in fact did create money. They printed and circulated their own banknotes, linked to gold at the standardized dollar/gold parity. The banknote itself showed the name of the bank that issued it. (Figure 2.1) This was the regular state of affairs in the United States until the 1930s. When people say that "banks create money," this was in fact the case a few generations ago. These rhetorical devices seem to persist for decade after decade, even after the real situation changes.

Figure 2.2: Banknote issued by the
Hongkong and Shanghai Banking Corporation, 2009

U.S. banks today do not print their own banknotes – although this practice does still exist, for example in Hong Kong. The Hong Kong currency has the name of the issuing bank printed on it. Today, only the Federal Reserve, as the present monopoly manager of the currency, can increase or decrease the amount of money (dollar base money) in existence. If you look at the U.S. dollar banknote today, you will see that it is actually called a "Federal Reserve Note." The issuing bank is the Federal Reserve.

Most supposed economic experts today have a poor grasp of even the simplest monetary principles. Is it any wonder that the currency systems they design and manage have a tendency to blow up periodically?

* * *

Traditionally, the question of how to implement a gold standard system was left up to the bankers, either individual commercial banks or the Federal Reserve. However, during the latter half of the twentieth century, it appears that bankers were not taught how to do this properly. The informal chain of intergenerational education was broken. One of the major reasons that the U.S. left the gold standard in 1971 was not because it wasn't producing excellent economic outcomes – this was after two of the most prosperous decades in U.S. history – but because the people in charge of maintaining the system made a series of chronic operating errors. The car worked, but nobody taught them how to drive it. The result was a car crash.

Part of the reason for this is that it is near-impossible to find any adequate explanation of how such systems work. Most of what you can read in books, by both the Keynesian economists and even the gold standard advocates themselves, is bunk.

Any paper currency has value today because of a limitation of supply. We all know that if a government started printing its currency willy-nilly, then the value of the currency would soon plunge to its commodity value. For a paper currency, that value is nil. To preserve this limitation on supply, a government also prohibits anyone else from printing the currency, known as "counterfeiting."

Simply having a limited supply of a currency doesn't give the currency value. You could have a very small supply – let's say $1,000 of currency in existence – but if nobody wants it, then the value of the currency will still be zero. For other people, the "$1,000 of Bob's Buxx"

36

you created last night on the laser printer is just worthless paper. There is no demand for the currency.

However, if you have a currency that is very much in demand, worldwide, then you can have an immense supply of currency, but the currency will still have value. At the end of 2011 there was about $1,067 billion of U.S. dollar banknotes and coins in existence. In addition, banks and other entities held reserve deposits at the Federal Reserve of an additional $1,534 billion, giving a total monetary base of $2,601 billion. Despite this immense sum of base money in existence, the U.S. dollar still maintained some value.

At the end of 2011, the Canadian dollar was worth about the same as a U.S. dollar. However, there were only about $61 billion Canadian dollars in existence in the form of banknotes and coins, plus another $2.5 billion in reserve deposits at the Bank of Canada. Why is it that the U.S. dollar and the Canadian dollar had about the same value, even when there were $2,601 billion of U.S. dollars in existence, but only $63.5 billion of Canadian dollars? The reason is that the demand for the U.S. dollar, worldwide, was also proportionally larger than that of the Canadian dollar.

For one thing, there were a lot more people in the U.S. (314 million), using U.S. dollars, than there were in Canada (35 million), using Canadian dollars. However, this alone does not explain why there were so many more U.S. dollars in existence. The U.S.'s population is about nine times larger, but there were about 17 times more U.S. dollars in existence (in the form of banknotes and coins) than Canadian dollars. We could hypothesize that each U.S. citizen is holding much more paper money than each Canadian citizen, but there doesn't seem to be any evidence of this. Indeed, the typical U.S. citizen doesn't hold many banknotes at all. Look in your wallet. How much money is in there? Probably, there is less than $100 – far less than the $3,398 of banknotes and coins in existence for each person living in the United States. (Businesses hold some too, but typically as little as possible due to risk of theft.) Most Americans use bank checks, credit or debit cards for transactions larger than $60 or so, and direct wire transfers for larger transactions.

If the typical American held as much currency as a typical Canadian, the total dollar banknotes and coins in circulation might be around $547 billion, not $1,067 billion.

This leads people to believe that most of the U.S. dollars in existence are actually outside the U.S. Perhaps 50% or more of the U.S. dollars in the world are somewhere out there, serving as an international currency. Foreign banks hold a significant portion of bank reserves at the Fed. Canadian dollars also serve as an international currency – certainly, there are some Americans who hold a few – but not nearly to such a degree.

It might also mean that, if the Canadian dollar were, for some reason, to become the preferred international currency, instead of the U.S. dollar, then perhaps the number of Canadian dollars in existence would balloon to about $600 billion or so to meet this worldwide demand.

Thus, on the side of supply, we have the monetary base. These are the total number of Canadian dollars in the world. On the side of demand, we have anyone in the world who wants to hold the Canadian dollar, either in the form of a banknote or in the form of bank reserves held at the central bank.

Why does demand exist for these currencies? The "demand" is the desire of a person to physically hold paper banknotes, or, if you are a member bank in the central bank clearing system, the desire to hold bank reserves recorded at the central bank. Look in your wallet. Are there some banknotes there? Why do you hold them? You want some to spend throughout the day. In other words, you want to use them as a tool to facilitate commerce. It's difficult to buy a sandwich for lunch using barter. Maybe you start to feel uncomfortable when the amount of paper money in your wallet drops below $40, and you go to the bank ATM machine and get more. On the other hand, you might feel that $500 in paper cash is too much, and then you go to your bank and deposit it in the bank. In effect, you loan the bank the money.

The bank doesn't store the money – literally paper money – in a vault. The bank also has a certain number of banknotes that it wishes to hold, to meet the needs of its business. If the bank has too few banknotes, it converts some of its bank reserves into paper money. In other words, it sends an order to the Treasury, saying "we want another $1 million dollars in twenties, please." The Federal Reserve deducts $1 million of bank reserves, and $1 million of banknotes are delivered to the bank. On the other hand, if the bank has too much money, it will send the excess money to the Treasury: "Here's $1 million in twenties." The Treasury takes the money, and the bank is credited $1 million in bank reserves at the Federal Reserve. If the bank then holds more bank reserves than it would like – which normally earn no interest – then the bank will either loan the money out or use it to buy some asset, such as a government bond.

The "demand for money" is the result of individual decisions. All paper money, and bank reserves, are held by someone, somewhere. Each person (or corporation or other institution) holds exactly as much as they want. If they have more or less than they want, they can act to rectify the situation. The demand for money can change for all number of reasons, due to the decisions of people to hold more or less currency.

The typical person holding currency in their wallet doesn't react to minute-to-minute changes in markets, or news developments. However, some people do. These are currency traders. Just as is the case for all other monetary transactions, all currency trading is done with base money. Sometimes, on the streets of some cities, this is done with paper currencies. However, for most large institutions, it is done with bank reserves. Let's say that you are a currency trader. At some point, you decide to sell $1 billion, and take the equivalent number of Japanese yen in return. What happens? Probably there is a bank acting as your intermediary. That bank must deliver $1 billion in base money to the buyer. Usually, there is another bank acting as the intermediary for the buyer. Let's say the seller is Person A acting via Bank A, and the buyer is Person B acting via Bank B. Bank A must pay Bank B $1 billion, possibly with paper banknotes, but most likely in the form of a transfer of bank reserves. The bank reserves held by Bank A decline by $1 billion and the bank reserves held by Bank B increase by $1 billion. At the same time, Bank B pays the equivalent sum of yen (probably in the form of bank reserves at the Bank of Japan) to Bank A, credited to Person A's account.

Person A, and consequently Bank A, "decreased their demand" by $1 billion U.S. dollars, for whatever reason, and "increased their demand" for the equivalent amount of yen. Using dollar base money to purchase another currency is inherently no different than using dollar base money to purchase any other good or service. The process is the same.

The value of the currency reflects, not surprisingly, the intersection of this supply and demand. On the one hand, we have the Canadian dollar, which has a relatively small total supply (C$63.5 billion), and a relatively small total demand. On the other hand, we have the U.S. dollar, which has a large supply (US$2,601 billion), and a relatively large demand. The point at which supply and demand intersect for these two currencies, in other words the value, was about the same. They had about the same value in the foreign exchange market.

A modern currency is a paper chit whose supply is limited, and for which there is some demand – the desire for people to hold the currency in their wallet, or in the form of bank reserves. The intersection of this supply, with the demand, produces the value of the currency.

The operating principle behind any kind of stable-value system, in other words a policy of maintaining the currency's value at a fixed rate to some target – which could be gold, another currency, or some other thing – is that the supply of currency (base money) is adjusted on a real-time basis so that the intersection of supply and demand is always at the target value. Supply has to be adjusted continuously, because demand is also changing continuously due to the decisions of people to acquire or disacquire base money, for their individual reasons.

In effect, we are adjusting the scarcity of money so that this paper chit has exactly the value that we want it to have.

When the currency's value is too high (supply is scarce in relationship with demand), then we supply more currency (base money). When the currency's value is too low (supply is excessive in relationship to demand), then we reduce the supply of currency.

Typically, this supply adjustment is accomplished by offering to buy or sell the currency, in unlimited quantity, at or near the parity price. For example, in a gold standard system, the currency issuer may be willing to trade $35 for an ounce of gold, or an ounce of gold for $35. Anyone who wishes to increase their holdings of dollars can go to the currency issuer, deliver an ounce of gold, and receive $35 in return. Anyone wishing to decrease their holdings of dollars can go to the currency issuer, deliver $35, and receive an ounce of gold in return.

In practice, acquirers and disacquirers will net out. Thus, if all acquirers want to increase their holdings of dollar base money by $1,344,457, and all disacquirers want to decrease their holdings of dollar base money by $2,338,973, then, in aggregate, people in general (all people worldwide) wish to reduce their holdings of dollar base money by $994,516. This excess aggregate supply is delivered to the currency issuer, and 28,415 ounces of gold is given in exchange. In this way, the currency issuer reduced the monetary base, or supply of currency, by $994,516, in response to the change in aggregate demand for the currency, at the parity value of $35 per ounce of gold. Obviously, if the currency issuer is willing to trade dollars and gold, in unlimited quantity, at the $35/oz. parity, then the value of the dollar can never deviate meaningfully from its gold parity.

This process is wholly automatic, and involves no decision-making by the currency issuer. The currency issuer never decides that "next month, the monetary base will increase by $10,000,000." Rather, the currency issuer reacts, automatically, to the requests of the market – the world as a whole – to acquire or disacquire base money, for use as a transactional tool.

Does this really work? Yes, it does, and in fact we use this principle all the time. Let's take the example of a gold bullion exchange-traded fund (ETF). This is an investment product that became quite popular throughout the world. The idea is that the ETF, which trades on the stock exchange, will have a value exactly linked to gold bullion.

We will use a specific ETF as an example, the SPDR Gold Shares, which is part of the State Street Global Advisors family of exchange-traded funds. The ticker for this ETF is GLD, on the New York Stock Exchange.

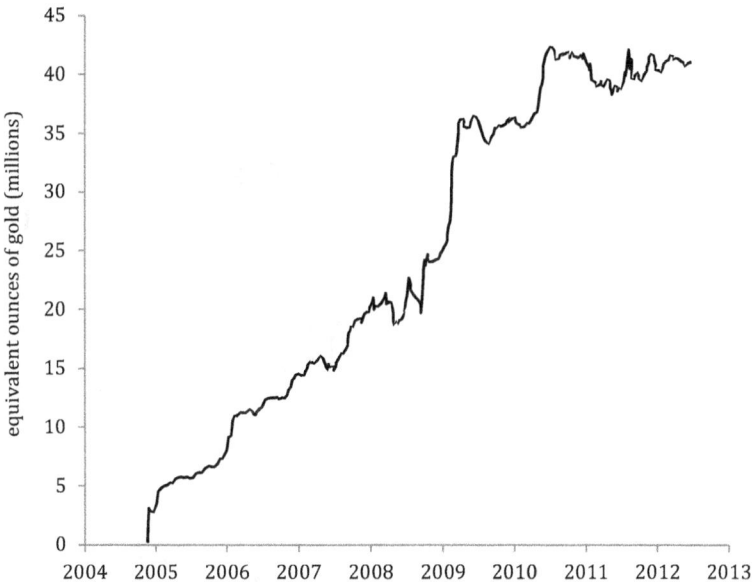

Figure 2.3: SDPR Gold Shares (GLD), Shares Outstanding (equivalent ounces of gold), 2004-2012

How do shares in this ETF (the equivalent of base money) come into existence?

When the value of the ETF is higher than the target parity value vs. gold bullion, the ETF manager sells new shares into the market. The number of shares outstanding expands. Supply increases. When the value of the ETF is lower than its target parity value vs. gold bullion, the ETF manager buys shares in the market. This reduces the number of shares outstanding.

As a result of this mechanism, the daily adjustment of the supply of ETF shares outstanding, the value of the ETF shares in fact tracks the value of gold bullion very closely (Figure 2.3).

If you took the shares of the GLD ETF and made them into paper share certificates (uncommon today but the norm in the 1960s), and you made these paper share certificates into "bearer shares" owned by whoever happened to be holding them (as opposed to most shares today whose ownership is recorded in a register of shareholders), then you would have something very much like a gold-based currency. However, they would be of rather large denomination – each share of GLD has a value that is pegged to approximately one-tenth of an ounce of gold.

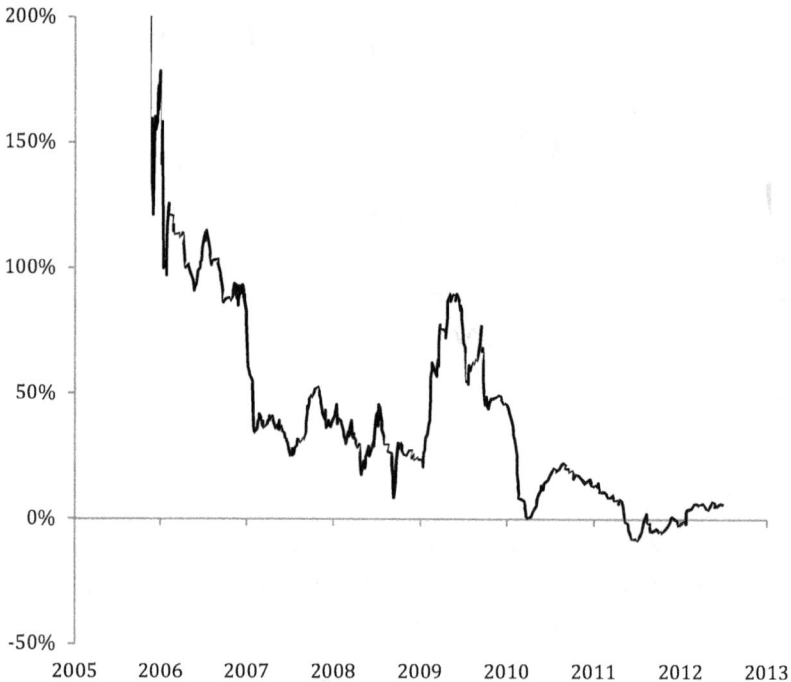

Figure 2.4: Year-on-year growth rate of shares outstanding of the SPDR Gold Shares (GLD), 2005-2012

Soon after the ETF's inception in November 2004, there were shares outstanding equivalent to 3.330 million ounces of gold. As of the end of 2011, there were shares outstanding equivalent to 40.335 million ounces of gold, an increase of about twelve times!

The supply of GLD shares increased by twelve times in the space of seven years. That is a lot. If you were to say to someone that "we have increased our supply of currency by twelve times in the past seven years," that person would probably conclude that the value of the currency collapsed. But that didn't happen at all. The value of GLD did not collapse, it remained exactly linked to gold at the specified parity rate. What happened is that GLD was very popular as an investment product. Thus, the demand for GLD increased by twelve times in seven years. To accommodate this increase in demand, while maintaining the value of GLD at its parity price, the ETF manager increased the supply by the equivalent amount.

Although one might assume that something that becomes so much more plentiful couldn't possibly maintain its value, in fact the dramatic increase in supply is the result of the mechanism by which the ETF maintains its value.

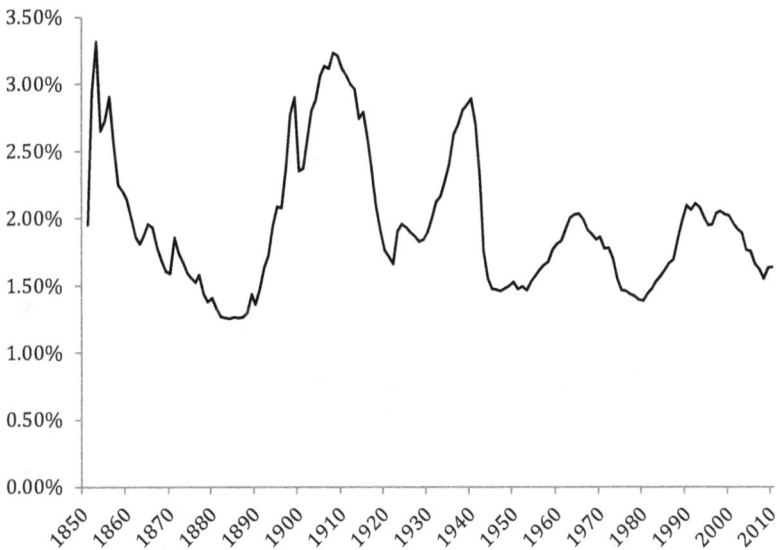

Figure 2.5: Percentage Increase in Aboveground Gold Per Year Due To Mining Production, 1850-2010

43

Indeed, this increase in demand was in part due to the fact that the trust's value was held at the bullion parity, by way of the ETF's daily adjustment of supply. The ETF obviously represented a reliably gold-based instrument, which can be bought and sold in a fashion that is easier and lower in cost than buying and selling gold bullion itself. These are attractive characteristics, which is why the ETF has been so popular than people were willing to hold shares in the fund with a value equivalent of 40.335 million ounces of gold.

What if the manager was incompetent, and the ETF's value varied wildly from its promised parity value? Obviously this is a loose cannon out of control. Demand would plummet, because nobody would want to own such a thing. Oddly enough, the result would be that the shares outstanding wouldn't grow at all, and indeed the trust would probably disappear eventually.

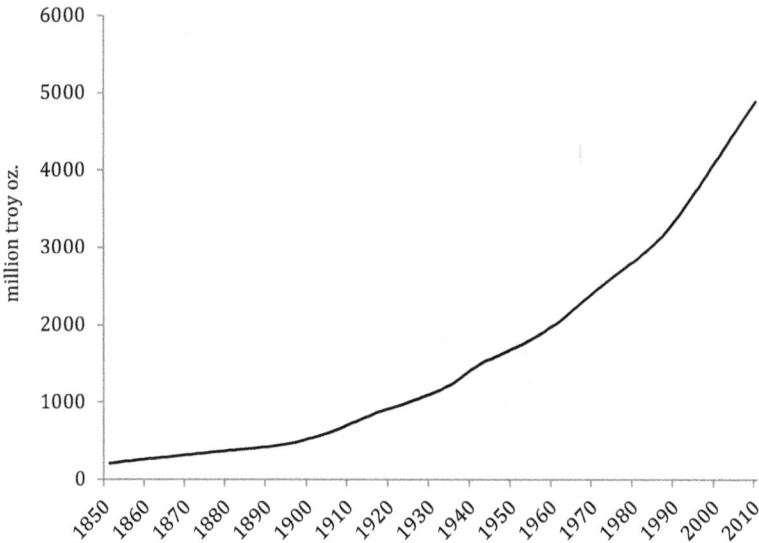

Figure 2.6: Estimated Aboveground World Gold Supply, 1850-2010

Figure 2.4 shows the growth of the shares outstanding in GLD in percentage terms. The shares outstanding had high growth for years, even in excess of 100%, but in late 2010-2012, the growth rate flatlined. Note that the growth rate of the shares outstanding for the SPDR Gold Shares had nothing to do with mining production (Figure 2.5). The amount of gold bullion in the world, during this time, increased about 2% per year from mining. The shares outstanding ("base money supply") of the ETF is related to the demand for the ETF, and the mechanism that matches that demand with supply (the daily adjustment in shares outstanding by the ETF manager), producing the result that the value of the ETF has been reliably fixed to gold bullion.

Let's look at a different ETF, the iShares Gold Trust (ticker IAU). This product is very similar to the SPDR Gold Shares (GLD) exchange-traded fund. However, its history is somewhat different (Figure 2.7).

The shares outstanding of this ETF did not flatline in 2010-2012, but continued to grow at a relatively brisk pace.

The rate of change of the shares outstanding of the iShares Gold Trust (IAU) is not at all linked to the rate of change of the shares outstanding of the SPDR Gold Shares (GLD). Why are they different?

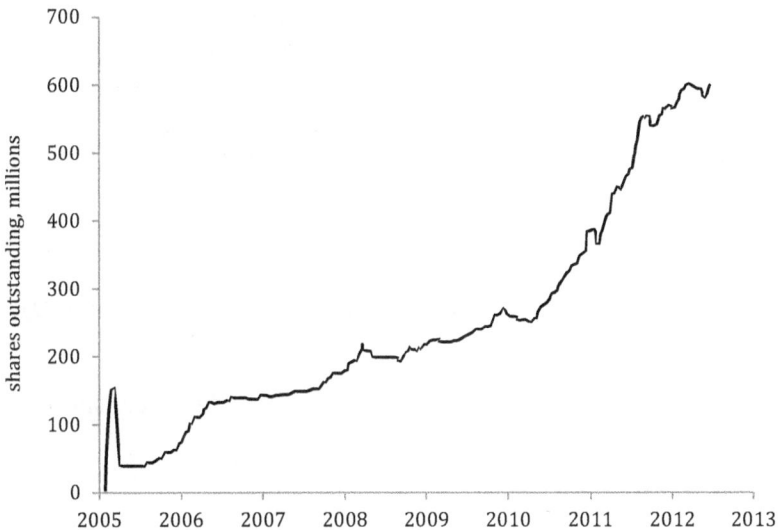

Figure 2.7: iShares Gold Trust (IAU), Shares Outstanding, 2005-2012

The answer is simply that the demand for each item was different. For some reason, in one month, people wanted to buy the SPDR Gold Shares (GLD), and in another month, they wanted to buy the iShares Gold Trust (IAU). Why? It's not important. Demand changes for all number of reasons. The change in the shares outstanding ("base money supply") of one fund or another can be very different, even when they are both reliably linked to gold.

Here we have two very similar exchange-traded funds. Both were based in the United States. Both were designed to have a market value that is linked to gold bullion, and in fact achieved this goal during the time period. In both cases, there were no restrictions of any type on buying or selling, or what could be termed "capital controls." Both operated with a similar mechanism – a daily adjustment of the shares outstanding, to keep the value of the shares in line with its gold parity value.

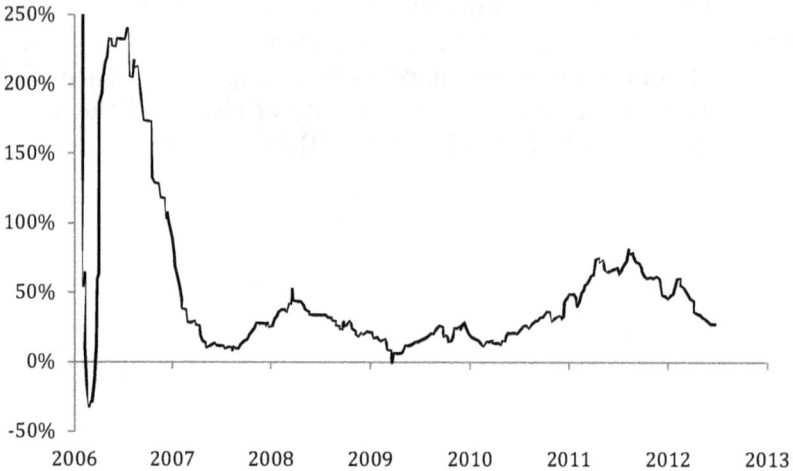

Figure 2.8: Year-on-year Growth Rate of iShares Gold Trust (IAU) Shares Outstanding, 2006-2012

Let's see what it looks like on a day-to-day basis. Figure 2.9 shows the shares outstanding (represented as equivalent ounces of gold) for GLD, on a daily basis, for a six-month period during the second half of 2010.

The shares outstanding changes every day. The trust manages the shares outstanding on a day-to-day basis, to keep the trust's value in line with its gold parity.

Figure 2.10 shows the same time period, for IAU – a very different result! The IAU trust managers also varied the shares outstanding of the trust on nearly a daily basis, although in this case, the result was steady growth rather than the more varied result for GLD. Both funds maintained their promised value parity with gold bullion.

In both cases, the shares outstanding is a residual. There is no committee that meets and decides, "how many shares outstanding shall we have next month?" It is the result of the automatic operating mechanism that keeps the value of the trust in line with its gold parity, by selling shares (thus increasing the shares outstanding) when the trust's value is in excess of the gold parity, and by buying shares (thus reducing the shares outstanding) when the trust's value is below its gold parity.

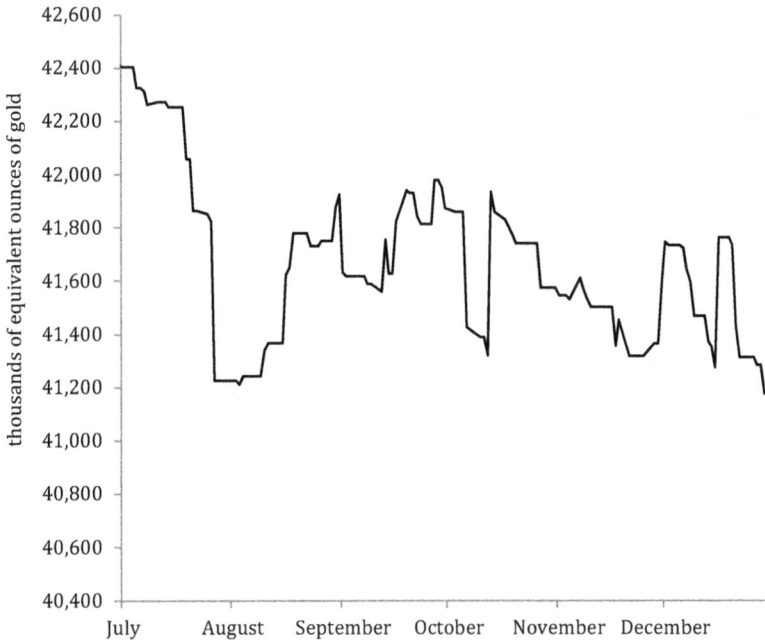

Figure 2.9: SPDR Gold Shares (GLD), Shares Outstanding (equivalent ounces of gold), 2010

On a given day, the gold parity (or net asset value, expressed in dollars) may be computed at $135.50 for the GLD trust. On this day, the trust managers will buy or sell shares, in unlimited quantity, at or near the parity price. In practice, a small "spread" is often used. The manager may agree to sell in unlimited quantity at $135.77 (0.2% over the parity), and also buy shares, in unlimited quantity, at $135.23 (0.2% under the parity). It is easy to see that, if the trust is willing to buy or sell in unlimited quantity at those prices, increasing or reducing the shares outstanding in the process, then the price of the trust cannot vary by more than 0.2% from the parity value. The shares outstanding at the end of the day is the result of the private market's willingness to transact with the trust at those prices.

These two exchange-traded funds are comparable to two different gold-based currencies, such as the U.S. dollar and British pound. The change in the base money supply for dollars can be very different than

47

that of pounds, for the same time period, because the demand for dollars may be very different than the demand for pounds. However, the managers of both currencies use a similar operating mechanism, the daily adjustment of the supply of base money, and both have the same goal, to maintain the value of their currencies at the specified parity value with gold bullion.

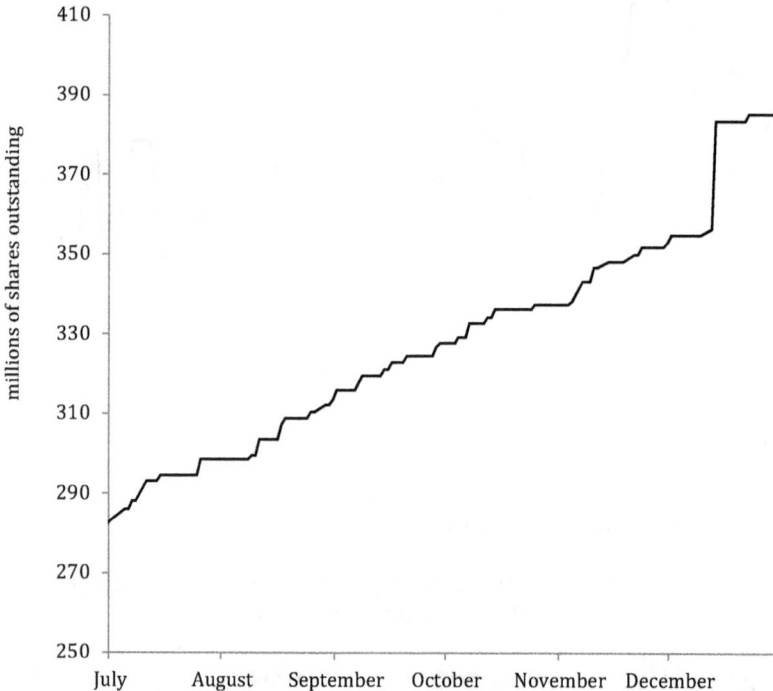

Figure 2.10: iShares Gold Trust (IAU), Shares Outstanding, 2010

One last example is shown in Figure 2.11: the ETFS Physical Gold Shares (SGOL).

Who are the private market buyers and sellers, and owners of these funds? It could be anyone. There is no requirement that the owners be U.S. citizens. These trusts are "international trusts," in the sense that they could be, and in fact are, owned by people and institutions from all over the world. The "demand" for the trust, as an investment vehicle, is a worldwide demand. The shares outstanding, or "supply" of the trust, is a reflection of that worldwide demand. The analogue for a currency is an "international currency," where a large number of the currency holders are foreigners. Any currency is inherently an "international currency," and could potentially be owned by anyone in the world, but in practice most people don't have any interest in owning the domestic junk fiat currencies of most countries. Nobody outside of Costa Rica feels a need to hold the Costa Rican colón, although they could if they wanted to. However, many people worldwide want to hold dollars or euros, and use them in their monetary affairs.

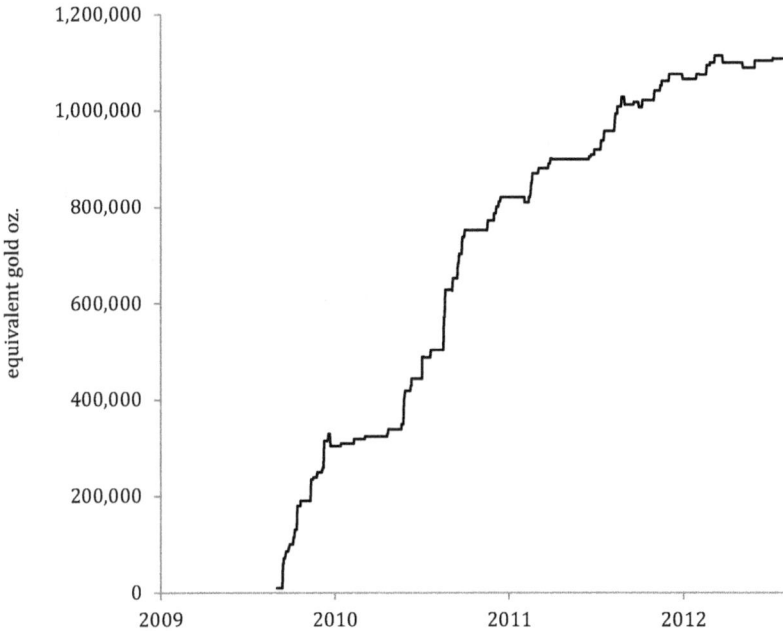

Figure 2.11: ETFS Physical Gold Shares (SGOL), Shares Outstanding (equivalent ounces of gold), 2009-2012

Figure 2.12 shows a chart of Hong Kong dollar base money, for the same time period during the second half of 2010.

Again, the result reflects the daily adjustment of base money supply, the natural outcome of the automatic operating mechanisms of Hong Kong's currency board system. Hong Kong's currency board system works very much like the gold bullion ETFs, and also much like a gold standard system. The only real difference is the target: the Hong Kong dollar's target is the U.S. dollar, and the ETFs' target, or the target of a gold standard system, is gold bullion. Gold bullion is the "standard of value," which is why these are known as "gold standard" systems.

49

The shares outstanding ("base money supply") of these ETFs has nothing to do with the domestic or international production of gold, or exports and imports of gold bullion. Their supply is wholly dependent upon demand for the trusts, as an investment device. Likewise, for a gold standard currency, the base money supply has nothing to do with gold mining production, or imports and exports of gold bullion, but rather demand for the currency as a monetary instrument, a useful tool for transactions.

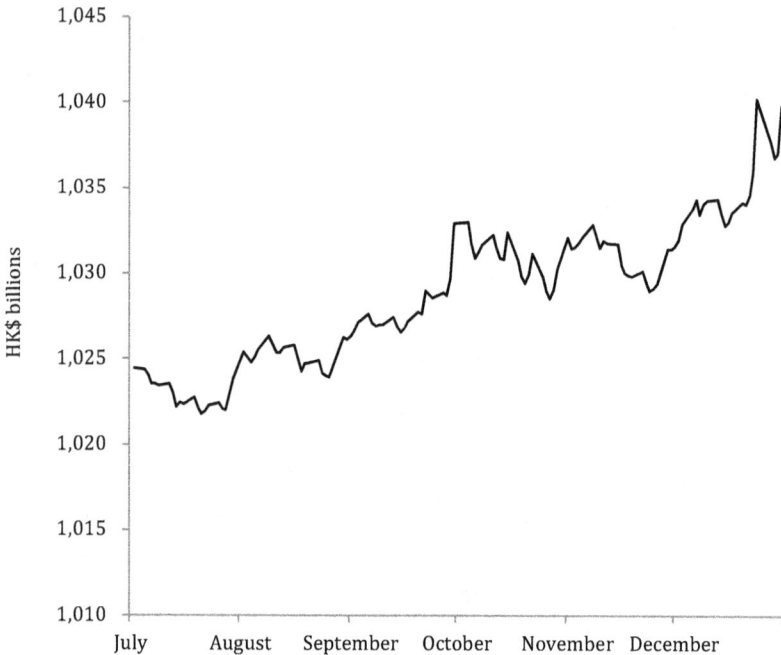

Figure 2.12: Hong Kong: Base Money, 2010

These trusts, in principle at least, are expected to hold a "100% bullion reserve" – in other words, gold bullion of a quantity corresponding to the equivalent shares outstanding. However, a gold standard system can be set up so that this is not a requirement at all. In fact, a "100% reserve" gold standard system has been virtually unheard-of over the past three hundred years.

Instead of a gold bullion ETF, consider a gold-denominated money market fund. This would be a fund that holds short-term debt instruments denominated in gold bullion, just as a dollar money market fund hold short-term debt denominated in dollars. For example, a company could borrow 100,000 ounces of gold, repayable

50

in six months. This is a short-term gold-denominated debt. (Such loans, sometimes called "leases," do exist today but are rather rare, used primarily by gold mining companies.) This debt could be owned by the money market fund, just as money market funds today hold short-term dollar-denominated debt. Interest is paid on the debt.

Instead of a debt denominated in actual gold bullion, the debt could be denominated in a gold-based currency. If the Thai baht were linked to gold at 1,000 baht per ounce, then a corporate debt for 10 million baht would be largely equivalent to a loan for 10,000 ounces of gold. A money-market fund that holds debt denominated in gold-based currency could in fact hold debt denominated in a wide range of currencies, as long as they were all gold-based.

This gold-denominated money market fund could even be synthesized, by using dollar-denominated debt and some form of gold/dollar swap agreement, forward contract, or futures contract.

This gold-denominated money market fund would hold no gold bullion. There is no metal in a vault. However, just as a dollar-denominated money market fund (which holds no dollar base money – dollar bills in a vault or deposits at the Federal Reserve) has a value that is consistently linked to dollars, a gold-denominated money market fund would have a value that is consistently linked to gold. Unlike the gold bullion ETFs, this gold-denominated money market fund would pay interest, because it is earning interest on its gold-denominated short-term loans.

A money market fund's shares outstanding (or assets under management), or its "supply," is, once again, determined by investors' desire to either invest or disinvest in the money market fund. It is determined by the "demand" for the fund among investors. Likewise, a dollar money market fund's "supply" or assets under management would rise and fall as a residual of investors' investment or disinvestment in the fund.

The shares outstanding of our gold ETFs, or gold-denominated money market funds, has nothing to do with economic conditions directly, such as GDP growth rates, unemployment, various price measures such as the Consumer Price Index, "purchasing power parity", balance of payments conditions, the trade deficit or current account deficit, savings rates, interest rates, government fiscal policy, tax policy, imports or exports of gold bullion into or out of the United States, or a dozen other things that could be named. All of these things may alter demand for the fund – in other words, investors' desire to invest or disinvest in the fund – but since virtually anything could potentially change investors' demand for the fund, there is no reason to single out specific influences.

There is no "price-specie flow mechanism." This is often found in college textbooks' description of historical gold standard systems. It doesn't exist.

The rate of change of shares outstanding in these ETFs can be very rapid. Often, the growth in shares outstanding over a year has been in excess of 50% or even 100%. This is because demand for the fund grew commensurably over that same time period, and the fund's managers accommodated that demand by increasing supply, at the specified gold parity.

Although the gold ETFs described have not yet had a long-term contraction in shares outstanding, the shares outstanding may contract rapidly over a short period. For example, between September 29, 2010 and January 25, 2011, the shares outstanding of the GLD fund declined by 5.8%, or an annualized rate of 23%.

If this was a currency, the currency managers might have some nervousness about seeing the monetary base increase by 50% over a year, or decline at a 23% annualized rate. People have the notion that the base money supply should grow at a slow, stable, single-digit rate. Also, some people assume that such dramatic changes in base money supply must have equally dramatic consequences for the economy as a whole.

This is not the case at all. The changes in the base money supply (shares outstanding in the case of an ETF) are the outcome of the mechanism that maintains the value of the currency at the specified gold parity. The purpose of the mechanism is to maintain a stable currency value. If the currency value is stable, as promised, then there will be no dramatic economic effects. If you were an investor in the GLD fund, you would notice no dramatic effects from these huge changes in shares outstanding. The important thing for you is that the fund's value maintains its proper gold parity. If you were capable of using GLD shares in payment, in effect using them as money, their usefulness as a monetary means of transaction would be unaffected by these dramatic changes in supply, as long as the value remained linked to gold bullion as promised. Likewise, users of a currency are not alarmed at all by such dramatic changes in base money outstanding, and indeed would hardly know that they exist. Very large changes in supply, arising from the normal and correct operation of an ETF or gold standard system that is being properly managed, are of little concern. However, very small changes in value, compared to the gold parity target, might be a sign that the ETF or gold standard system is not being operated properly, and are thus a matter of great concern. Large changes in value, compared to the parity target, are cause for panic.

* * *

Often, an economy will have a slow, stable increase in base money with a gold standard system, typically reflecting the rise in nominal GDP. However, at other times, the supply and demand for a currency can vary wildly. For example, it is quite common to see very dramatic increases in base money supply when a currency goes from being perceived as low-quality to being perceived as higher-quality. This might mean going from a floating fiat currency to a gold standard system, or perhaps simply from being a low-quality floating fiat currency to a better-quality floating fiat currency.

For example, the Russian ruble suffered a catastrophic fall in value in 1998. In 2000, the ruble's value was stabilized again (Figure 2.13).

From 2000 to 2007, the ruble's value was quite stable vs. the U.S. dollar, even showing a persistent rising trend. During this period, the ruble monetary base was growing at a brisk clip, averaging about a 35% increase per year (Figure 2.14).

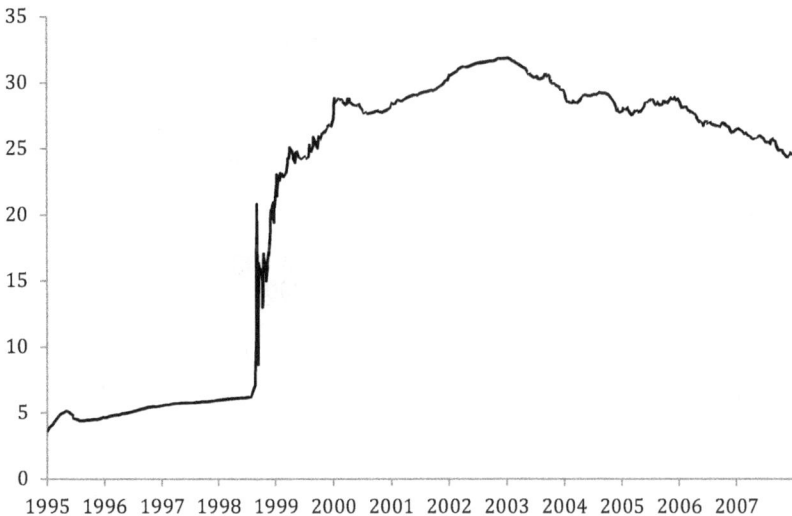

Figure 2.13: Russia: Rubles per U.S. Dollar, 1995-2007

How was it that the ruble monetary base could increase by a whopping 35% per annum, for year after year in 2000-2007, but the currency didn't lose value? The answer was that the ruble had been largely abandoned during the 1998 crisis. Russians didn't want to use rubles. As the currency became more stable and reliable, and as the economy expanded, people wanted to hold more and more rubles. The central bank accommodated this increase in demand with an increase in supply, such that the currency's value remained stable vs. the dollar. The currency became more popular, just as the gold bullion ETFs' shares outstanding grew dramatically as they became popular.

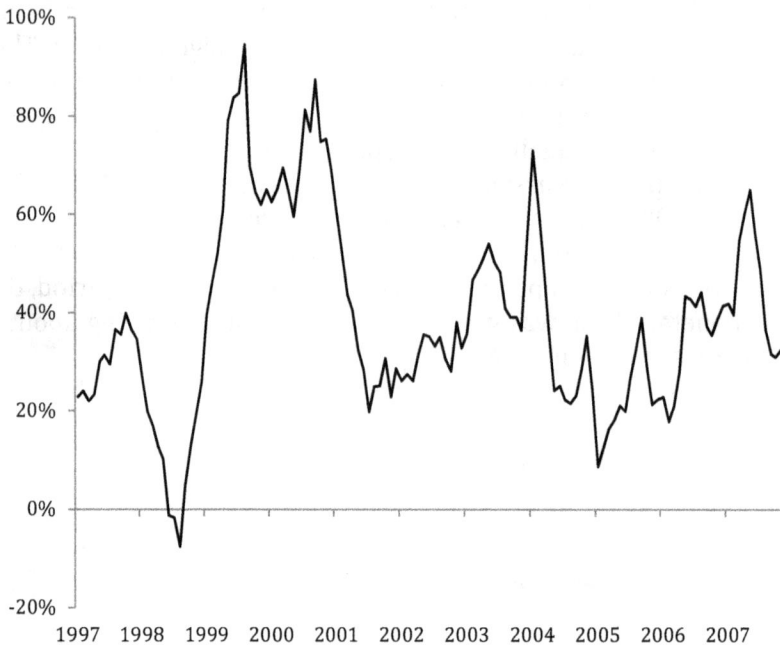

Figure 2.14: Russia: Year-On-Year Percentage Change in the Monetary Base, 1997-2007

In late 1998, the ruble's value collapsed by about a factor of five, from 5/dollar to 25/dollar (Figure 2.15). Did the monetary base also increase by a factor of five? Actually, it hardly changed at all from a year earlier (Figure 2.14). The collapse in value was mostly due to a collapse in demand, in turn motivated by the fact that the ruble's value was falling quickly with no effective response by the currency manager. The analogy to a gold bullion ETF is if the market value of the shares fell dramatically compared to the promised bullion parity.

Seeing that the ETF was not being managed properly, people would sell the shares aggressively, thus "reducing their demand" for the shares. The ETF would become very unpopular.

Most of the devaluation took place by the end of 1998. There was a little more slippage during 1999, and then stabilization in 2000 (Figure 2.15).

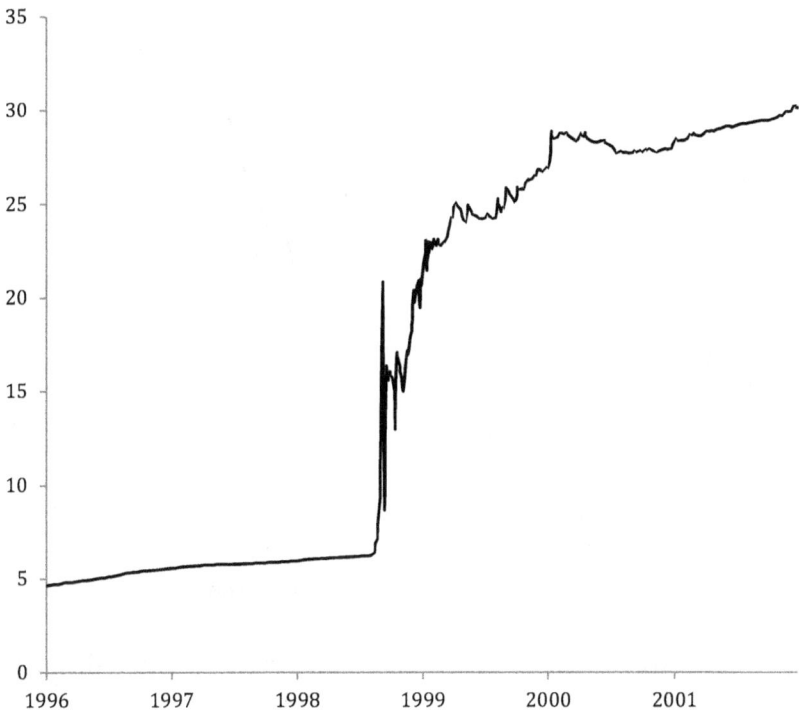

Figure 2.15: Russia: Rubles per U.S. Dollar, 1996-2001

However, the monetary base had little to no growth in 1998, with only a small expansion towards the end of the year. In 2000 and 2001, when the ruble's value was stabilized, the monetary base had immense growth (Figure 2.16).

The interplay between the supply and demand of a currency can be quite complex, and often does not at all follow a simple linear relationship, or expectations based on rudimentary understanding.

Dramatic reductions in base money supply are less common. One reason might be that a currency is perceived as being at risk. The government might talk about devaluing the currency, or perhaps the government is at risk of default on its debt. Naturally, people would be less willing to hold such a currency, and thus demand shrinks.

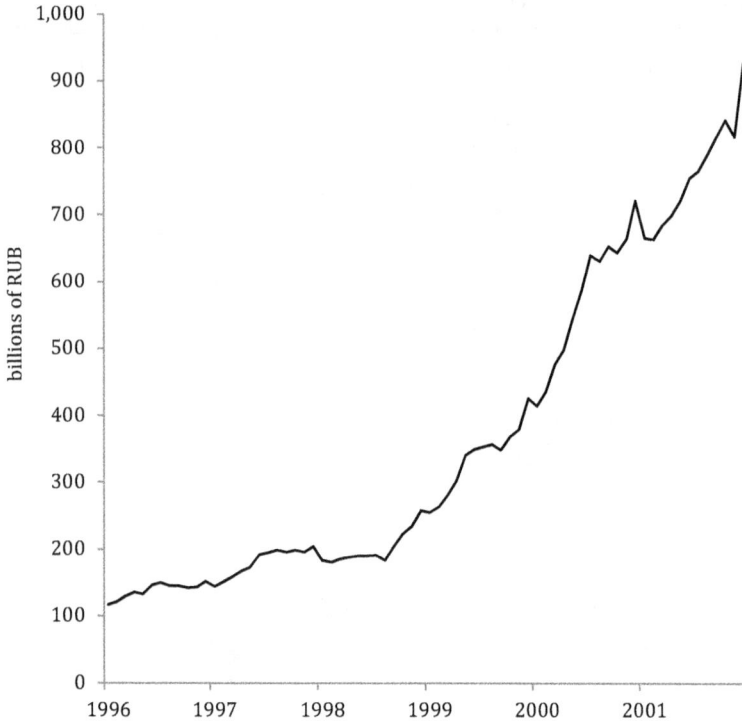

Figure 2.16: Russia: Monetary Base, 1996-2001

A gold standard system in operation would respond to this shrinkage of demand by shrinking supply, just as a gold bullion ETF would react by shrinking shares outstanding (or assets under management). Many people would be nervous that such a dramatic shrinkage of the monetary base would have economic consequences, but again, that is not the case. If the currency remains at its gold parity, there would be no particular economic consequences. Indeed, the reason to shrink the supply is to avoid the economic consequences that would ensue if supply were not adjusted properly. If demand declined dramatically, without a consequent shrinkage in supply, the value of the currency would fall below its gold parity. This would alarm people, and demand would shrink even further as it became apparent that the currency managers had abdicated their responsibility to maintain the gold standard parity by way of proper supply adjustment. The currency would plunge further, with all the usual negative results.

When a government starts to talk about devaluing the currency, perhaps in hopes that it will help resolve an unemployment problem, or a problem of overindebtedness among some group of voters, or is in danger of defaulting on its debt, that creates a general crisis atmosphere which is very bad for business. This could be blamed on the shrinkage in the monetary base resulting from the normal operations of the gold standard mechanism. However, the actual reason is the threat of destructive government policy.

In 1933, the U.S. dollar was devalued from $20.67/oz. to $35/oz. This took place at a steady pace throughout the year of 1933 (Figure 2.17).

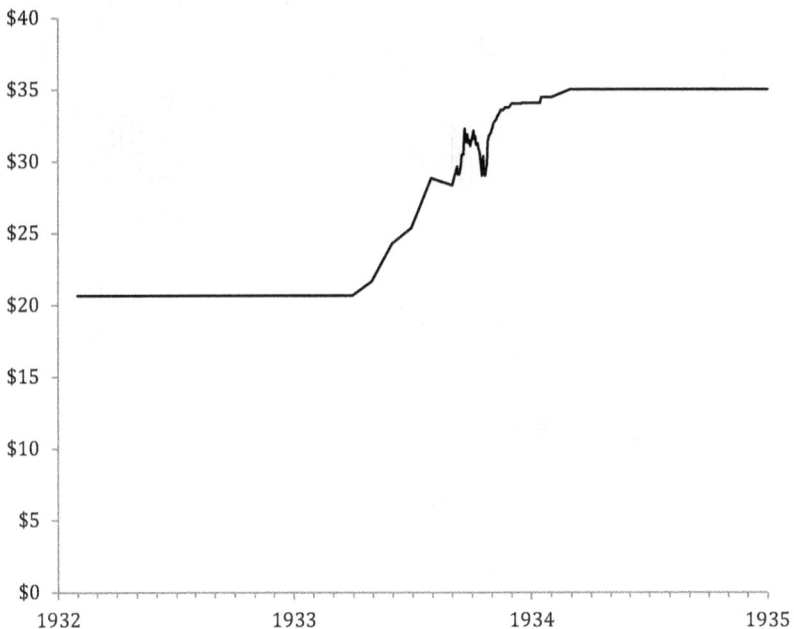

Figure 2.17: U.S.: Dollars per Ounce of Gold, 1932-1934

However, the dollar monetary base did not expand much during 1933 (Figure 2.18). The fall in the value of the dollar came via the decline in demand for a currency that was being devalued.

In 1934, the monetary base began to expand again, after the dollar was repegged to gold at $35/oz. near the beginning of the year. Why? Probably, people saw that the dollar was being managed with a gold standard system again, instead of being devalued into oblivion or remaining as a chaotic floating currency (as had happened to the

British pound a few years earlier). This made the currency more popular, and the automatic mechanisms of the gold standard system naturally accommodated this increase in demand. (Demand also increased because the dollar had a lower value, and thus it took more of them to buy things.)

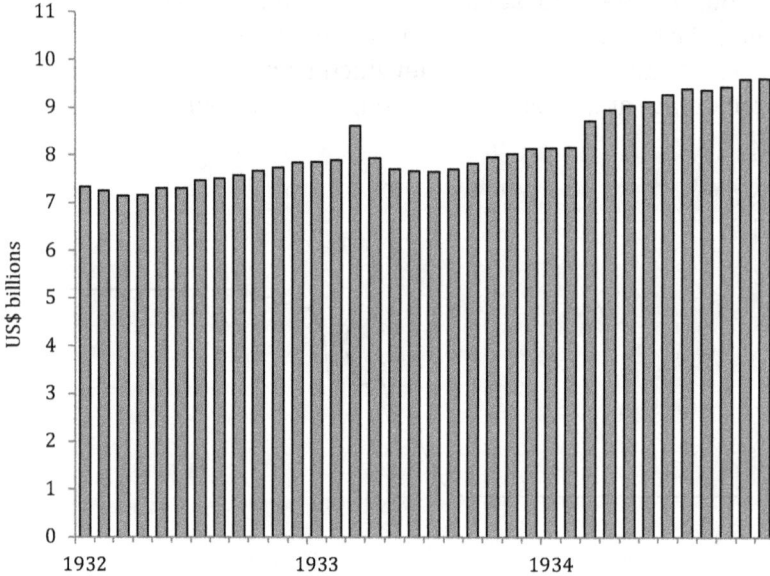

Figure 2.18: U.S.: Monetary Base, 1932-1934

An even more dramatic example comes from the German hyperinflation of 1920-1923. Figure 2.19 shows the beginning stages of this event, ignoring for now the clownish "billion mark banknote" period of 1923.

In Figure 2.19, the total German mark base money supply of 1913 (annual average) is normalized at 1.00. The value of the paper mark, compared to its prewar gold parity, is also normalized at 1.00. In January of 1919, after the war's end, total base money had expanded by 5.69x compared to its 1913 average, but the value of the mark had fallen such that it took 1.95 paper marks to buy a gold mark (or the equivalent amount of gold bullion). Thus, the value of the paper mark was slowly cut in half over five years, a modest depreciation (13% per year on average) that most Germans were probably barely aware of, especially with the concerns of wartime at the forefront. The British pound had a similar decline in value during the same period.

Between January 1919 and February 1920, the mark's value collapsed. This was related to the signing of the Treaty of Versailles in June 1919, which committed the German government to unpayable reparations expenses. In February 1920, it took 23.6 paper marks to buy the amount of gold bullion equivalent to one prewar gold mark. In other words, the value of the paper mark collapsed by a factor of twelve in this fourteen-month period.

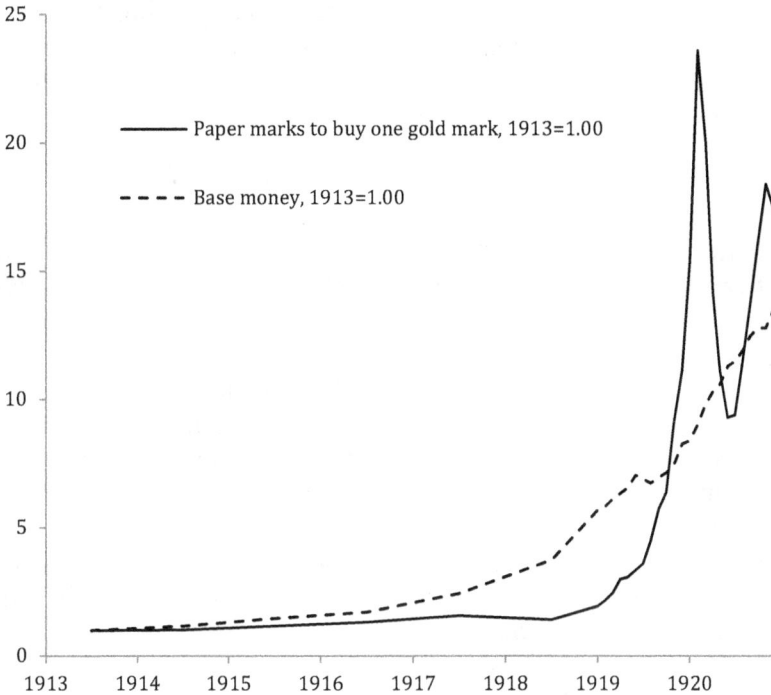

Figure 2.19: Germany: Value of Paper Mark and Base Money, 1913-1920

However, during this period, the monetary base expanded by only 58%. This is still a large number, but it is not that much more than the roughly 38%-per-year expansion of the monetary base from 1913 to early 1919, which did not have any catastrophic consequences.

Then, in 1920, the paper mark's value exploded higher, such that in June 1920 it took 9.3 paper marks to buy the gold bullion equivalent to a prewar gold mark – more than doubling in value from its February 1920 lows. However, the monetary base continued to expand during this time. In 1921, the hyperinflation properly began. The mark ended that year at only 1/45th of its prewar value.

* * *

We have been looking at things from something of a "stock" perspective – the total demand for a currency and the total supply. The same issues can be looked at from a "flow" perspective. On any given day, some people will want to sell their shareholdings in a gold ETF (their individual demand is shrinking), and other people will want to buy shares in the fund (their individual demand is growing). Of course, they expect to do this transaction at or very near the fund's gold parity value.

One day, sellers want to sell 500,000 shares in the fund, and buyers want to buy 800,000 shares in the fund, assuming a transaction price at the parity value. The sellers sell 500,000 shares to the buyers. This leaves buyers who want to buy an additional 300,000 shares in the fund.

If the trust did not alter the shares outstanding on a daily basis, these buyers could only be satisfied by somehow finding people willing to sell an additional 300,000 shares to them. This would be done by bidding a higher price. At perhaps 2% over the parity value, either more sellers would appear or buyers would leave the market, unwilling to pay the higher price. The market would "clear," with buyers and sellers balancing. However, as a result, the trust's share price would rise beyond its gold parity value. In this case, the clearing of the market, or balancing of buyers and sellers, is achieved by a change in price, or deviation from the parity value.

This is how most markets work. Typically, a corporation has a fixed number of equity shares outstanding (at least in the short term). The market price of the stock goes up and down to a point at which the number of buyers and sellers match. The same is true of heads of lettuce; on a given day or week, the number of heads of lettuce available for sale is fixed, and the price moves up or down to the point at which the numbers of buyers and sellers match. The market clears. An attempt to "control prices" by some sort of regulation or coercion results in a market that does not clear. Eventually, buyers, who still want to buy but not at the mandated price, and sellers, who still want to sell but not at the mandated price, find some other way to do so.

In the case of the ETF, the trust managers step in, on a daily basis, to resolve this imbalance. The trust managers are willing to sell the additional 300,000 shares desired by the buyers, at the promised gold parity. Thus, supply matches demand at the parity value, by way of a change in the number of shares outstanding. The clearing of the market is achieved by a change in supply, or shares outstanding, rather than a change in price.

Quite a lot can be learned by thinking through how these gold bullion ETFs operate. They are directly analogous to how gold standard currency systems operate. From there, consider the operations of a gold-denominated or gold-based-currency-denominated money market fund – similar gold-based investment products that do not hold any gold bullion. Historically there has been a lot of variation in how gold standard currency systems are set up. However, they all have the same policy goal, which is to keep the value of the currency at its gold parity target. They also have the same basic operating principle, which is a daily adjustment of supply, to match demand at the parity price.

Chapter 3:
The United States' Experience with a Gold
Standard System

When the United States was formed in 1789, it was not particularly apparent that the country would become the most successful of the 19th and 20th centuries. The former colonies had been wracked by eight years of war with the British. The currency, the Continental Dollar, had collapsed in hyperinflation. The government that issued it, the Continental Congress, itself proved to be unviable, going through three incarnations in only fifteen years. Appalled by the collapse of their fiat paper currency, the Founding Fathers insisted that, henceforth, the U.S. government would get out of the money-printing business, its activities limited only to minting standardized full-weight gold and silver coins as a public service.

The Coinage Act of 1792 established the value of the dollar to be equivalent to either 371.25 grains of pure silver, or 24.75 grains of pure gold. The system was bimetallic. Both gold and silver were used as currency.

Coins were alloyed with 10% copper to increase durability, known as "standard" gold or silver for coin use. In terms of troy ounces, the gold value of the dollar was $19.39/oz. The ratio between gold and silver was set at 15:1, reflecting the market values of the metals at the time.

The Act set forth a punishment for anyone who attempted to change the value of the currency:

Section 19. And be it further enacted, That if any of the gold or silver coins which shall be struck or coined at the said mint shall be debased or made worse as to the proportion of the fine gold or fine silver therein contained, ... every such officer or person who shall commit any or either of the said offenses, shall be deemed guilty of felony, and shall suffer death.

The population of the United States in 1790 was 3.9 million people, not counting Native Americans. The population of the United Kingdom in 1801 was 10.5 million, and the population of France in 1801 was 29.4 million. The largest cities in the United States were towns by European standards. New York had 33,131 people in 1790. Philadelphia had 28,522. Boston had 18,320. Newport, Rhode Island had 6,716.

Greater London had 1,011,157 people in 1801. Paris had 546,856 within the central city in 1801, and more within Greater Paris. Compared to the great capitals of Europe, with their cathedrals and accumulated grandeur of centuries, the United States was barely more than a string of campsites on the edge of wilderness. In France in 1789, king Louis XVI was culminating centuries of rule by some of the most opulent and grandiose aristocrats in European history. Mozart soared above the music world of Vienna; his beloved opera *The Magic Flute* was completed in 1791. The young Beethoven moved to Vienna in 1792.

Despite this modest beginning, the new United States had the Magic Formula: Low Taxes and Stable Money. Capitalist countries that follow this formula tend to do extraordinarily well, and the United States embodied this ideal to an extent hardly seen in all of history. The Revolutionary War was, in large part, inspired by the desire to escape British taxation. Many who migrated to the American colonies had fled the oppressive taxes of various European states. In the Americas they could live nearly tax-free. For the entirety of the nineteenth century, until the legalization of the income tax in 1913, the U.S. Federal government funded itself from import tariffs. (This system still exists in some Caribbean financial havens, where the primary form of taxation is import tariffs.)

In 1789, only adventurous hunters and trappers crossed the crest of the Appalachians. In 1775, Daniel Boone traversed the Cumberland Gap and established the first settlement in Kentucky. Further western settlement was delayed during the war years. Most of the North American continent was officially owned by France and Spain. The first official traverse of the continent had to wait until 1804, when the Lewis and Clark expedition set off for the Pacific. The expedition was commissioned by Thomas Jefferson to explore the Louisiana Purchase, which he bought from Napoleon in 1803. (Napoleon needed the money to put down an uprising in Haiti, and wanted extra funds to prepare an invasion of Britain.) Lands west of the Louisiana Purchase were not officially added to the United States until the 1840s.

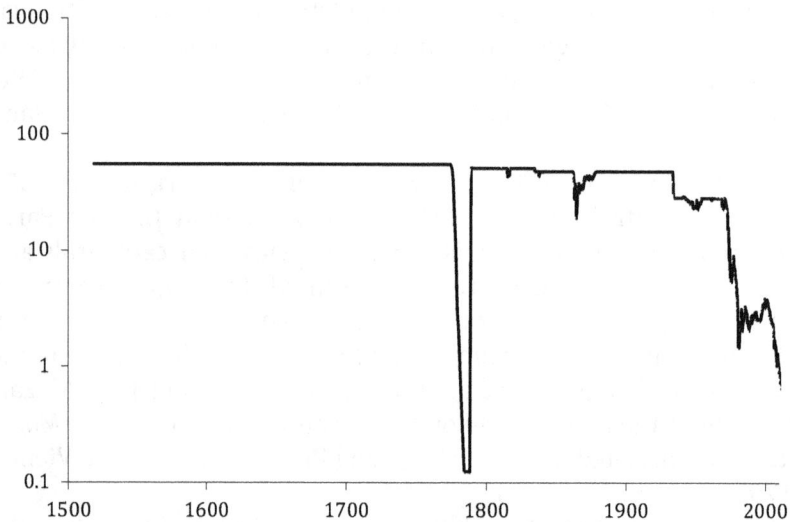

Figure 3.1: Value of 1000 "Thalers" in Gold Oz., 1513-2010
logarithmic scale

The economy of the new United States was based primarily on subsistence agriculture. Trade consisted mostly of crude natural resources, such as furs, timber, fish, and tobacco, which were exported to Europe. Some had become wealthy on the resource trade; many of these fortunes were lost in the years of war and hyperinflation. As the United States began, the majority of Americans, to European eyes, were barely better off than the primitives with whom they shared the continent. The black slaves were worse off.

What we know today as the "dollar" originated in the Joachimsthal region of Germany as a silver coin in the year 1518. This standardized silver coin became popular throughout Europe, issued by many mints and governments, but all "thaler" coins contained the same amount of silver. Europe was on a "thaler standard" long before the United States was formed. One of the most common forms of thaler coins, especially among the American colonies, was the Spanish thaler, sourced from the silver mines of Mexico. This Spanish-made thaler became the template for the U.S. dollar (Figure 3.1). Until the mid-1870s, silver and gold traded reliably in a ratio of about 15 or 16 to 1. Both silver and gold coins were used, primarily gold for larger denominations and silver for smaller, known as a "bimetallic" system. Thus, a silver basis was functionally equivalent to a gold basis, as a standard of value, and thaler/dollar coinage was an effective gold standard system from its inception in 1518. The original German thaler was a common element in the German coinage system until 1907.

In 1834, the official value of the dollar, in terms of gold, was adjusted slightly downward to reflect the fact that silver's value was slightly lower than the official 15:1 ratio established in the Coinage Act of 1792. The effect of this was to make gold more prominent within the bimetallic system. The new gold parity was 23.2 grains of gold per dollar, or $20.67 per ounce. The new official silver/gold ratio was 16:1. The United States officially adopted a "monometallic" gold-only system in the Gold Standard Act of 1900. Silver coins officially became token coins, much like our base metal coins today whose contained metal value is generally less than their face value. The U.S. was somewhat laggard in this; Britain adopted a monometallic gold-only system in 1816.

During the gold standard era in U.S. history, 1789 to 1971, the U.S. government deviated from gold standard principles on two major occasions (Figure 3.2). One was during the Civil War, when the Federal government printed United States Notes (paper money), also known as "greenbacks," to pay for war expenses. By the end of the war, the dollar's value was about half of its prewar gold parity. After the war's end, a long period of correction ensued, and the dollar was officially returned to a gold standard system in 1879, at the prewar parity of $20.67/oz.

The second exception was a devaluation of the dollar in 1933, from $20.67/ounce to $35/oz. The gold standard system was reinstated in 1934, and continued as official policy until 1971.

Three minor episodes are worth noting. During the War of 1812, the combination of a suspension of redeemability, and the introduction of Treasury Notes by the Federal government as a funding strategy, led to an episode of dollar weakness, particularly among Southern banks. This was remedied after the war's end, in the 1817-1819 period. During World War I, the Treasury pressured the then-new Federal Reserve to help finance large deficits with the printing press. Federal Reserve Notes flooded forth. Redeemability was suspended, and the dollar's value dropped from its gold parity. This deviance was corrected in the 1920-21 period, and the value of the dollar returned again to its $20.67/oz. parity. Lastly, during World War II and some time afterwards, the Treasury again pressured the Federal Reserve to cap interest rates and allow easier funding of very large wartime deficits. When the war ended and the budget deficits disappeared, the Fed remedied this gold parity deviation again, particularly following an accord with the Treasury in 1951.

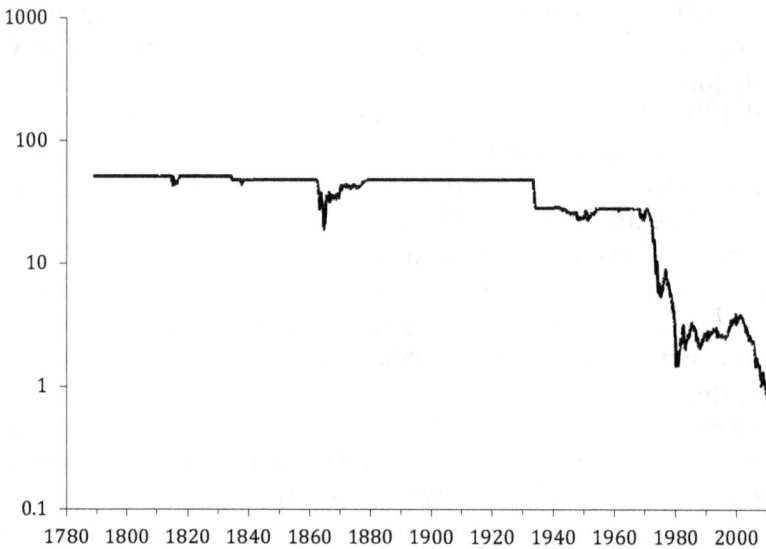

Figure 3.2: U.S.: Value of $1000 in Gold Oz., 1789-2012
logarithmic scale

In 1900, the population of the United States had reached 76.2 million. The continent had been settled from one coast to another, forming a contiguous state larger than any except for the empire of Russia. The original thirteen states had grown to forty-five. The United States had, more than any other country, imitated and expanded upon the Industrial Revolution that began in Britain. Britain was still the leader of the European world, presiding over a globe-spanning empire of unprecedented reach. British-style capitalism, British banking, British monetary management, British industrial innovation, British law, British scholarship, and British statesmanship were the examples the rest of the world imitated. (Germany, France and Italy retained their

66

leadership in the fields of fine art, artisanal crafts, cuisine, and other niceties of civilization.) The British pound was the world's premier international currency.

British ideals found even more ardent expression in the former British colonies of North America. The minimally aware observer could see that the United States, once considered an "emerging market," was in the process of surpassing Britain by most measures of economic development. Based on the crude estimates of GDP available today, the annual per-capita GDP of the British citizen was 11.77 ounces of gold in 1900. The per-capita GDP of the U.S. citizen was 13.08 ounces of gold. The population of Britain in 1901 was 30.5 million. Greater London had expanded to 6.2 million. New York was home to 3.4 million. However, the United States still took a subsidiary role in world affairs, content, for the most part, to follow the British and European example. The British Royal Navy ruled the seas, while the United States' navy ranked fifth in the number of ships. London reigned as the world's premier financial center. A milestone for New York's rising prominence was marked when, in 1904 and 1905, the duty of raising money for a series of large loans for the government of Japan was split evenly between London and New York firms.

By 1970, the United States dominated world affairs to a degree not seen since the empire of Rome. On a global basis, its influence was unprecedented. British and European leadership in virtually all matters had transferred to the United States. The U.S. dollar was the premier international currency. U.S.-style capitalism was the model for the world (although many intellectuals preferred the Soviet Union or Cuba). U.S. banking, U.S. monetary management, U.S. industrial innovation, U.S. law, U.S. scholarship, and U.S. statesmanship were the examples the whole world followed. To the dismay of many sophisticates, the world also embraced U.S. music, fine arts, popular crafts, architecture and fashion. The creative mind of United States industry seemed a fountain of incredible miracles: Telephones, radio, electricity, television, refrigerators, synthetic fibers, plastics, transistors, vaccines, and antibiotics flowed forth from U.S. factories, into the hands of the swelling middle class. American men walked on the moon. Buildings scraped the sky. Superhighways crisscrossed the land. Nuclear energy promised to be so abundant that it would be "too cheap to meter." Average middle-class families took vacations via jet airplanes, owned multiple automobiles, watched color television, expanded their houses, and lived in a state of material opulence unimaginable to the overworked factory laborers of 1900. Academics discussed the "end of work;" projecting trends twenty or fifty years into the future, there seemed nothing else to do but enjoy more free time. The U.S. was described as the center of a soft empire that included Western Europe itself, all of Latin America, Japan, the Philippines, and other parts of Asia. Large U.S. military bases sat quietly in nominally-independent countries worldwide. The United States alone accounted for 35% of world GDP. U.S. annual per capita GDP had risen to an astonishing 140.9 ounces of gold. (It was the highest the U.S. ever achieved.) Britain's per-capita GDP in 1970 was 63.7 ounces, not even half that of the U.S.

The United States had followed the principle of a gold standard for 181 years. During that time, it evolved from a not-very-promising experiment in government among a handful of unruly subsistence farmers, to the most powerful, wealthy and successful country in the history of the planet. Which brings up the question: if a gold standard system is a path to economic disaster, as so many Mercantilist economists claim today, how did that happen?

* * *

One of the best indicators of monetary and macroeconomic conditions is the yield on long-term government bonds (Figure 3.3).

Reflecting general distrust of the new United States – the Continental Congress had hyperinflated its war debts away – yields on U.S. Treasury bonds were rather high for the time. Yields around 6% in 1800 were roughly three percentage points above typical bond yields for the highest-quality gold-based debt, around 3.25%, as was to be the case for British bonds throughout the 19th century.

The dollar devaluation of the Civil War unsettled bondholders, but after the war's end in 1865, Congress was clearly intending to bring the dollar's value back to its prewar parity. This made Treasury bonds a nice speculation; not only was a 6% yield quite good for a bond eventually linked to gold, but it could be bought with devalued dollars, which were expected to rise in value (and did).

The reinstatement of the gold standard in 1879 confirmed bond bulls' hopes. By this point, the United States was a growing industrial powerhouse, which had retained its commitment to gold standard principles even after a catastrophe like the Civil War. The risk premium collapsed, and until World War I, yields on U.S. Treasury bonds were in line with the world's best credit, the British government's Consol bond.

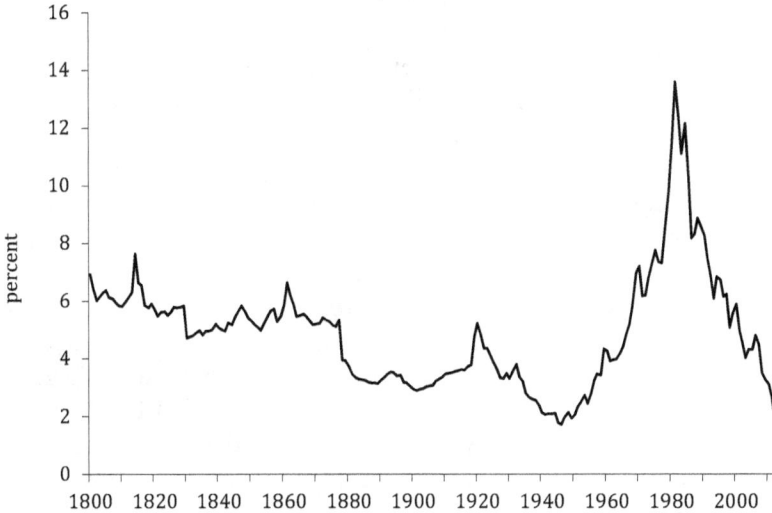

Figure 3.3: U.S.: Average Annual Yield on Ten-Year Treasury Bond, 1800-2012

The Great Depression and the outbreak of World War II drove yields to extraordinarily low levels, as investors everywhere (including Europe) sought to avoid risk by any means possible. Although the dollar was devalued in 1933, it nevertheless remained the most reliable currency in the world. The British pound was devalued in 1931, but it did not return to a gold standard system, and essentially floated until 1944.

During the 1950s and 1960s, government bond yields rose steadily. They had fallen to extremely low levels in 1949, a year of recession in the United States and a rather bad year worldwide, as China fell to communism and both Germany and Japan were consumed in hyperinflation. Risk-aversion, by now a habit after twenty years of turmoil, was investors' primary interest. The bountiful 1950s and 1960s led investors toward business expansion rather than risk avoidance. However, the Bretton Woods commitment to a gold standard was always rather weak, as Mercantilist money-manipulation ideas became more and more prominent. Already by 1960, many people felt the conflict between Classical and Mercantilists principles would lead to a breakup of the system. This indeed happened in 1971, so it is no surprise that, anticipating eventual currency devaluation, government bond yields continued to rise during the 1960s to quite high levels.

Particularly after the resumption of the gold standard in 1879, and until World War I, the United States enjoyed a wonderful time when yields on long-term government bonds (and, by extension, high-quality private-sector debt) were extremely low, around 3.25%, and also extremely stable. The volatility of bond yields was, by today's standards, nearly nonexistent. The market recognized that gold indeed served as a superlative standard of stable value – that it was money *par excellence*, as Karl Marx wrote in 1867. Currency stability in turn engendered economic stability, and provided the reliable foundation for all financial and economic activity.

After World War I, neither the United States nor the rest of the world ever enjoyed the kind of placid monetary environment that had existed pre-1914. The final rupture in 1971 followed 57 years compromised by war and Mercantilist influence, when the Classical principles of the pre-1914 world gold standard were never again implemented with the same clarity, commitment and discipline.

* * *

It is often said that there were more, and more difficult, recessions during the gold standard years than under today's Mercantilist floating currency arrangement. It should be no surprise that such claims are made; the whole purpose of Mercantilist monetary policy is to resolve recessions, and the Mercantilists are eager to promote the idea that their system is superior to the Classical alternative.

Today's official arbiter of recession, the National Bureau of Economic Research, provides dates of recessions back to 1854. When reviewing this record, it must always be remembered that today's economic statistics, from government agencies staffed by tens of thousands of employees, mostly did not exist prior to World War II. The period before 1914 is particularly data-light. Thus, these assessments are made from exceedingly sparse data. Also, the NBER itself, populated by postwar Keynesian economists, has a natural incentive to make things look worse that perhaps they were.

With these things in mind, we find that the NBER records fifteen recessions between 1854 and the outbreak of World War I. Some of these took place during the Civil War and the floating-currency period that followed. Thus, let us focus on the period after the resumption of the gold standard in 1879. Here, we find nine recessions in thirty-four years, from 1880 to 1913. This is a rather large number, raising the question of whether what the NBER means by "recession" for that period is the same as what we mean today. With so many setbacks, it seems a wonder that any progress was made at all.

Despite these apparent difficulties, per-capita GDP, in terms of ounces of gold (equivalent in those days to nominal dollars), rose 95% between 1880 and 1913. Per-capita GDP, measured in ounces of gold, is lower after 42 years of Mercantilist floating fiat currencies than it was in 1970. Much lower.

Industrial production tells much the same story. Over forty-two years, from 1870 to 1912, industrial production in the United States rose by 682%. In the 42 years of floating currencies since 1971, industrial production rose by 159%. Even this result was achieved mostly during the Great Moderation period of 1982-2000, when monetary conditions most closely resembled the stable money ideals of the Classical period. From 1970-1982, industrial production rose a mere 21%. During 2000-2012, industrial production rose a grand total of 7%.

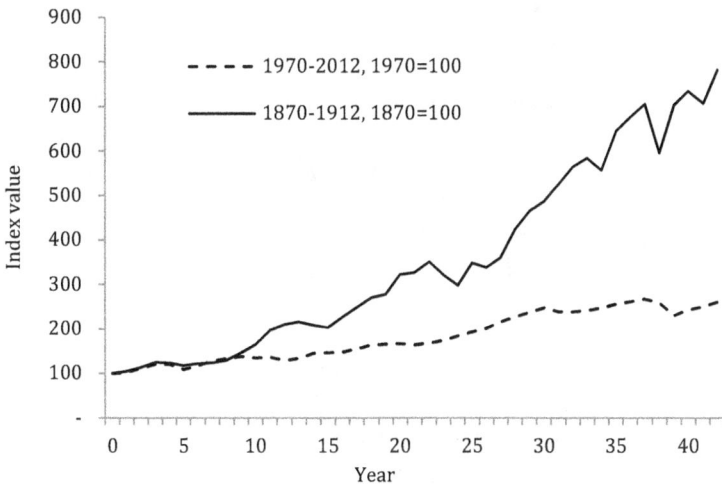

Figure 3.4: U.S.: Industrial Production, 1870-1912 and 1970-2012[1]

Today, the 1950s and 1960s are remembered as a time of extraordinary growth and wealth creation. During those decades, industrial production rose at a compounded annualized rate of 4.8%. During the 1870-1912 period, it rose by 5.0% annualized. By this measure, the 1870-1912 period was one of the finest stretches of prosperity the United States ever experienced.

The period from 1865 to 1914 was the great era of railroad building in the United States. The amount of railroad mileage added during this period is, even by today's standards, nothing short of incredible. From 1870 to 1913, an average of over five thousand miles of railroad were added per year. In the peak year of 1887, over 13,000 miles of railroad were opened. This was done entirely with hand tools and physical labor, before diesel-powered heavy equipment, before power tools, and before electricity. The U.S. population in 1890 was 63 million. Somehow, this was accomplished despite the supposed chronic recessions of the time. For comparison, from 2007 to 2010, 8,060 miles of new rail were added in China, or a rate of 2,700 miles per year. This was with all modern advantages including heavy equipment, power tools, electricity, and a population of 1,340 million in 2010.

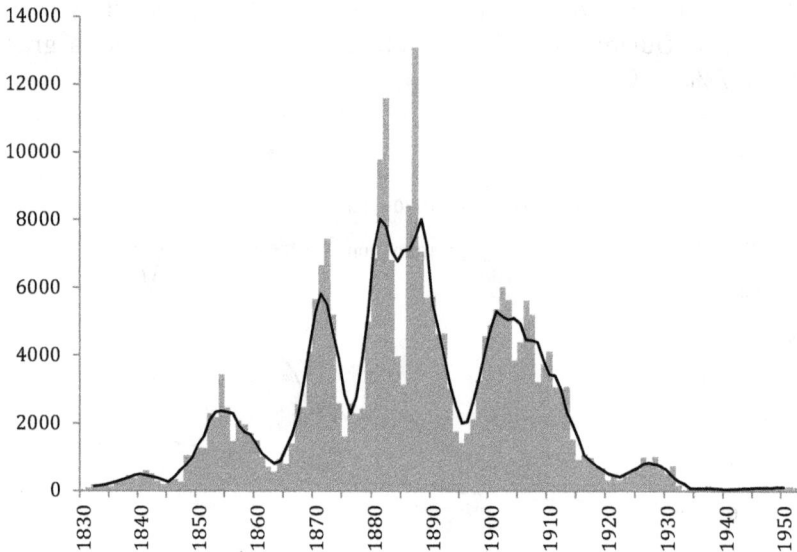

Figure 3.5: U.S.: Miles of Railway Built Per Year, 1830-1950[2]
with five-year moving average

Some recessions were exacerbated by various threats by the Democratic Party to, in effect, devalue the dollar via the "free coinage of silver." Beginning in the mid-1870s, the value of silver, which had maintained a 15 or 16 to 1 ratio with gold in the open market for centuries, plummeted in value such that, in the mid-1890s, it took about 33 ounces of silver to buy an ounce of gold. The U.S. went to *de facto* monometallism in 1873, but U.S. law still officially regarded sixteen ounces of silver as equivalent in value to an ounce of gold.

Thus, by allowing "free coinage," 33 ounces of silver, worth roughly $20 on the open market, could be made into coins worth roughly $40. In effect, it would have been a devaluation of the dollar by 50%.

Not surprisingly, these threats of currency devaluation (beginning in the 1870s but intensifying with the Sherman Silver Purchase Act of 1890), upset financial markets repeatedly. Democrats swept into power in November 1892, taking both houses of Congress and the presidency. A financial panic ensued soon after, the Panic of 1893. Fortunately, president Grover Cleveland was a staunch gold advocate, and nothing was done. This did not sit well with many party leaders. In the 1896 Democratic primaries, the incumbent Cleveland was replaced by the fiercely pro-silver William Jennings Bryan, thus raising again the issue of dollar devaluation. Financial markets trembled. Bryan lost the 1896 election to William McKinley, a gold-standard man. The U.S. policy of monometallism was made official in the Gold Standard Act of 1900. With monetary insecurity no longer a factor, the economy boomed.

The 1880s and 1890s were also a time when agricultural output expanded to an astonishing degree. This was driven by the railroad expansion, which made it possible to transport agricultural goods from huge swaths of potential farmland. Without the railroads (and the canals that preceded them), farm products could only be moved within a very small radius of perhaps twenty miles, with horse-drawn carts.

Between 1870 and 1895, the total acreage devoted to the ten largest crops increased by 111%. Total crop production increased by 119%. Similar things were happening around the world, as places like Australia, Africa, Brazil and Argentina also enjoyed a railroad (and steamship) boom, bringing immense new swathes of agricultural land into the embrace of the world economy. The result was a worldwide glut of agricultural products, and falling prices.

Thus, the 1880-1896 period was also a time when the common capitalist pattern of overinvestment was followed by a period of correction. Falling prices led to losses; losses led to less investment. The Democratic Party's insistence on dollar devaluation reflected the needs of farmers who had borrowed money to buy land and put it into production. The farmers couldn't pay their mortgages. (Some farmers may have even borrowed a little more aggressively, convinced that their debts would be devalued away.)

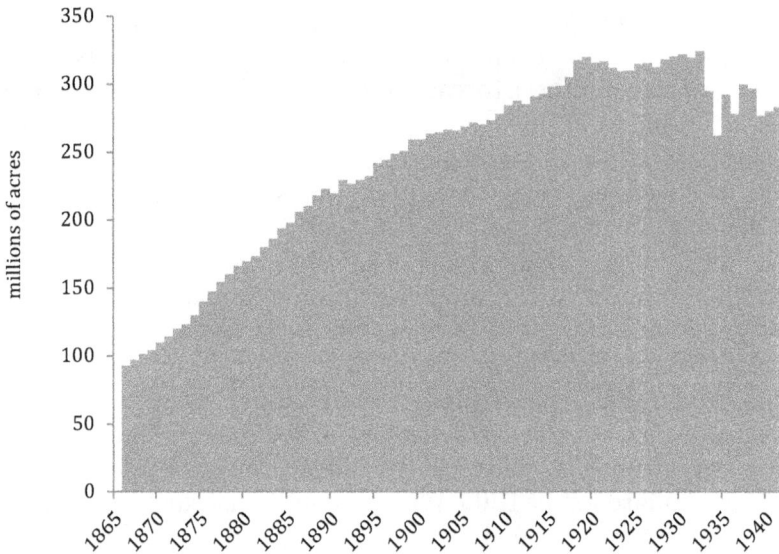

Figure 3.6: U.S.: Ten Major Crops, Total Acreage,
1865-1940

Another factor of the time was the recurrence of the liquidity shortage crisis. At certain times of the year, particularly around harvest season, the demand for base money would suddenly spike higher. In other words, all banks would be experiencing withdrawals of cash simultaneously. This reflected the common practice, of the time, of paying agricultural workers a full years' salary at once, in the form of banknotes, following the sale of the crop. Demand for banknotes would surge. A solution had been found decades before by the Bank of England – a "lender of last resort" that would make short-term loans to banks, at a penalty interest rate, if this occurred. The Bank of England deftly handled such a crisis in 1866, the last such liquidity-shortage crisis in British history.

However, the United States did not have an institution such as the Bank of England that effectively played this role. The situation was exacerbated by regulations such as reserve requirements (imposed by the National Bank system), which prevented banks from using what cash they had, lest their cash reserves fall below the regulatory limit. This issue culminated in a crisis in 1907. J.P. Morgan famously resolved the crisis by gathering bankers together, and insisting that they collectively ignore their reserve requirements. "Use your reserves!" he bellowed: "That's what they're for!" This freed up

74

enough cash to meet the demand. Nevertheless, the episode led to the creation of the Federal Reserve in 1913.

The Federal Reserve was supposed to prevent such crises. However, it was to do so within the context of the gold standard system, just as the Bank of England had since 1866 and indeed earlier. There was no inherent conflict between this form of "19th century central banking" and the gold standard system. The Bank of England performed both roles until 1914. The Fed itself, although it was increasingly dominated by a Mercantilist agenda, nevertheless worked alongside the gold standard system for 58 years, from 1913 to 1971. The crisis of 1907 was the last liquidity-shortage crisis in U.S. history.

Overall, the recessions of the pre-1914 period generally resembled the recessions of the Bretton Woods era of the 1950s and 1960s – temporary perturbations in a strong upward growth trajectory. The result would have been even better if it had not been marred by the threats of dollar devaluation in the 1890s, or if the seasonal liquidity-shortage issue had been resolved earlier, as it had in Britain. Despite these flaws, the 1880-1914 period was a time of incredible wealth creation, along with the 1920s, 1950s and 1960s. They were the best eras in the United States' long journey to becoming the world's most powerful economy.

* * *

Discussions regarding "prices" or "the price level" in the pre-1940 era must always begin with a discussion of exactly which prices are being referred to. The Consumer Price Index, as we know it, began to be compiled by the Bureau of Labor Statistics in 1940. Prior to that, the most common price index used is the BLS wholesale price index, which began to be compiled in 1919 with backdating to 1914. Prior to 1914, the most commonly used price index is a series compiled by two academics, George Warren and Frank Pearson, and published in 1933. This index is known as the Warren-Pearson index.

The Warren-Pearson index is basically a raw commodity index, similar to today's Commodity Research Board Continuous Commodity Index. The Warren-Pearson index is based on prices in New York City. It is not a nationwide index, which is particularly significant given that, due to the transportation difficulties of the pre-1914 era, substantial regional differences in commodity prices should be expected. The Warren-Pearson index's composition for the year 1889 was:

Farm Products	25%
Foods	25%
Building Materials	10%
Textiles	10%
Metals and Metal Products	10%
Fuel and Lighting	10%
Hides and Leather	4%
Spirits	3%
Miscellaneous	1%
House Furnishings	1%
Chemicals and Drugs	1%

A look at the price of commodities in the United States, compared to gold, shows no clear upward or downward trend (Figure 3.7). Periods of relatively high prices generally correspond to wars. A plateau in the 1795-1815 period aligns with the Napoleonic Wars in Europe. Another jump higher was related to World War I. World War II created another surge in prices, to a plateau that was maintained during the 1950s and 1960s.

If we exclude those wartime periods, we find a gentle drift from extended periods of lower prices to extended periods of higher prices. Commodity prices made a low in 1843 and 1897, but that only returned them to the levels of 1749-1776. During the 1920s, prices are higher than the long-term average, although no higher than they were for an extended period in 1795-1817, and also around their levels during the 1950s and 1960s.

These periods of higher and lower prices likely represent overall supply-demand characteristics for commodities. The Napoleonic Wars began in 1803 and continued to 1815, creating demand for commodities throughout Europe. (The War of 1812, with the British, began because the United States was enthusiastically selling war materials to France.) During the 1920s, commodity prices may have been elevated due to the destruction of commodity-producing capacity in Europe during World War I, and also the demand for commodities for postwar rebuilding.

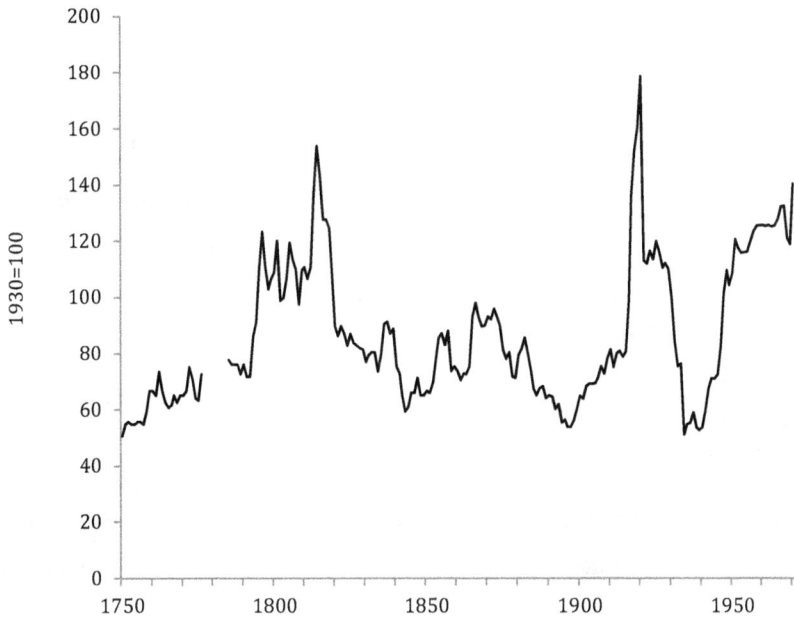

Figure 3.7: U.S.: Price of Commodities in Gold Oz., 1750-1970[3]

The 1950s and 1960s were also a time of relatively high commodity prices (compared to gold), especially metals, perhaps due to post-World War II rebuilding and rapid industrial expansion worldwide at the time. Food prices began the 1950s at a high level but, during the 1960s, steadily fell due to the increase in production brought about by the "green revolution" in chemical fertilizers and hybridized seeds, which increased per-acre yields dramatically.

From 1910 to 1940 – a time when the U.S. population grew by 43% – production of the twelve largest crops barely changed at all (Figure 3.8). This would be expected to cause greater relative scarcity of agricultural products, and thus higher prices.

All in all, the record of commodity prices in the United States during the gold standard era, prior to 1971, reflects what one might expect to see if gold was, as promised, a stable measure of value. Although there were times of somewhat higher and somewhat lower commodity prices, these were likely reflections of the natural supply and demand characteristics of the commodities themselves, not changes in the value of gold.

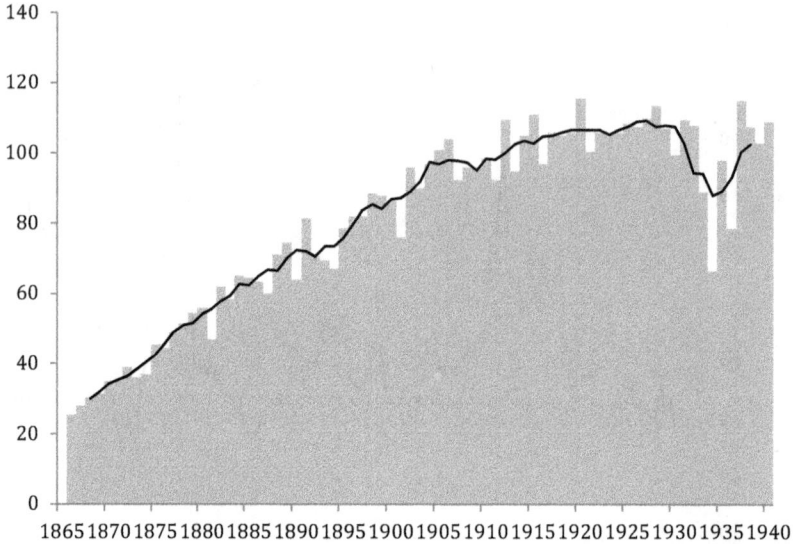

Figure 3.8: U.S.: Index of Production of Twelve Major Crops, 1865-1940
with five-year moving average

Unfortunately, a great many observers have embraced the fallacy that commodity prices are supposed to be perfectly flat, and that any change in commodity prices is attributable to changes in the value of gold. This is nonsense. Commodity prices should reflect the supply and demand of commodities, ideally expressed in terms of a benchmark of stable value. Prices are supposed to change. It is the change in prices that puts a halt to the excessive expansion of commodity production, likely the case in the 1880s and 1890s, and then provides the profit impetus to increase production when that is appropriate. If the price of commodities rises by 30% during some time period, that does not at all mean that the value of gold fell by 30%. It probably meant that the market value of commodities rose by 30%, compared to a stable measure of value.

A second common fallacy is to use these commodity price indices as if they represented today's Consumer Price Index. The CPI is a heavily damped, slow-moving index. A rise of the CPI of 10% in a year, or a decline by 3%, might indicate a major monetary event, or major macroeconomic turmoil. However, commodity prices today regularly vary by that much in a year, or even a week, with no particular significance (Figure 3.9). Thus, we sometimes hear that, with a gold standard system, "prices fell by 25% during the decade," as if that represented an economic event that would cause the CPI to fall by

25% today. This is merely lazy misrepresentation, often to purposefully mislead the gullible.

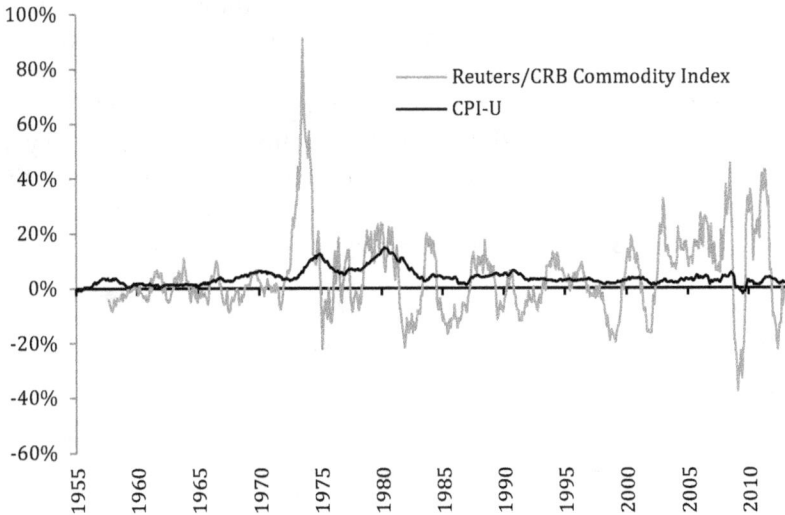

Figure 3.9: U.S.: Year-On-Year Change of the Reuters/CRB Commodity Index and CPI-U, 1955-2012

As one would expect, on an apples-to-apples comparison, commodity prices actually became more volatile after the end of the gold standard and transition to floating currencies in 1971. Claims of "price volatility" pre-1913, and "price stability" post-1971, are mostly just an artifact of measuring two different things.

Unfortunately, there is no final arbiter as to whether changes in commodity prices represented changes in commodities' value, or in the value of gold. If there were something even more stable in value than gold, against which gold could be compared, we would simply use that as a measure of value and monetary basis, instead of gold. No such thing has ever been found. Overall, the commodity price history of the pre-1971 period is very good. It indicates that gold indeed served as a reliably stable measure of value, as the Classical economists expected it would. The happy result was seen in the performance of the U.S. economy itself. During the gold standard era, the United States became the economic wonder of the world.

* * *

The purpose of a gold standard system is to produce a currency whose value is linked to gold, via an operating mechanism that matches the supply of currency with the demand for currency. During the 19th century, the U.S. economy expanded by an enormous degree, and, not surprisingly, the total amount of base money expanded as well. In 1775, the estimated total amount of base money in circulation in the American Colonies was $12 million, mostly in the form of foreign-made bullion coins. In 1900, the total amount of base money in circulation was $1,954 million, an increase of 163 times. During this time period, the amount of aboveground gold in the world increased by an estimated 3.4 times due to mining production.

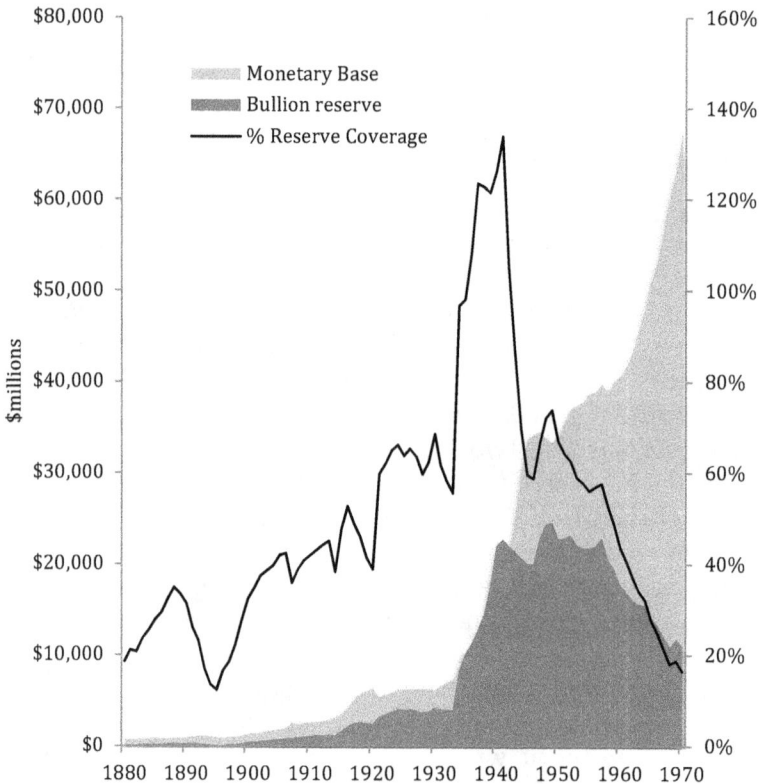

Figure 3.10: U.S.: Monetary Base, Gold Bullion Reserve, and Reserve Coverage Ratio, 1880-1970

From 1880 to 1970, the final ninety years of the gold standard policy in the United States, the monetary base increased by ninety times. In gold terms (adjusting for the devaluation in 1933), the monetary base increased by fifty-three times. During this period, the amount of gold bullion held in reserve against base money outstanding varied from around 10% in the mid-1890s to around 135% during World War II (Figure 3.10).

In actual practice, the gold standard systems in use in the United States could expand to any degree, alongside the economy as a whole, within the framework of a stable gold parity – in much the same way as the shares outstanding or assets under management of an ETF can expand or contract as needed. The gold standard system did not "restrict growth" in any way. Certainly no system that "restricted growth" would have allowed the United States to become the world's most successful economy during that time period.

Base money supply had nothing to do with mining production, imports or exports of gold bullion, the "balance of payments," relative price levels, interest rates, or any other such thing. The mechanism was a currency-board-like system as described previously (Figure 3.11).

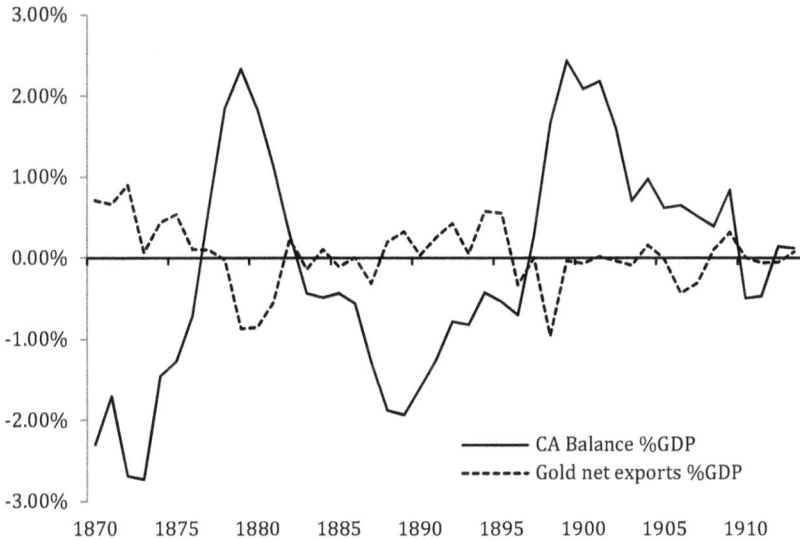

Figure 3.11: U.S.: Current Account Balance and Net Gold Exports, Percentage of GDP, 1870-1913[4]

Bullion reserve coverage was never 100% or higher, except for a brief time around World War II. This did not cause any particular problems.

(The devaluation of 1933 made the existing gold reserves more valuable in dollar terms, leading to a dramatic increase in effective bullion reserve coverage.)

The growth rate of base money did not have some smooth, steady curve, but rather had periods of rapid growth and periods of quiescence. This was a reflection of base money demand; in other words, people's changing interest in holding more or less base money.

Much of what has been written about how the gold standard system worked in the United States is complete fiction. It was a very simple system, and easy to understand. In practice, when the proper operating principles were observed, it worked exactly as promised.

Chapter 4:
Britain and Holland's Experience with Gold
Standard Systems

I. Britain

In the 1680s, the intellectual atmosphere of England was still saturated by the Mercantilist economic ideas that had circulated throughout the 17th century. This changed because, on June 10, 1688, a son was born to England's King James II. The new prince displaced the daughter Mary, a Protestant, as the heir apparent to the English throne. After Mary's birth, James II had converted to Catholicism, and his attempts to Catholicise British institutions had caused much dissent. His belief in French-style absolute monarchism threatened the hard-won authority of Britain's Parliament. With the son's birth, many in Parliament feared that Britain, Protestant since Henry VIII's infamous divorce in 1532, would turn Catholic and veer towards absolute monarchy. This raised the threat of civil war, which everyone was anxious to avoid so soon after the bloody English Civil War of 1642-1651.

A coalition within Parliament invited the daughter Mary and her husband, the Dutch prince William of Orange, to make a military invasion and claim the English crown, thus insuring that the country would remain Protestant. In November 1688, William crossed the English Channel with a large invasion fleet, and after only two minor clashes, James' regime collapsed. In February 1689, Parliament declared William the new monarch, in the process also declaring its own power as superior to the king's. Parliament was relieved that so little blood had been shed, and the event became known as the Glorious Revolution.

At the time, the Classical ideals of sound money were best expressed by the Dutch. The Dutch guilder had been reliably gold-based since the founding of the Bank of Amsterdam in 1609, for the express purpose of producing a high-quality currency to facilitate trade. After decades of excellent management, the Bank of Amsterdam's reputation grew to be so great that a Bank of Amsterdam bank deposit or deposit receipt was actually more valuable than the equivalent bullion coin. The Dutch guilder became the world's premier international currency, and Amsterdam became the world's premier financial center.

As King William III established himself in London, he brought with him a friend, the philosopher John Locke. Locke had fled to Amsterdam in 1683, under suspicion of involvement in a plot to assassinate King Charles II of England. There is little evidence that he was involved in the scheme, but his writings arguing for Parliamentary supremacy and against absolute monarchism were considered revolutionary at the time.

James II sought refuge with Louis XIV in Catholic France. This coincided with Louis XIV's ambitions to expand into parts of Germany and the Spanish Netherlands. Thus began the Nine Years' War (1688-1697), which involved much of Europe in an effort to contain France's ambitions. Within this arena, James II attempted to regain control of Britain, personally leading armies into battle in Ireland and Scotland. This was followed soon after by the War of the Spanish Succession (1701-1714), in which Britain fought alongside a Grand Alliance to prevent Louis XIV from potentially unifying Spain and France.

The wars cost money. In 1694, the Bank of England was founded, to provide a £1.2 million loan to King William III to fund the war. The loan was at 8% – which must have galled William, because in Holland, governments borrowed at 3-4%, reflecting the high reliability of the currency. However, even this rate was charitably low for the time, and probably reflected a concession on the Bank's part in return for its creation and charter. At first, William borrowed from small-scale goldsmiths at rates up to 30%. The previous year, in 1693, William borrowed £1 million at 10% for sixteen years, with additional lottery benefits that brought the effective coupon to 14% per annum. The Bank loaned the government the money in the form of paper banknotes, radically increasing the use of banknotes instead of coinage within Britain.

In 1695, a discussion developed regarding whether the British pound should be officially devalued, reflecting the worn nature of most coins. In an extensive report, William Lowndes, secretary to the Treasury, argued that it was the king "to whose regality the Power of Coining Money, and determining the Weight, Fineness, Denomination and Extrinsick Value there of doth Solely and Inherently Appertain." Lowdnes had the weight of British history and legal precedent on his side, at least as far back as Henry VIII, who had essentially devalued his debt away. Locke, however, asserted that the values of gold and silver were fixed by natural law and could not be changed by king or Parliament. For Locke, changing the value of money was akin to a plan "to lengthen a foot by dividing it into Fifteen parts, instead of Twelve ... calling them inches." Devaluing the currency, particularly so soon after substantial sums of it had been lent to the government "will weaken, if not totally destroy the public faith when all that have trusted the public and assisted our present necessities upon Acts of Parliament in the million lottery, Bank Act, and other loans, shall be defrauded of 20 per cent of what those Acts of Parliament were security for." Backed by William III, Parliament sided with Locke. In 1697, a recoinage was undertaken, to insure that the coins in circulation indeed contained the metals that they were supposed to. Due to details regarding the ratio of silver and gold specified, gold became the effective basis for the British pound henceforth.

Thus began Britain's great era on a gold standard system. The principle of £3 pounds, 17 shillings and 10 pence (£3.891667) per troy ounce of gold began with Locke, and continued until 1931 – a 234-year stretch in which Britain adhered to the Classical ideal of money that was as reliable and unchanging as possible. (The pound's value was equivalent to 7.992 grams of gold, or 0.2570 troy oz.) The influence of Dutch principles via William III and Locke did not entirely swing British economic thinking, which remained primarily Mercantilist for several decades afterwards. John Law's book was written even after the government's monetary policy had clearly swung from a Mercantilist to a Classical basis. Mercantilist thinking continued in Britain up through the sophisticated soft-money proposals of James Denham Stuart in the 1760s, in which an all-knowing "statesman" would guide the economy by way of careful centralized management of currency and credit supply. Fortunately, the British government itself ignored all such arguments. It wasn't until the triumph of Adam Smith, beginning in 1776, that British intellectuals fully embraced Classical principles of money.

Britain too exemplified the Magic Formula ideal. Although excise taxes (sales taxes) were often high, there was no income tax until the outbreak of war with France in 1798. The other major taxes were tariffs, a window tax (a primitive form of a property tax on buildings), and a land tax instituted in 1692. However, the land values on which the land tax was based were never adjusted. They remained at the 1692 levels for most of the 18th century, amounting to a steady decline in effective tax rates.

Britain eventually eclipsed Holland as the world's financial center, and the British pound became the world's premier currency. British capitalism and contract law formed the foundation of the Industrial Revolution, which first appeared in Britain in the 1770s. Throughout the 19th century, Britain was on the forefront of technological advancement and industrial expansion, this enabled by the large sums of capital that could be amassed via Britain's sophisticated financial system. The surging economy and galloping technological advances allowed Britain to field the world's most powerful navy. This became the basis for the British Empire, the grandest in the world at the time. The Empire was at times brutal; but its success also reflected recognition of Britain's superlative statesmanship. Even Britain's most cruel and ruthless expansionists, such as Cecil Rhodes in southern Africa, brought wonders in their wake. The spectacular bridge across the Zambezi river in western Zimbabwe was part of Rhodes' plan to connect a railroad from Capetown, South Africa, to Cairo, Egypt. Zimbabwe's black educated class today attends universities that Rhodes founded.

As time passed, and Locke's promises seemed more and more secure, interest rates on Britain's government debt declined. Britain's years of warfare began to wind down, with a peace treaty signed between France and Britain in October of 1711 – in effect, the failure of Louis XIV's expansionist ambitions. In that year, a coalition of government lenders agreed to be paid 6% on their aggregate holdings of debt. In April 1713, the Treaty of Utrecht formally ended years of warfare between Britain, France, Spain and others. Louis XIV died in 1715. By the 1720s, long-term British government bonds traded at a yield of 3.0%-3.5%. In 1749, most outstanding British government debt was consolidated into a new issuance of government bonds of infinite maturity, the famous Consols. The first issuance of Consols had a coupon of 3.0%, and for a time until 1755, traded above par.

The days of King William III borrowing at 14% were long gone. Britain replicated what Holland had done. As the government adhered to the principle of keeping the currency as stable as possible, at its parity of £3 17s 10d per troy ounce of gold, the British pound became widely regarded as the world's best currency, and the British Consol was the world's best bond.

The remainder of the eighteenth century had a series of smaller wars. Stuart invasions were repelled in 1715-1716 and 1745-1746. War with Spain consumed 1717-1720 and 1739-1748. The War of Austrian Succession took place in 1740-1748, and the Seven Years' War in 1755-1763. Being able to fund these wars at 3% rates by way of the expanding London financial industry helped put Britain at the forefront of Europe by the end. In the 1760s, Britain's empire included the Americas, Canada, Florida, Gibraltar, and numerous smaller holdings, while influence in India increased.

Forty more years of difficulty followed, beginning with the American Revolution in 1776, and ending with the defeat of Napoleon at Waterloo in 1815, after over twenty years of intermittent wars with the French.

As a result of the Napoleonic Wars, the Bank of England suspended redeemability in 1797. The Bank could have maintained the value of the pound at its gold parity by the use of purchases and sales of non-bullion assets. However, although there was no official policy of deviating from the gold standard, in practice the pound's value drifted downward. The British pound had become a floating currency. The nadir was touched in August 1813, when the pound's value had declined to 70.8% of its prewar parity value, or £5 10s per ounce of gold. It returned to nearly this low in February 1815, after Napoleon's escape from Elba, when the value of the pound sank to £5 7s per ounce of gold. Overall, the decline in pound value during the war years was modest. The drop in the pound's value from 1797 to 1813 averaged 2.1% of depreciation per year, much gentler than the changes in currency value we experience regularly today. Nevertheless, for people accustomed to a century of stable currency value, it was deeply disturbing.

The war's conclusion at Waterloo in 1815 prompted the government to resolve the floating pound issue. The value of the British pound was gradually raised back to its prewar parity at £3 17s 10d per troy ounce of gold, and the gold standard was officially resumed in 1821.

Britain's government took another important step at this time. Decades of near-continuous warfare had left immense government debts, totaling £876 million in 1815 (estimated by some at over 200%

of GDP). The interest on the debt alone accounted for more than half of government spending in 1815, and was more than total government spending in the last year of peace, 1792. After the war's end, the debate raged whether the income tax, introduced in 1798, should be continued, to help pay down the debt, or whether it could be abolished. The proposal to eliminate the income tax was enormously popular, and in 1816 it was eradicated.

The rising value of the pound, and its deflationary consequences, was one reason for some economic difficulties in the years 1815-1825, particularly among agricultural producers. Thankfully, these recessionary factors were mitigated by the positive effects of the elimination of the income tax. The combination of low taxes and a gold-based currency formed the foundation for a century of breathtaking success. The Magic Formula was again in action. The 19th century was a time of peace on the European continent, although the Europeans continued to scuffle with each other along the edges of their expanding world empires. Until 1914, Britain enjoyed a marvelous upward march of progress and prosperity that left it the premier country in the world, even as it was challenged toward the end of the century by the even more impressive accomplishments of the United States, Germany and Japan.

Benefiting from this long period of growth, Britain's government generally ran budget surpluses, such that the national debt had fallen to £650 million in 1914. However, this debt was now supported by a much larger economy. The estimated debt/GDP ratio had fallen to a manageable 26%.

Although Britain had risen to the pinnacle of world prominence, beginning in the 1870s, economic growth began to slow. Partially, this was due to a series of bad harvests in Europe, which led to rising tariffs across the continent (and the world) as a form of economic support. The idea of "protecting domestic businesses" with higher tariffs during a recession was quite popular in the latter 19th century, although the tariff wars – a form of tax increase – usually made the collective situation worse. The income tax was reintroduced in 1842, in response to budget deficits. Repealing the tax again became a major political topic. Both of the leading political figures of the latter 19th century, Benjamin Disraeli and William Gladstone, promised to repeal the income tax in the 1874 election. At the time, it was generating only 7.8% of the government's revenue. Disraeli won; the tax stayed. Although the economy was expanding rapidly, the benefits flowed mostly to a few while a large underclass was overworked, underpaid, and at risk of sliding into abject poverty if they should suffer any personal setback. Karl Marx had argued, in the *Communist Manifesto* of 1848, that a progressive income tax, at a high rate, was necessary to help right this imbalance. Reflecting more moderate socialist views then gaining in popularity, tax rates slid modestly higher, while government services gradually expanded.

The British Empire continued to grow and reached its peak in 1922. At that point, it consisted of 33.7 million square kilometers of land, or 22.63% of the world's total land area, and around 20.0% of the total population of the world.

With the outbreak of World War I, the Bank of England again suspended the redeemability of its banknotes; again this was supposed to be a temporary measure; again, there was no official adoption of a floating currency policy; again, the value of the pound sank from its prewar gold parity, and floated on the open market. As was the case in a lesser way in 1797-1815 as well, the Bank of England aided government war financing by making direct loans to the government. The result was an increase in notes and coins in circulation from less than £200 million before the war's outbreak in 1914, to more than £580 million in 1919.

Again, after the war's end, the pound's value was raised back to its prewar parity. However, this time the British government maintained its wartime tax rates, which had soared higher during the war for excise taxes, property taxes and income taxes. The top income tax rate rose from 6% to 30%, where it remained after the war. Again, the rise in the pound's value, to its prewar parity, introduced recessionary pressures on the economy, in addition to the issues of demobilization and a major drop in government spending. However, unlike in 1816 when these factors were substantially mitigated by the elimination of the income tax, this time the high wartime taxes remained. The trend towards socialism continued, and a barrage of new welfare programs were introduced soon after the war's end.

The gold standard was officially resumed in 1925, at the prewar parity. The venerable pound was again worth Locke's original value, from 228 years previous. However, the economy was doing badly, with unemployment in excess of 10%. In 1926, a General Strike lasting nine days took place. The poor economy was partially blamed on the resumption of the gold standard. Mercantilist views had been rising in influence since the end of the 19th century, along with interest in statism and socialism in general. In the midst of this intellectual climate, Classical principles of monetary management lost some of their luster, and the age-old arguments of the Mercantilists – that unemployment and other economic problems could be solved, at no real cost, with the magic of monetary "management" – gained new followers. The eventual result was the devaluation of the British pound in 1931 in response to the economic difficulties of the Great Depression. The post-WWI gold standard, in the end, lasted only six years.

The devaluation of 1931 led to thirteen years of a floating pound, officially coming to an end with Britain's participation in the Bretton Woods agreement in 1944. (In practice, the pound was linked to the dollar in 1941.) Britain again had a gold standard policy, with the pound worth $4.03 (or £8.68 per ounce of gold). After World War II, Britain again labored under even higher taxes. The British economy was a persistent laggard during the 1950s and 1960s, even as the war's losers, Germany and Japan, made huge advances. The poor economic conditions inspired the British Mercantilists (especially dominant in Keynes' home country) to fiddle with the currency in an effort to deal with unemployment. This "domestic monetary policy" was completely contrary to the proper operating mechanisms of a gold standard system. The result was a devaluation to $2.80 in 1949 (£12.50/oz.), and then to $2.40 in 1967 (£14.58/oz.).

After 1971, the British pound floated along with the rest of the world's currencies. Some governments – notably Germany, Switzerland and Japan – did not share the United States' enthusiasm for currency deprecation, and consequently, the value of their currencies rose vs. the dollar during the 1970s. Britain, however, was even more enthusiastic about Mercantilist "easy money," and in 1985 the British pound was worth only $1.30.

* * *

Britain's great success with gold-based money is perhaps best illustrated by the history of British interest rates during the gold standard era (Figure 4.1).

In the 1690s, and indeed the entirety of the seventeenth century, businesses typically borrowed at rates in the mid-teens, if not higher. Thus, the 8-10% rates at which the 18th century began, just after the recoinage of 1697, already represented considerable improvement from the situation that preceded it. As it became clear that Britain's commitment to Locke's gold parity was sound, even with the demands of wartime, yields fell to Holland-like levels in the mid-3% range for long-term government debt, and stayed there for two centuries.

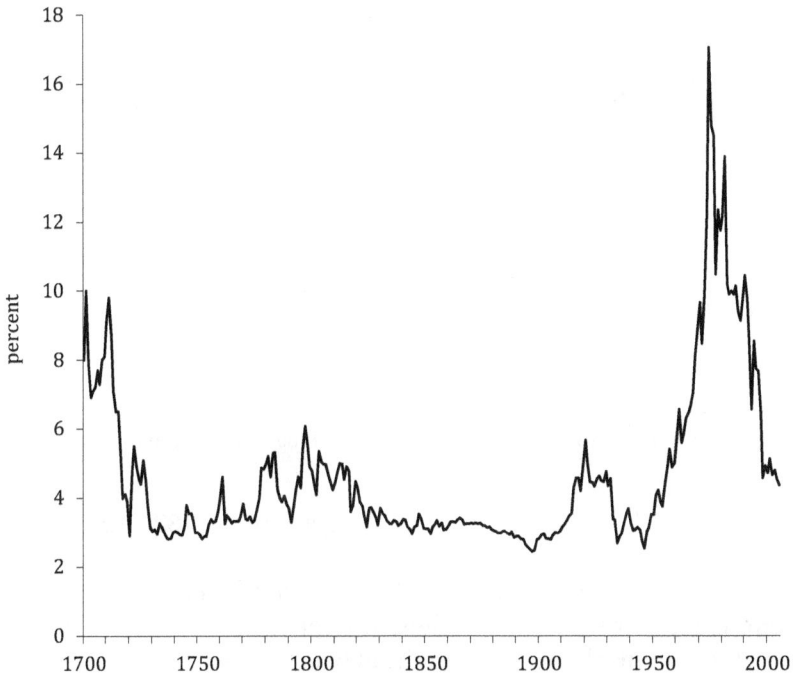

Figure 4.1: Britain: Yield on 2.5% Consol Bond, 1700-2005

Yields rose in response to the difficulties of the American Revolution, and again during the 1797-1821 floating pound period of the Napoleonic Wars. After the reinstatement of a gold standard in 1821, Britain began a truly extraordinary century, where yields were not only low, but very stable. The average yield on the Consol bond (of infinite maturity) during the 1821-1914 period was 3.15% (Figure 4.2). Even more astonishing, however, is that the Consol's yield spent the entire century within about a half percent (fifty basis points) on either side of this average. Britain's real-life experience with a gold standard system was not only acceptable, it was as close to perfection as anyone could dream of in an uncertain world.

Since 1914, and the rise of Mercantilist influence that followed World War I, none of the hundred-plus central banks in the world have ever been able to replicate this performance – even as they swear day and night that they are committed to monetary and macroeconomic stability.

Figure 4.2: Britain: Yield on 2.5% Consol Bond, 1821-1913

After 2010, yields again fell to relatively low levels, but that was accomplished with an unprecedented degree of direct government involvement in markets. This condition was not likely to be sustained for very long – certainly not for a century – and may be looked upon later as a precursor to a currency and credit tempest that makes the 1970s look like a mild summer rainshower.

* * *

The history of commodity prices in Britain, in terms of gold, stretches back much further than the Warren-Pearson index. Over a four-century period, British commodity prices, expressed in ounces of gold, were extraordinarily stable over the long term (Figure 4.3). Over shorter time periods they vary, but that is to be expected for any commodity market, particularly considering the pre-industrial conditions and constant warfare of the time. Commodity prices made a higher plateau in the 1800-1820 period, reflecting the Napoleonic Wars. A dip in the 1890s again corresponds to soaring production worldwide. Commodity prices were considerably more volatile during the 20th century. This was due to the emergence, for the first time, of global synchronized macro events, notably the two World Wars, the Great Depression, the worldwide boom of the 1950s and

1960s, the 1970s synchronized currency devaluation, and the Great Moderation of the 1980s and 1990s.

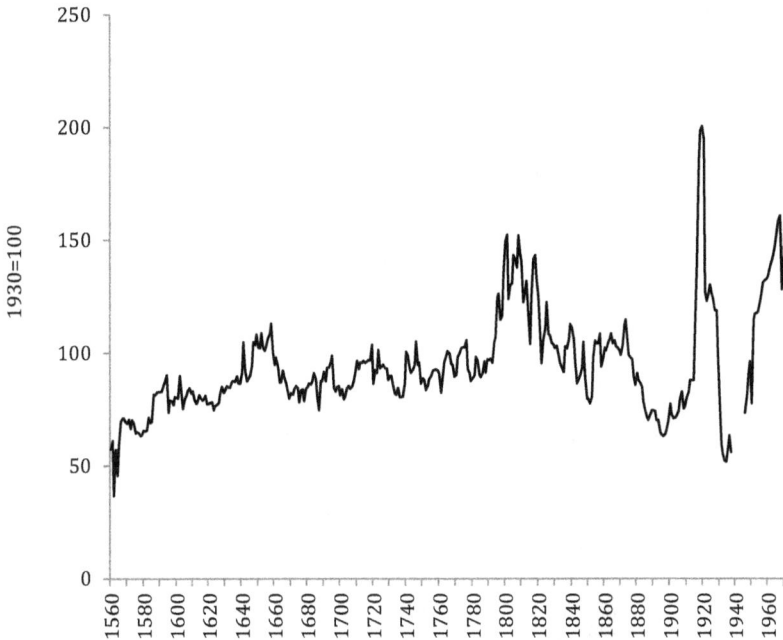

Figure 4.3: Britain: Commodity Prices in Gold Oz., 1560-1970[1]

Our investigations can be extended further with another series, illustrating the prices of commodities in gold oz. in Britain from 1400-1640 (Figure 4.4). As these price indices are not easily compatible, they are presented separately.

There is no final arbiter by which one can say that these commodity price swings represent changes in the real value of commodities, as represented by a measure of stable value, instead of changes in gold's real value itself. Nevertheless, the result is again generally what one would expect to see if, indeed, gold was an unchanging measure of value, as the British experience with interest rates also indicates. In other words, there is little evidence here contrary to the conclusion that gold indeed served as the Monetary Polaris, the one thing that does not change in value, the quality above all others that makes gold desirable as the basis for monetary systems.

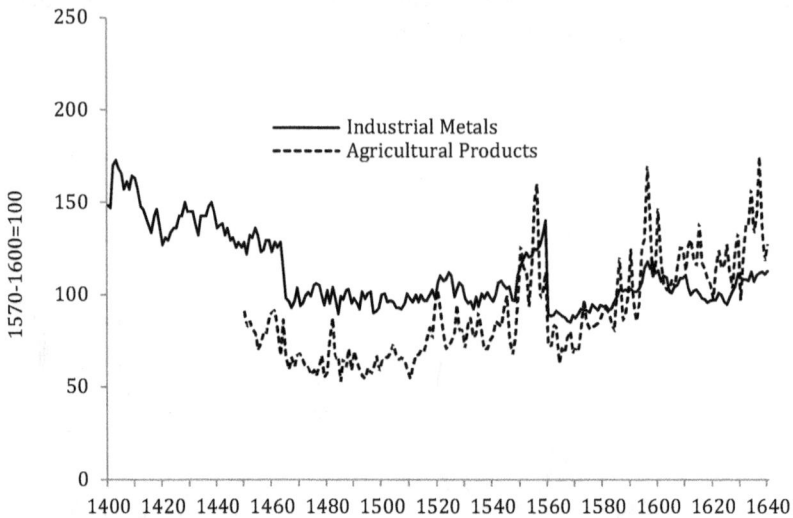

Figure 4.4: Britain: Commodity Prices in Gold Oz., 1400-1640[2]

Certainly, the result was far better than has ever been achieved with Mercantilist principles. The record of the many various attempts at currencies that were not based on gold (or silver) is one of eventual collapse and failure. "Paper money eventually returns to its intrinsic value – zero," said Voltaire in 1729. Nothing has changed since then. In a study of 775 floating currencies by Michael Hewitt in 2009, the average life of a floating paper currency was found to be 27 years. [3]

$$* * *$$

The Bank of England's balance sheet for the years 1720-1913 illustrates the practical implementation of a gold standard system during that time (Figure 4.5). The period also includes the wartime floating currency episode beginning in 1797, and the resumption of the gold standard in 1821 – an excellent example of a major country returning to a gold standard system after a long hiatus.

Again, there was never a 100% bullion reserve policy. Bullion reserves varied wildly from year to year (Figure 4.6). The Bank of England managed its assets quite actively until the Bank Charter Act of 1844, when new regulation was imposed and management became much more stable. Changes in gold bullion holdings did not necessarily correspond to changed in base money at all. Base money (banknotes outstanding and deposits, but not including bullion coins in this case) varied considerably from year to year, once again not showing any smooth growth curve but rather, like the gold bullion ETFs examined previously, reflected the variability in the public's demand for base money as an instrument for monetary transactions.

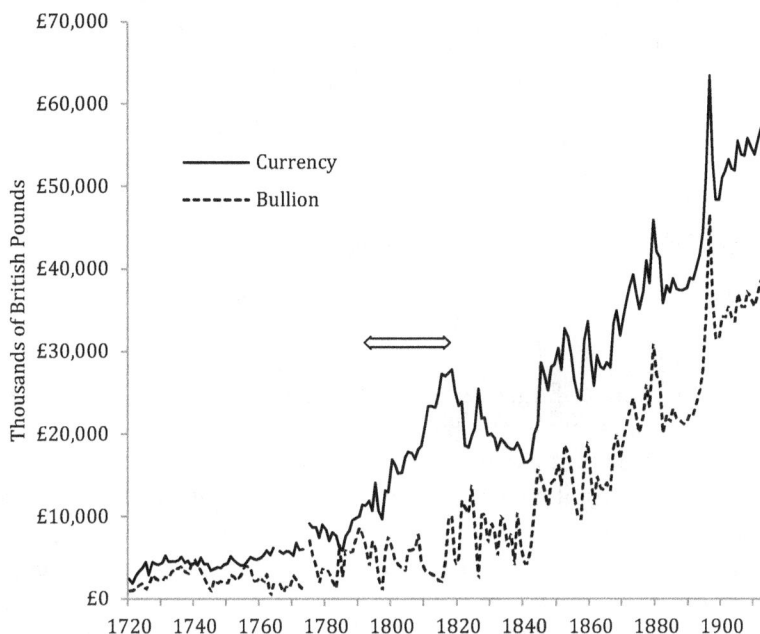

Figure 4.5: Britain: Bank of England, Currency in Circulation and Bullion Reserve, 1720-1913[4]
arrow denotes floating currency period

There was no relation to mining production, imports or exports of bullion, the "balance of payments," relative price levels, interest rates and so forth. Despite the dramatic changes in balance sheet composition, the practical result (excepting the floating-currency period) was placidity: the British pound maintained its promised gold parity, and produced one of the greatest eras of monetary and macroeconomic stability the world has ever seen.

Total banknotes in circulation increased from £2,480,000 in 1720 to £55,094,085 in 1913, an increase of 22 times. During this time period, estimated total world aboveground gold supplies increased from 112 metric tons in 1720 to 776 metric tons in 1913, or 6.9 times.

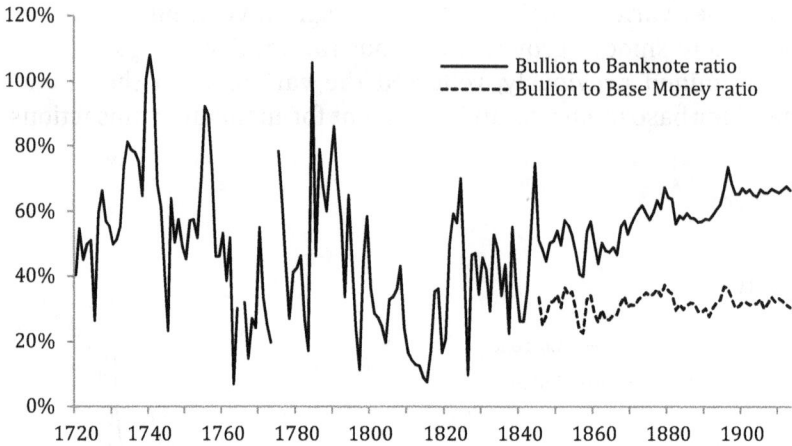

Figure 4.6: Britain: Bank of England, Gold Bullion Reserve Ratios, 1720-1913

By 1844, the Bank of England was operating in essence like a modern central bank. Deposits at the Bank of England served much the same function as deposits at a central bank today, as a form of base money.

Compared to total base money including deposits at the Bank, the bullion reserve ratio was stable around 30% (Figure 4.6). The remainder of reserve assets was made up of roughly equal proportions of government bonds, non-government bonds (corporate and perhaps foreign sovereign), and direct lending and discounting.

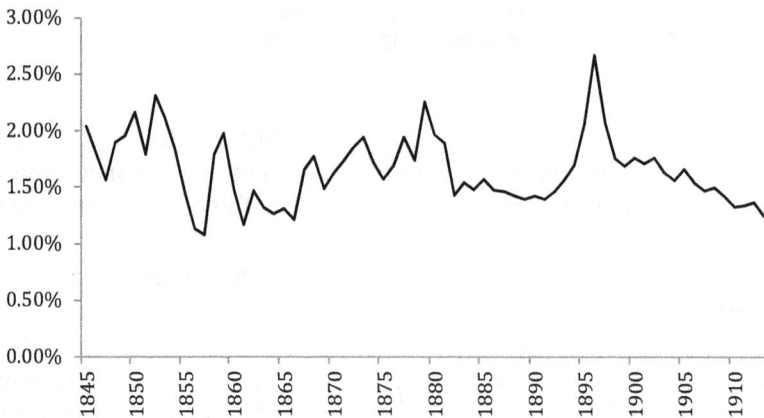

Figure 4.7: Britain: Bank of England, Gold Bullion Reserves as a Percentage of World Aboveground Gold, 1845-1913

Although the British pound was the premier international currency of the world, and the basis for numerous subsidiary currencies linked via currency-board arrangements, the total bullion holdings of the Bank of England were only a small portion of total world aboveground gold supplies, averaging about 1.5% during the 1844-1913 period (Figure 4.7).

Just as is the case with bullion ETFs, and with present-day currency boards, the Bank of England's base money supply was adjusted on a daily basis to match supply and demand for base money, at the designated gold parity of £3 17s 10d per ounce of gold.

This adjustment was accomplished with changes in all types of assets, including gold bullion, government bonds, other types of bonds, and direct lending and discounting.

II. Holland

The Netherlands' great era of success began with its independence from the collapsing Spanish empire in 1585. Spain, in its decline, had crushed its mercantile class with a combination of excessive taxes and, in the midst of incessant government financial demands, chronic currency debasements. The industrious Dutch naturally found Spanish rule oppressive, and, after decades of unrest, the revolt against Spanish rule began in 1572. The fall of Antwerp, then the largest city in the Netherlands, marks the beginning of *de facto* Dutch independence in the north in 1585, although the wars with Spain continued until peace and independence were formally secured in 1648. Many in Antwerp fled to Amsterdam in the north to escape hostilities, making Amsterdam the most populous city of the new independent Netherlands.

Freed from Spain's oppressive taxation, and with a sound gold-based currency formalized in 1609 with the creation of the Bank of Amsterdam, the Magic Formula was in place. Holland's economy boomed. In 1602, the Dutch East India company was formed, the world's first multinational corporation. The company's creation was financed by the issuance of shares, and trading of the shares established the world's first modern stock exchange. In time, Holland became the premier financial center in Europe. With little to offer in terms of natural resources, even as simple as arable land, the economy turned toward trade and manufacturing, supported by a sophisticated financial system. Although the technological innovations of the Industrial Revolution were still a century away, Holland of the 17th century has been called the first modern capitalist economy. Domestic manufactures of textiles exploded, and the country also became a center for shipbuilding, sugar refining, and papermaking. The Dutch East India Company took over Europe's only trade link with Japan in 1640 (replacing the Portuguese, whose missionary Catholicism was problematic to the Shogun), and eventually managed trade and colonial holdings throughout Asia. In 1621, the Dutch West India Company was established, and quickly built a sizeable business along the triangular slave and sugar trade, between Europe, Africa, Brazil, the Caribbean and the American colonies. In 1670, the Dutch merchant marine totaled 568,000 tons of shipping capacity, about half of the European total. Not only was Amsterdam the center of global trade, it became the center of trade within Europe as well. Holland became the wealthiest country in Europe.

The value of the Dutch guilder was 605.61 milligrams of gold, or 51.3584 guilders per troy oz. With the establishment of a sound gold-based currency, interest rates in Holland sank to familiar gold-standard levels around 3.5% for best-quality credits. In 1603, the City of Amsterdam paid 6.17%-8.33% on its borrowings. By the 1660s, this had fallen to 3.0%-4.0%. In 1700, the government paid 3.0%-3.75% on its long-term debt. In 1650-1675, interest rates on private commercial loans were 3.0%-4.5%. In 1700, private commercial loans could be had for as little as 1.75%-2.0%, at shorter maturities. These low gold standard interest rates were a great advantage in financing many commercial ventures, and the envy of businessmen in other countries throughout Europe.

The financial system grew increasingly sophisticated to meet the demands of Holland's world trade. The insurance industry grew to provide risk control for merchants' many sailing voyages, and later expanded into life insurance. Joint stock ownership was applied even to individual ships, split between sixteen merchants to diversify risk. Trade credit expanded. Foreign exchange trading became a major business for bankers. Commodity exchanges flourished. By the 1680s sophisticated derivatives markets had been created, including put and call options, futures contracts, margin buying of stocks on the stock exchange, and nascent stock-index trading. An active market in public debt emerged.

The population of the Netherlands was 1.5 million in 1600, and grew to 1.9 million in 1700 – about the population of today's San Antonio, Texas. Amsterdam's population began the 17th century around 50,000; in 1700, it was around 200,000 (Tacoma,

Washington). By today's standards, this is tiny. Yet, this modest community of merchants, bankers and manufacturers financed a historic explosion of art and artisanry. Their business profits paid for the paintings of Rembrandt (1606-1669) and Vermeer (1632-1675), and many other scenes of their friends, wives, children, and everyday life. The volume of quality work was enough to later form a cornerstone of museum collections around the world. Architecture reached its zenith, along with accomplishments in sculpture and literature.

The Dutch Empire expanded along with commerce and finance. As the Spanish/Portugese empire crumbled, many imperial possessions fell into the hands of the rising Dutch. Brazil was captured from Portugese rule in 1637, accompanied by conquests throughout the eastern shore of South America, and islands in the Caribbean. Portugese trade settlements in Africa were conquered, along with outposts throughout Asia in today's India, Sri Lanka, Singapore, Malaysia, Indonesia and Taiwan. Trade along the Hudson River in North America began in 1609, and Albany was established in 1614. A fortified town at the mouth of the Hudson, New Amsterdam, was created in 1625 to ward off threats from nearby English and French colonies. In 1643, a settlement was established at Valdiva in southern Chile. In 1652, a colony was founded at Cape Town, South Africa. The Dutch Empire eventually also included settlements in today's Australia, Iran, Iraq, Pakistan, Yemen, Bangladesh, Oman, Burma, Thailand, Cambodia, Vietnam, China, Japan, Netherlands Antilles and Aruba, Guyana, Virgin Islands, Tobago, Colombia, Suriname and Ghana. It was the world's premier empire, until Dutch naval supremacy was eclipsed by Britain's at the beginning of the 18th century.

Holland's fall from prominence in world affairs was precipitated by outside forces, not surprising for a small and potentially vulnerable country that had punched well beyond its weight class. European markets, particularly that of France, were abruptly closed beginning around 1670, dealing a harsh blow to Holland's many trade endeavors in Europe. In 1672 the Franco-Dutch war began, in which France, Sweden and Britain teamed up against the Dutch Republic. The absolute monarch Louis XIV saw the Dutch as trading rivals and an obstacle to French expansion. Louis also wanted to gain the alliance of Britain, which itself wanted to limit the influence of the Dutch navy. It was a testament to Holland's power that it was able to fend off this combined assault. The war lasted until 1678, leaving the Dutch government with huge debts. Britain's Glorious Revolution, a few years later, was congruent with a Dutch strategy of breaking this British-French alliance. Holland was soon involved again in decades of chronic warfare (now in alliance with William III's Britain), with the Nine Years' War (1688-1697) and War of the Spanish Succession (1701-1714). The result was that the Dutch government's debts increased still further up to 1713.

Tax rates soared higher to pay war expenses and the ensuing debts. Holland became known as a poor place to invest, due to high taxes. Dutch capital went elsewhere. The Magic Formula was lost. The country did not suffer the kind of collapse that Spain had experienced, but the laggard economy was surpassed by its larger European neighbors, notably Britain. The Fourth Anglo-Dutch War (1780-1784), tangentially related to the American Revolutionary War, put Holland on a sharper path of decline. The Dutch navy, once the world's most powerful, had been neglected since 1712 due to budget pressures and economic stagnancy. It was no match for the British Royal Navy. Many of Holland's imperial holdings worldwide transferred to the expanding British Empire. The war was a disaster for Holland at home as well, particularly economically.

Tax rates rose even higher. The Dutch East India Company, which managed much of Holland's Asian empire, went bankrupt in the mid-1780s and was nationalized in 1796. The Bank of Amsterdam defaulted on some obligations in 1781, declared itself insolvent in 1790, and was nationalized. It finally closed in 1819. In 1810, the public debt was forced into default, a consequence of the Netherlands' annexation into Napoleon's Imperial France.

Despite these many difficulties, the Dutch retained strong discipline over their money, and kept it linked to gold at the original parity value. Yields on perpetual government bonds were quoted at 2.51% in 1762. Even in 1786, while the economy was spiraling into decline, government debt traded around 3.0%. The final disasters of the 1790s made even government bonds an obvious credit risk, and in 1798 their yields were quoted in the 6.42%-6.95% range.

Chapter 5:
The World's Experience with Gold Standard
Systems

The world's major commercial centers have always used gold as money, typically alongside small-denomination monies including silver, copper, bronze (roughly 88% copper and 12% tin), or some other commodity such as cowrie shells or cocoa beans. The Sumerian civilization of Mesopotamia (3500-1800 B.C.) used gold and silver as money, although small-scale commerce was also done with standardized rings made of shell. The Sumerians even traded warehouse receipts for gold among each other as a form of payment. These warehouse receipts were recorded in cuneiform clay tablets. Gold-based representative money predates paper. When the Spanish conquistadores discovered and then looted the New World, they were thrilled to find that the Incas and Aztecs also mined and hoarded gold and silver. The Aztecs used gold as money in regular commerce, in the form of standardized figurines (a decorative sort of ingot), and quills of feathers filled with gold dust. Cacao beans (chocolate) served as small-scale money. The Incas' Soviet-style command economy did not have any form of money, as it is known in market economies. However, rulers amassed huge quantities of gold and silver, which they used to purchase alliance, receive and pay tribute to neighboring states, and reward generals for military service.

The King James Bible mentions gold 417 times, and silver 320 times. The first mention is in Genesis 2:11-12, only a few sentences after the world is created: "The name of the first [river] is Pison; that is it which compasseth the whole land of Havilah, where there is gold; and the gold of that land is good."

For roughly two thousand years, 2700-700 B.C., gold and silver were used throughout Mesopotamia and the Near East as money in bullion form. This required regular weighing for transactions, but had the advantage of being devaluation-proof. A standard Sumerian unit of silver was a "shekel," a combination of the Sumerian words "she" (wheat) and "kel" (a unit similar to a bushel), indicating a value analogous to one "kel" of wheat. Indeed, Sumerian cuneiform tablets indicate that: "the price of one gur of barley is one shekel of silver." Rings and coils of silver used for payment, in standardized shekel weights, date from as early as 2700 B.C.

The Code of Hammurabi (1772 B.C.), a Babylonian legal code, indicated several penalties to be paid in gold, measured in units called "mina" (equivalent to sixty shekels). For example:

> 138. If a man wishes to separate from his wife who has borne him no children, he shall give her the amount of her purchase money and the dowry which she brought from her father's house, and let her go.
> 139. If there was no purchase price he shall give her one mina of gold as a gift of release.
> 140. If he be a freed man he shall give her one-third of a mina of gold.

The first gold and silver coins in ancient Greece and Lydia date from the 7th century B.C. India's oldest coinage dates from the 7th-6th centuries B.C. It was made of silver. Chinese bronze "coins" in the shape of a stylized spades and knives began as early as 1200 B.C. Chinese gold coins date from the sixth or fifth century B.C. The coin (a standardized, simplified unit of precious metals) was simply one way of trading in gold and silver, which had previously traded in other forms based on bullion weight.

In roughly 100 B.C, the Chinese historian Sima Qian wrote: "With the opening of exchange between farmers, artisans, and merchants, there came into use money of tortoise shells, cowrie shells, gold, qian (bronze coins), dao (knives), and bu (spades). This has been so from remote antiquity."

The Chinese are also credited with inventing paper, apparently by one Cai Lun in 105 A.D. The first record of Chinese paper money dates from 140 A.D. Unfortunately, we do not know what came of it.

The British pound originally referred to a Tower pound weight (240 pennyweights, about 350 grams) of silver, in any form. It was simply a representation of weight. For many centuries, there was no standardized coin or ingot corresponding to this measure. The Tower pound itself derived from the Arabic dirham, a silver coin common in the Middle East. The dirham also served as the basic unit of monetary unit of the Hanseatic League, a trade group of medieval Germany and northern Europe. Even into the 20th century, silver bullion was used as money in China, based on weight. If necessary, silver coins and ingots would be sawn into pieces to provide correct payment, and this was perfectly acceptable. In the American colonies, gold and silver coins from any country, or bullion in any form, were acceptable as payment based on the weight of contained metal.

In the 1970s, the mining corporation Anglo-American engaged archaeologists to examine ancient gold mining sites in the Zambezi river valley of South Africa. Extensive mining areas were found with shafts up to fifty feet deep. Stone objects and charcoal remains established dates of 35,000, 46,000 and 60,000 B.C. In 1988, a team of archaeologists dated nearby settlements at an age of 80,000-115,000 B.C.

The world has always used gold as money. The worldwide gold standard of the late 19th century, from roughly 1850 to 1914, was a refinement, harmonization and modernization of this ageless principle.

Interest rates on loans denominated in gold and silver have always been very low for the best credits. Over a four-century period, the United States, Britain and Holland all experienced long-term government bond yields in the 3.0%-3.5% range – at times even below 3.0% – for extended periods of time. This was no fluke. In the sixteenth century, the Bank of St. George, of Genoa, issued a gold-based perpetual bond (again, infinite maturity) that traded at a yield of 3.0% in 1523; 2.875% in 1525; 3.875% in 1542; 2.5% in 1573; and 3.25% in 1590. Records of the market prices of long-term *prestii* government bonds of Venice in the 14th century show that they typically traded with about a 5.5% yield during times of peace.

Prior to the Renaissance, which coincided with the lifting of bans on the payment of interest imposed by the Christian church (originally in 325 A.D. at the Council of Nicaea), one needs to go back to Rome for further information on gold- and silver-based market yields in the Western world. During the rule of Octavian (27 B.C. to 14 A.D.), when Rome's economy, financial sophistication, and monetary quality was at its peak, businesses commonly borrowed at 4%-6%, on a gold or silver basis.[1]

By 1850, Britain and the Bank of England already had over 150 years of experience not only with gold and silver coins, but with the common use of standardized banknotes and the sophisticated financial systems that accompanied them. Britain was also, since 1816, on a strictly monometallic system. Silver coins were still used, but only as token coins. Gold, and gold alone, was the basis of the monetary system. This was a new development made possible by the widespread use of paper banknotes. Until then, some form of money needed to be used for small denominations, as gold bullion is useful only for unusually large transactions. The result was bimetallism. Although silver's value remained in a very tight ratio with gold, silver's slight variation in market value caused all manner of problems as commitments could be paid in either gold or silver. Also, the use of metal coins in general was quite problematic, as normal coin wear meant that coins often did not contain the promised metal value. This became still more problematic on the international level, as each country had its own version of bimetallism, which changed from time to time, its own means of addressing coin wear, banknotes issued by a myriad of small private issuers, and so forth.

The creation of standardized, reliable banknotes solved both of these issues. Increasing use of bank deposits as a replacement for direct cash holdings also proved most convenient. In this and all related matters, the world looked to Britain for guidance. In the mid-1870s, silver was both *de facto* and *de jure* demonetized worldwide. Australia adopted a monometallic standard in 1852, and Canada in 1853. An international conference in 1867 was held to standardize the bimetallic systems then common. The Latin Monetary Union was formed in 1865 between France, Belgium, Italy and Switzerland (other countries later joined informally) to standardize the bimetallic systems then in use. The official ratio of silver to gold was set by the Latin Monetary Union at 15.5 to 1. (The United States had an official silver:gold ratio of 16:1 at the time, meaning that exchange rates between the U.S. dollar and members of the LMU would vary depending on whether one was trading silver or gold; complicated arbitrage situations arose.) Germany adopted monometallism in 1871. The Latin Monetary Union shifted to a *de facto* policy of monometallism in 1873, which became official in 1878. The United States embraced *de facto* monometallism in the Coinage Act of 1873, and formally adopted monometallism in the Gold Standard Act of 1900. During the 1870s, silver's value fell from the close relationship it had maintained with gold for centuries, and was no longer usable as a small-denomination proxy for gold even among those that wished to do so. Humanity itself decided, on some level, that silver was no longer money (Figure 5.1).

With all countries on a monometallic standard, currency exchange – and, consequently, international trade and investment – became vastly simplified. Currencies were just different names for gold, easily converted at fixed exchange rates. The switch to monometallism was accompanied, in some cases, by the adoption of a currency board linked to the British pound, raising Britain's role in the center of the world monetary system of the time.

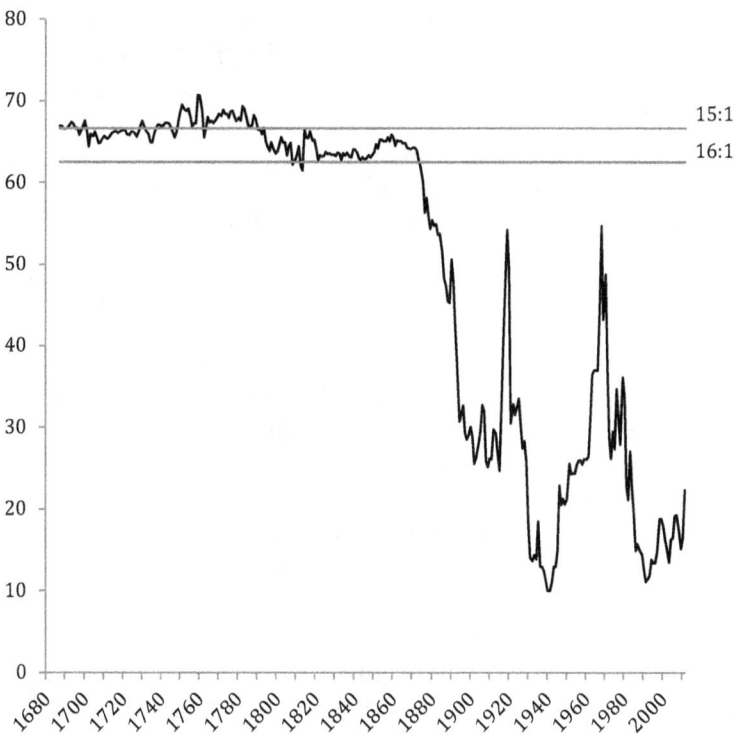

Figure 5.1: Value of 1000 oz. of Silver in Gold Oz. in London, 1687-2011[2]

Some countries not only made slight adjustments to existing bimetallic systems, but introduced major currency reforms upon the British or U.S. model. Particularly after 1870, Europe enjoyed a period of peace until 1914. During this time, governments reinstated gold standard systems that were suspended during wartime. The United States did so in 1879, following the floating of the dollar in 1861 due to the Civil War. The U.S. dollar was also made more uniform and unified by the introduction of the National Bank System, such that a "dollar" from each issuing bank was effectively interchangeable. France had maintained the principle of the gold parity established by the Bank of France in 1803; in practice, it was suspended due to wartime during the Second Empire period under Napoleon III. France's gold standard system was reinstated in 1878, reflecting political stability following the establishment in 1870 of the Third Republic, which lasted until 1914.

The Meiji Restoration in Japan of 1868, replacing the medieval Shogunate established in 1600, led to the introduction of the unified Japanese yen in 1871. The original value of the yen was equivalent to one U.S. dollar. The gold-based yen replaced a menagerie of hundreds of minor currencies. The unification of Germany in 1871, assembled from dozens of small states, led to the introduction of the unified German mark in 1873. The standardized, gold-based mark replaced myriad minor currencies then in use throughout Germany.

The establishment of the Kingdom of Italy, in 1861, unified a number of smaller states on the peninsula, and led to the introduction of the unified Italian lira that same year. Spain's peseta was introduced in 1869, after years of turmoil leading to the Glorious Revolution of 1868. After a few more years of settling down, constitutional monarchy was re-established in Spain and produced a period of relative stability that lasted until 1931. After a protracted struggle for independence from the Ottoman Empire, the autonomy of the newly independent, modern Greek state was first recognized by the Great Powers (Britain, France and Russia) in 1829, and a new monarchical government was introduced in 1832 with the Treaty of London. The modern Greek drachma dates from 1832. China's modern yuan originated in 1889, when it was established equivalent to one Mexican silver peso (the original basis of the U.S. dollar as well).

Each country had its own particular approach as to how their gold standard systems were established and operated, and its own timetable, reflecting the specifics of each country and its internal political situation. Gold and silver had always been the monetary basis of Europe and the world, but in the latter half of the 19th century, a more unified and organized monetary system emerged as one country after another established the beginnings of modern standardized currencies. Throughout this time, Britain and the British pound served as the example to emulate.

Countries that had a poor record of currency management in the 20th century generally also had difficulties in the 19th century. Nevertheless, after various upsets, they returned over and over to a gold standard system. This included Spain, Argentina, Brazil, Italy, Chile and Greece. (These behaviors seem to persist in the culture and political system.)

As central banks, patterned after the Bank of England, and unified systems such as the U.S.'s National Bank system became more common after 1850, the bullion holdings of central banks increased. However, this was matched by a reduction in the use of gold coins. In essence, people traded their coins with the central bank for banknotes. This was a practical trend, as banknotes do not suffer natural wear, their quality is not in question, and they are infinitely subdividable.

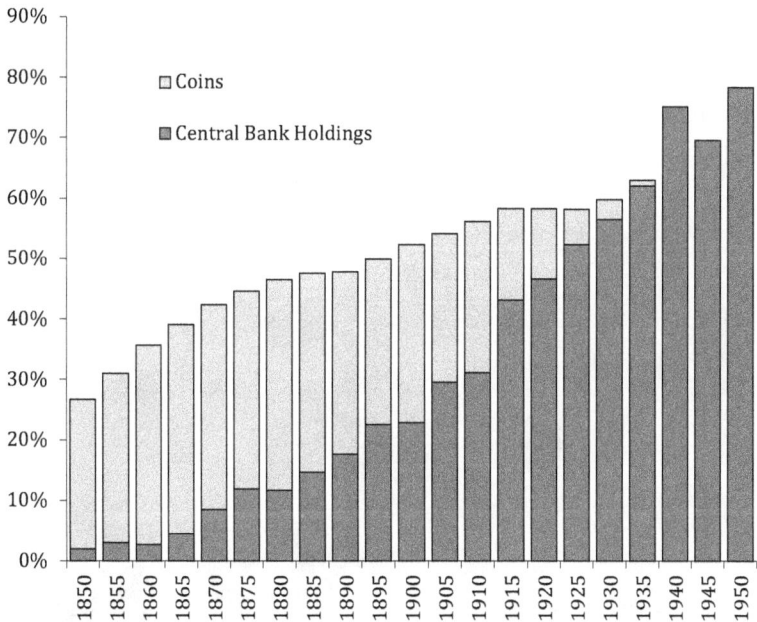

Figure 5.2: Monetary Gold as a Percentage of Total Aboveground Gold, 1850-1950[3]

Thus, the total percentage of aboveground gold in monetary use did not increase substantially between, for example, 1880 and 1935. (Figure 5.2) During the Bretton Woods period, after World War II, central banks' gold holdings generally remained static on an absolute basis, and declined as a percentage of total aboveground gold (Figure 5.3).

The latter 19th century was a time of high and rising tariffs worldwide, impeding trade within Europe. However, it was also a time of global empire, and trade within an empire was often without impediment. Capital flowed freely, particularly between the European centers of empire and territorial holdings. The first great age of globalization began. Foreign investment, as a percentage of GDP, rose from 7 percent in 1870 to 18 percent in 1914. In 1950, after two World Wars and the Great Depression, this ratio had fallen to 5 percent. The 18 percent level was not reached again until 1999.

In 1870, the ratio of world trade to GDP was ten percent, and it rose to 21 percent in 1914. In 1938, it had fallen back to nine percent. It did not reach 21 percent again until 1996.

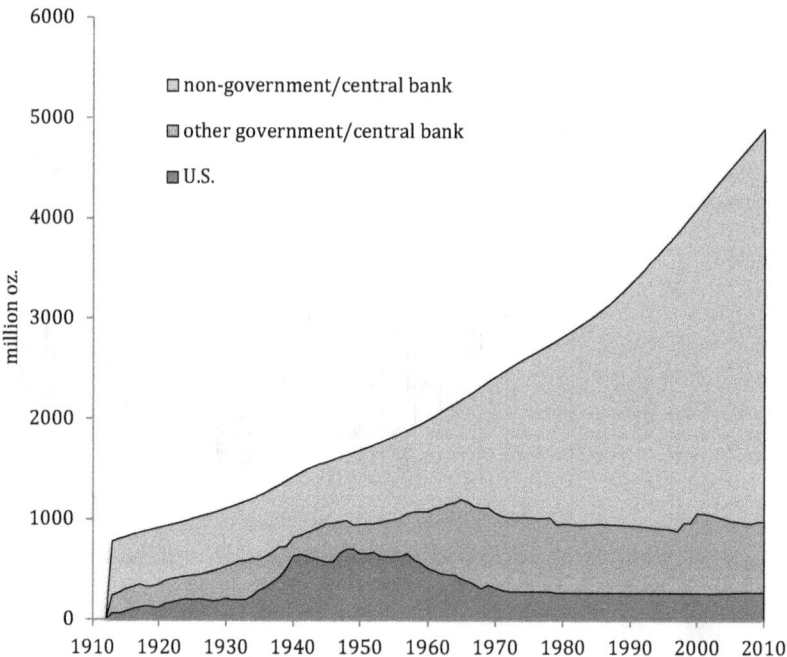

Figure 5.3: Central Bank Gold Holdings, 1913-2010[4]

Interest rates worldwide converged to low levels. British debt was perceived to have the lowest risk of either credit default or currency devaluation. Other governments' debt traded with a small risk premium. Yields on French government debt were around 15% when the Bank of France was established in 1800, with the purpose of re-establishing a gold standard system in France. Yields on French rentes had fallen to 8.73% in 1816; 4.89% in 1855; 3.14% in 1890; and 3.00% in 1902.

Government bond yields in the Netherlands were 6.7% in 1814; 4.36% in 1850; and 3.26% in 1900. Belgium's government paid 5.0% in 1840; 4.02% in 1870; and 2.92% in 1900. Germany's government paid 5.72% in 1820; 3.86% in 1840; and 3.46% in 1900. Sweden's government paid 5.96% in 1868; 3.57% in 1875; and 3.82% in 1900. The magic that Rome had created in the 1st century, Holland had created in the 17th century, and Britain had created in the 18th century, spread to the entire globe in the 19th century. Corporations found that they could borrow at rates only a little higher than the best quality government bonds. In 1880, just after the reintroduction of a gold standard system in 1879, U.S. high-grade railroad bonds traded with a 4.46% yield. In 1900, the yield was 3.18%.

The world was effectively unified with a single currency – gold – and enjoyed all the advantages to trade and finance that creates. Not only was it a single currency, it was the best possible currency. Unlike recent "currency union" projects like the eurozone, there was no need for fiscal coordination, political union, or some central governing body. Each country could choose to participate unilaterally, on its own terms, and maintain policy independence in all other spheres.

No major country maintained a "100% reserve" gold standard system, in which gold bullion is held in a vault for each equivalent unit of currency outstanding. Combining both gold and foreign reserves (bonds denominated in foreign gold-based currencies), in 1900 the reserve ratio for Britain was 42%; Germany, 50%; France, 67%; Belgium, 35%; Netherlands, 60%; Denmark, 70%; Finland, 77%; Norway, 61%; Russia, 72%; Austro-Hungary, 68%. Obviously, the reserve ratios for gold bullion alone would be below these levels, perhaps well below. (The remainder of reserve assets was domestic debt.)

Trade was still problematic due to high tariffs. In 1904, standard tariffs for manufactured products were 25% in Germany; 27% in Italy; 34% in France; 35% in Austria; 73% in the United States; and 131% in Russia. This reflected tax systems that were heavily skewed toward indirect taxes. Direct taxes (income taxes) were just beginning to be introduced, at low rates. Nevertheless, capital flowed freely throughout the world, without the problems of unpredictable exchange rates or government capital controls. The liquidity shortage crisis, a problem in earlier decades, was apparently resolved by the maturation of "lender of last resort" techniques at the Bank of England. A crisis in 1866 was resolved in this manner, and Britain never suffered another liquidity shortage crisis. The Bank of England's example as a "lender of last resort" was imitated at similar central banks throughout the world.

Europe's colonial holdings provided, in the terms of the day, "a source of raw materials and a destination for finished products" – in other words, trading partners for the industrialized European core. Empires expanded dramatically toward the end of the 19th century, as governments sought to increase their effective free trade zones. Between 1884 and 1900, the British Empire expanded by 3.7 million square miles and 57 million people; France added 3.5 million square miles and 36 million people; Germany annexed one million square miles and 17 million people. The United States digested its Western territories, and soon expanded to the Philippines, Cuba, Alaska, Hawaii, Puerto Rico, Guam, the Solomon Islands, and a soft empire throughout Latin America including a portion of Panama. Japan grabbed the Korean peninsula, Formosa (Taiwan), and a chunk of Mongolia. Belgium developed the Congo. In 1880, European colonies included 9.5 million square miles and 312 million inhabitants. In 1913, they totaled 20.3 million square miles and 525 million inhabitants. It was the first great era of "emerging markets," as European empires brought with them European governance, and thus European monetary, financial, administrative and legal systems, sewing these regions into the global economy. For better or worse, European industry and agriculture spread throughout Asia, Africa, Latin America, the Middle East, and Europe's eastern hinterlands.

In 1849, there was not a single mile of railway in India, then part of the British Empire. In 1880, India had 9,000 miles of track. In 1929, there were 41,000 miles of railroad in India, built by British engineers, British capital, and Indian labor. The first railroad in South Africa (another British territory) opened in 1860. South Africa's rail network later reached 12,000 miles of track, not including extensions which were intended to eventually reach all the way to the 3,000-mile rail network of British-controlled Egypt. By 1901, over 12,000 miles of railway had been laid in British-held Australia. In 1895, China's Qing dynasty had became so weak that it was forced by the European powers to allow rail construction, with additional concessions such as settlement and mining near the rail lines. By 1911, there were over 5,500 miles of rail line in China. In 1899, France began Vietnam's

North-South railway; in 1904, work began on the Sino-Vietnamese railway, connecting France's holdings in Indochina with China's heartland.

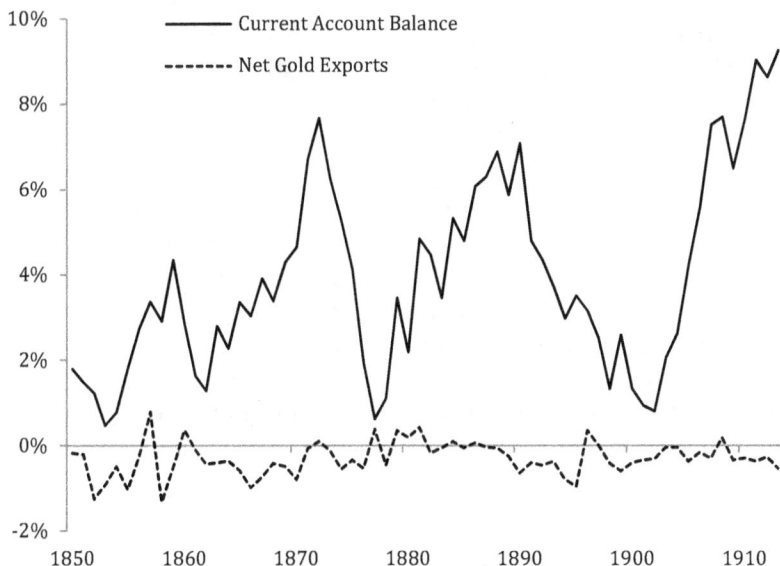

Figure 5.4: Britain: Current Account Balance and Net Gold Exports, Percent of GDP, 1850-1913[5]

By 1870, steamship technology had developed to the point that it was economically viable to replace sail for commercial transport. From expanding port cities, new steamship networks connected these railway systems, and the products they carried, to markets worldwide. Between 1850 and 1900, individual steamships grew ten times larger in size, as world shipping ballooned. Total shipping tonnage from British-held Singapore, to take one example, rose from 375,000 tons in 1860 to 5.7 million tons in 1900, an increase of 15 times.

This immense investment and development was financed by European capital, which could be raised cheaply and in large volume, mostly in the form of bonds denominated in Europe's gold-based currencies. Joint stock companies were deregulated in Britain in 1863. The number of joint stock companies in Britain expanded from 691 in 1863 to 7,000 in 1914. Investment trusts (mutual funds) became popular in the 1880s and 1890s. Net foreign investment was commonly above 6% of GDP in Britain, and before World War I climbed to an incredible 9% of GDP (Figure 5.4). Twice as much

British foreign investment went to Africa as went to Europe; four times as much went to Latin America. In 1914, 44% of global foreign investment was coming from Britain. From 1880 to 1914, British exports of goods and services averaged around 30% of GDP. (In 2011, it was 19.3%.) France accounted for 20% of Europe's total net foreign investment, Germany 13%. Belgium, the Netherlands and Switzerland also contributed substantial net foreign investment.

Despite claims that the gold standard systems of the era forced the "balance of payments" into balance, this was not the case at all (Figure 5.5). Another term for "net foreign investment" is a "current account surplus," which for some countries (like Britain) was extraordinarily large and persistent over decades. Of course these capital flows must go somewhere; countries that had a net inflow of capital (including the United States) thus had "current account deficits," another word for the same thing. The world gold standard system empowered these capital flows, because people could invest worldwide with little risk of currency fluctuation. In other words, the gold standard system helped produce "balance of payments imbalances," a bizarre term for global investing, and not particularly problematic when exchange rates are stable.

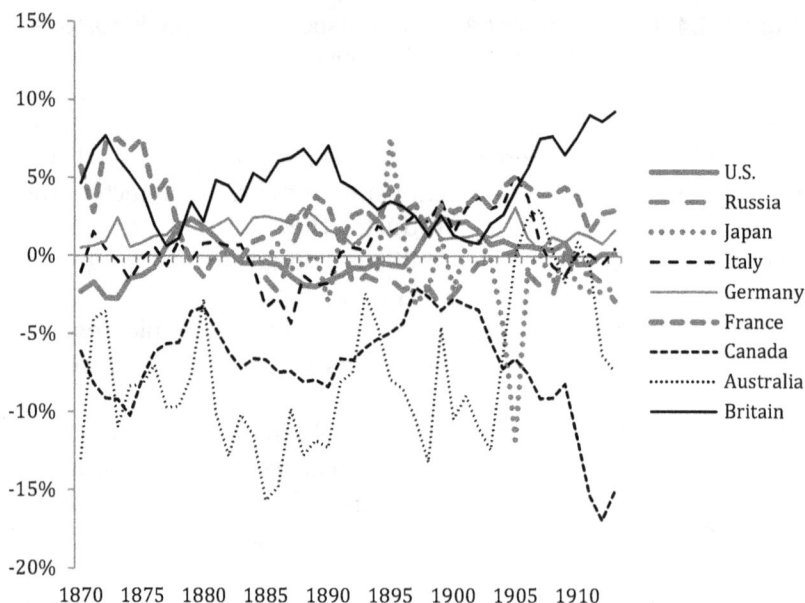

Figure 5.5: Current Account Balances as a Percent of GDP, 1870-1913[6]

Capital sought its highest return. During this time, that was often in the emerging markets, where small investments could lead to great increases in productivity. A consequence of capital flowing overseas was that it was not invested at home. In Britain in particular, complaints arose that a slower pattern of growth was being caused by low levels of domestic investment. This in turn led to greater domestic pressures for social welfare programs, and higher taxes to pay for them. The higher taxes made British domestic investment still less attractive.

Governments embraced the Classical ideal of Stable Money. They did not try to manage their economies by jiggering their currencies. The system was entirely sustainable, successful throughout, and ended only because of the outbreak of World War I. In 1914, Britain had followed gold standard principles for 217 years. If not for the war, the world gold standard could have lasted another 217 years, and in 1910, people expected that it would.

It was the finest expression of monetary perfection the world has ever seen. After World War I, governments attempted to re-establish the world gold standard of the pre-1914 era, and mostly succeeded for a few years in the late 1920s. However, this soon disintegrated during the difficulties of the early 1930s. The Bretton Woods conference of 1944 established another world gold standard system, this time with the United States in a leadership role instead of Britain. Unfortunately, that system was marred by various attempts to combine a Mercantilist "domestic monetary policy," typically involving interest rate manipulation, with a Classical gold standard policy. It could only be maintained with heavy capital controls, and even then major currencies had periodic devaluations. The Bretton Woods system's internal contradictions were too much. It lasted only a brief time, and collapsed in 1971-1973 despite worldwide peace and prosperity.

The floating currency system arrangement since 1971 is not rightly called a system at all. There was no international conference, like that at Bretton Woods, New Hampshire, to establish some new framework of cooperation. Today's arrangement is mostly chaos, the unpredictable consequences of central banks trying to manipulate their currencies on an improvisational day-to-day basis using an ever-shifting kaleidoscope of Mercantilist rationalizations.

This has consequences. Eventually, the consequences will be great enough that governments worldwide will again embrace the Classical principles of Stable Money. At that time, a new world gold standard will emerge, which will again serve as the foundation for global commerce and investment. Perhaps, with all of the advancements in technology and understanding, it will be even more perfect than the world gold standard of the pre-1914 era.

Chapter 6:
Example #1: The "Making Change" System

Let's begin with the simplest practical gold standard system, the "Making Change" system.

This system is almost identical to the gold-based exchange-traded funds described earlier.

The basic mechanism of the system is a lot like making change. Give me a dollar and I give you four quarters. Give me five one-dollar bills and I give you a five-dollar bill. In this case, it is: give me gold bullion and I give you the equivalent smaller-denomination banknotes; give me banknotes and I give you bullion.

One problem with using gold coins themselves in trade is that their denomination is too large. The smallest practical gold coin is about a tenth of a troy ounce, or about 3.1 grams. It would be a very small coin. However, even a coin of this size has a rather high value. In 2011, the average value of the dollar was $1,571 per oz. of gold. A tenth-ounce coin was worth about $157. The largest denomination used in regular daily transactions in the United States is the $20 bill. Usually, for amounts over $50, a bank check, credit card or debit card is used. A coin worth $157 in 2011 wouldn't be a very useful currency, and that would be the smallest denomination in a monetary system that used gold coins alone. Even if you did want to pay for something that cost more than $157 with this gold coin, there would be no way to make change. (Note that, although one rarely sees denominations of more than $20 in the United States, fully 75%, by dollar value, of all U.S. dollar banknotes in existence are in the form of $100 bills. They are probably being used for large cash transactions and as a store of value, both within and outside of the U.S.)

Historically, the problem of small denominations was solved with the parallel use of silver coins, the "bimetallic" system. This was possible because the market value of silver was very closely linked to gold, in a ratio of about 15:1 or 16:1. This ratio remained stable for hundreds of years, and indeed the historical record shows that this stable silver:gold ratio persisted as far back as Roman and Greek times, if not earlier. Copper or bronze coins served when even silver was of too high a denomination for small-scale use.

In the mid-1870s, the longstanding link between silver and gold ruptured, rendering traditional bimetallism impossible. Governments transitioned to effective monometallism during this time.

Full-weight commodity coins have always been a problematic form of money. They naturally wear down over time, or could be intentionally clipped, so the contained metal and thus the value of each coin would be different. Often, individual coins would have to be weighed in each transaction to determine their value. Chinese coins had holes in the middle so they could be sorted according to wear and grouped on loops of string. This was cumbersome to say the least. It was much simpler to have standardized banknotes, whose value was always exactly the parity specified, for example 1/20.67th ounce of gold in the case of the dollar, and which could be redeemed for exactly that amount of gold bullion on demand.

For these reasons, the bimetallic, full-weight coinage system, which was the primary system in the United States around 1800 for example, is no longer practical today.

In the Making Change system, the currency issuer (such as a central bank) offers to trade gold bullion for base money (banknotes or bank reserves recorded as deposits at the currency issuer) at a specified parity – for example, 1,000 currency units per ounce of gold. We will call these arbitrary currency units "goldenbucks," abbreviated "G\$." The currency issuer takes no discretionary action. It simply offers, to anyone willing, to either take one ounce of gold bullion and give G\$1,000 in base money, or to take G\$1,000 in base money and give one ounce of gold bullion. Each transaction is initiated by some private market entity.

You could also call this a "100% reserve" or "warehouse receipt" system. However, those terms mean different things to different people. To encourage people to look at these methodologies with a fresh viewpoint, we will use some fresh terminology.

Let's begin with a system that starts with no outstanding base money in circulation. This is analogous to the gold-based ETFs shown earlier, which began with effectively no shares outstanding.

The currency issuer's balance sheet looks like this:

Assets		Liabilities	
	none		none

Just as a gold-based ETF is interesting as an investment device, this new currency is interesting as a medium of transaction, or a monetary device. Thus, someone wants to own some. They want to hold it in their wallet, and then, when the time comes, use it in some transaction. They come to the currency manager with an ounce of gold, and receive G$1,000 in return. Unlike a one-ounce gold coin, you could buy coffee with this new currency, and receive correct change. The currency manager "makes change," taking the "large denomination" gold bullion and offering "small denomination" banknotes and coins, or bank reserves.

Assets		Liabilities	
Gold bullion	1 oz.	Base money	G$1,000

They tell their friends, and their friends tell their friends, and pretty soon lots of people have begun to acquire and use this new currency. The "demand" increases.

Assets		Liabilities	
Gold bullion	1,000 oz.	Base money	G$1,000,000

How do they obtain this new currency? Probably not by bringing an ounce of gold to the currency issuer directly. There would likely be some intermediary, like a bank or currency exchange dealer. For example, the bank could make a market in various currencies and goldenbucks. The bank could take U.S. dollars in trade and give goldenbucks in return. The bank then takes these U.S. dollars, buys gold bullion, and gives the gold to the currency issuer, in this way acquiring goldenbucks for sale. Along the way, the bank makes a little money in fees and so forth. This is a good business.

The most common way for a typical person to acquire currency is as payment for employment, or goods and services sold. After a payment, the person's bank account shows a balance of G$756. The person then withdraws G$100 from the bank account, from an ATM machine perhaps, thus acquiring G$100 in paper banknotes. The banking system must obtain these banknotes in some fashion, and the only way to obtain them is to bring gold bullion to the currency issuer and receive goldenbucks in return.

Perhaps the head of the currency issuer is embroiled in a sex scandal, which makes people nervous about the future operations of the currency issuer and the reliability of the currency. Thus, to be safe, they decide to return some of their goldenbucks to the issuer and get gold bullion instead. In other words, the "demand" for the currency decreases. People don't want to hold as much as they did before. The currency issuer receives base money and offers gold bullion. The currency issuer's balance sheet looks like this:

Assets		Liabilities	
Gold bullion	500 oz.	Base money	G$500,000

After a while, it becomes clear that there was no real danger to the currency, and that the system is in fact quite reliable. Thus, the popularity increases again.

Assets		Liabilities	
Gold bullion	2,000 oz.	Base money	G$2,000,000

Over time, people in neighboring countries start to hear about the new goldenbucks, and want to start using them instead of their local junk fiat currency. The currency becomes a popular international currency.

Assets		Liabilities	
Gold bullion	10,000 oz.	Base money	G$10,000,000

Unfortunately, the government can't get its deficit under control, leading politicians to begin making remarks that the currency manager should start buying government bonds with the printing press. This leads to widespread selling of goldenbucks worldwide.

Assets		Liabilities	
Gold bullion	7,000 oz.	Base money	G$7,000,000

As government bond yields rise, the housing market collapses, leading to mortgage defaults and bank insolvency. International holders of goldenbucks reduce their holdings further, but domestic residents, fearing bank collapse, withdraw deposits from banks and hold a greater amount of cash. To meet deposit withdrawals, banks need a greater supply of banknotes. They acquire this by selling assets, using the proceeds to buy gold bullion, and trading the gold bullion with the currency issuer for base money.

Assets		Liabilities	
Gold bullion	12,000 oz.	Base money	G$12,000,000

And so it may go on, through many such situations and events. Throughout, the policy of the currency issuer is simple: it will accept gold and give base money, or it will accept base money and give gold, at the parity rate. As long as the assets and liabilities of the currency issuer are kept in balance, as shown in the example, the currency issuer will always be able to meet its commitments. In the worst case scenario, where all existing base money is brought to the currency issuer in trade for gold – there isn't a single person in the world willing to hold a single goldenbuck – the very last base money would come in when the very last gold bullion went out. The currency issuer would have no assets and no liabilities, and the system would quietly go dormant. The currency would cease to exist. However, even at the very end, the currency manager kept its promise to deliver gold bullion on demand, and the currency remained at its 1000:1 parity with gold bullion.

Assets		Liabilities	
	none		none

* * *

The previous example is of a system that starts from zero, with no assets and no liabilities. What about a country with an existing currency, where the government would like to transition to a Making Change-type gold standard system? Let's use a real-world example: New Zealand. This is a simplified version of the Reserve Bank of New Zealand's balance sheet, at the end of 2011:

Assets (NZ$)	
Government securities	$3,177m
Short-term loans	$50m
Short-term loans (in foreign currency)	$6,096m
Marketable securities (in foreign currency)	$13,206m
Total	$22,529m

Liabilities and Capital (NZ$)	
Currency in circulation	$4,894m

Government deposits	$4,165m
Deposits of other institutions	$7,134m
Short-term loans (in foreign currency)	$1,163m
Long-term loans (in foreign currency)	$2,586m
Share capital	$2,587m
Total	$22,529m

New Zealand dollar base money is the currency in circulation, plus deposits at the Reserve Bank, which include deposits of the government and deposits of other institutions (banks). The total is NZ$16,193 million. The reserve assets include both domestic government securities (denominated in New Zealand dollars), and substantial foreign reserves in the form of marketable securities (foreign government bonds), plus loans to banks denominated in foreign currencies.

There is also a bit of "share capital." In other words, total assets are slightly larger than total liabilities (base money), with the difference recorded as the "capital" of the Reserve Bank. The presence of assets in excess of liabilities reinforces the ability of the currency issuer to meet all obligations. Within the Making Change system, if all base money in existence was brought to the bank in exchange for gold bullion, then the bank would be able to meet all bullion redemption and also have something left over.

The history of the New Zealand dollar (Figure 6.1) is fairly typical. It is a floating currency, nominally independent of the U.S. dollar, but in practice, the exchange rate with the U.S. dollar tends to stay within a well-established band. Governments find that they cannot let the exchange rate vary too far or too quickly from the major international currency, because of the turmoil that results to the terms of trade for businesspeople.

If New Zealand wished to adopt a Making Change gold standard system, it would sell reserve assets equivalent to the monetary base of NZ$16,193 million, and then, with the proceeds of the sale, purchase gold bullion. Let's say this occurred at the end of 2011. At that time, the value of the NZ$ was about US$0.77, and the value of the US$ compared to an ounce of gold was 1/1530th of an ounce, or 1530:1, or $1,530/oz. Thus, the value of the NZ$ monetary base, in gold terms, was 8.15 million ounces of gold, and the value of the New Zealand dollar, in terms of gold, was NZ$1,987/oz. This is a bit of a silly number for a new gold parity, so let's round to NZ$2,000/oz., which translates into 8.10 million ounces of gold. We will pay off the

120

foreign currency loans, and put the rest of the assets into domestic government bonds.

Figure 6.1: New Zealand: Value of New Zealand Dollar in U.S. Dollars, 1971-2011

From that point onward, the Reserve Bank of New Zealand would operate a Making Change-type gold standard system as described previously. For example, it would offer to either buy or sell gold at NZ$2,000/oz., in unlimited quantity, in the process adjusting the monetary base by the equivalent amount. (The various lending and borrowing in foreign currencies would probably no longer be necessary, and naturally disappear.) The Reserve Bank could also introduce a small "trading band," for example, offering to sell at 1% over the parity price (NZ$2,020/oz.) and offering to buy at 1% under the parity price (NZ$1,980/oz.), which would reduce the number of transactions the Reserve Bank would be involved in without materially affecting the operation of the Making Change system.

Assets (NZ$ millions)	
Gold bullion	8.10 million oz.
Government securities	$2,587
Total	$18,780

Liabilities and Capital (NZ$ millions)	
Currency in circulation	$4,894
Government deposits	$4,165
Deposits of other institutions	$7,134
Share capital	$2,587
Total	$18,780

* * *

The Making Change gold standard system is, to be sure, a very simple system, but even so, it is worth thinking about in more detail how it works. The currency issuer does not simply "sell gold at G$1,000." If a currency issuer simply sold gold at a price of G$1,000 (the parity price), but did not adjust the goldenbucks monetary base, the value of goldenbucks would vary from the parity. If the value of goldenbucks fell below the parity, to a market value of perhaps G$1,200 per ounce of gold (a value of 1/1,200th ounce of gold), then what would happen if the currency issuer sold gold at G$1,000? It would simply sell all the gold it owned, at a price below the market price. It would look something like this:

Assets		Liabilities	
Gold bullion	12,000 oz.	Base money	G$12,000,000

Holders of goldenbucks come to the currency issuer to buy gold bullion for G$1,000. However, the currency issuer does not change the amount of goldenbucks base money outstanding. (This is known as "sterilization.")

Assets		Liabilities	
Gold bullion	11,000 oz.	Base money	G$12,000,000

Because the supply of goldenbucks base money is unchanged, people continue to take more excess goldenbucks to the currency issuer in return for gold bullion.

Assets		Liabilities	
Gold bullion	10,000 oz.	Base money	G$12,000,000

By now, people have begun to realize that the currency issuer is not managing the currency properly, by reducing the base money supply when gold bullion is sold. This leads to a further decline in demand for goldenbucks, and accelerated purchases of gold from the currency issuer. The currency issuer actually increases base money outstanding, thinking this will help resolve the emerging economic crisis.

Assets		Liabilities	
Gold bullion	8,000 oz.	Base money	G$14,000,000

As the currency manager continues to fail to support the value of the currency, by way of a reduction in base money outstanding, and in fact goes the other way by expanding base money, a full-blown currency panic ensues.

Assets		Liabilities	
Gold bullion	4,000 oz.	Base money	G$15,000,000

At this point, to preserve dwindling gold bullion assets, the currency manager suspends sales of gold bullion. All remaining pretensions of maintaining a gold standard system are abandoned, and the currency becomes a floating fiat currency, which promptly declines to a third of its previous value.

This scenario might seem unlikely. How could anyone be so stupid? And yet, variations on this scenario happen all the time. The Making Change system is not just a matter of "selling gold at G$1,000." Rather, it is a system for managing the base money supply of goldenbucks, by way of sales and purchases of gold bullion at the parity price. It is these changes in the base money supply of goldenbucks that maintain their value at the parity price. When the market value of goldenbucks is marginally below the gold parity, then people will tend to trade their goldenbucks with the currency issuer for gold bullion. When the market value of goldenbucks is marginally above the gold parity, then people will tend to bring gold bullion to the currency issuer in trade for base money. The whole purpose of this system is to manage the base money supply of (otherwise worthless) goldenbucks, adjusting their relative scarcity so that their market value is equivalent to the gold parity. The system of offering to buy or sell bullion at the parity price acts as a signal, which tells the currency manager when to either increase or decrease the goldenbucks base money supply, and by how much.

Obviously, it won't work if you don't manage the supply of goldenbucks in the prescribed fashion. Simply selling something for less than it is worth, whether it be gold bullion or luxury cars, results in the seller selling all the available inventory. If you sell brand-new Mercedes S550 sedans (worth about $95,000) for $20,000 each, does that make the dollar worth 1/20,000th of an S550 sedan? It has no effect on the dollar's value at all.

If the Federal Reserve sold Mercedes S550 sedans for $20,000 each, in hopes that this would support the value of the dollar, this would actually have an effect on the dollar's value. The dollar's value

123

would go down, because nobody wants to hold a currency managed by idiots.

Figure 6.2: Thailand: Baht per U.S. Dollar, 1981-2011

This technique, of managing the base money supply directly as a means of managing a currency's value, can be used in the context of the Making Change system, or in a looser, ad-hoc framework common today. Either way, the basic results are the same. Let's look at some real-world examples of success and failure.

Figure 6.2 shows the value of the Thai baht, the currency of Thailand, compared to the U.S. dollar. The baht was roughly stable against the dollar from about 1985 to 1997. However, the exchange rate wiggled a bit. This was not an exact parity value, maintained by daily automatic adjustments, as is the case for our ETF or Making Change examples. It was more ad-hoc and informal than that. In 1997, the value of the baht vs. the dollar collapsed (the rising line indicates that it took more and more baht to buy a dollar). This was the Asia Crisis of 1997-1998. This dislocation was inadvertent; the Bank of Thailand wished to maintain the policy of keeping the value of the baht around 25 baht per dollar, but failed to do so. Figure 6.3 shows the 1997-1998 disaster in greater detail.

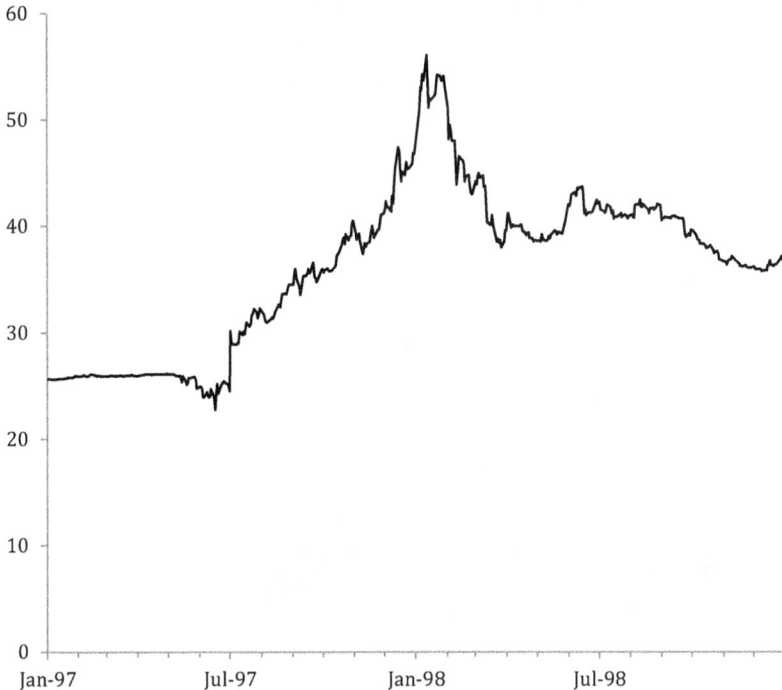

Figure 6.3: Thailand: Baht per U.S. Dollar, 1997-1998

The monetary base did indeed contract a bit in July and August of 1997, but that was largely a correction of the expansion in June. From a broader perspective, allowing for a bit of monthly variation, the monetary base hardly changed at all during this entire episode (Figure 6.4). We can conclude a few things from this: the Bank of Thailand took little meaningful action to support the value of the baht with reductions in the monetary base; but also, that the dramatic decline of the value of the baht was not due to excessive expansion of the monetary base. The reason for the decline was, in essence, a drop in demand for baht due to the continuing mismanagement of the currency by the currency manager. When the value of the baht varied from its dollar link by a little bit, people got worried, and when it varied by a lot, they panicked.

Figure 6.5 shows the value of the baht monetary base, as represented in U.S. dollars, according to the average exchange rate of the two currencies during the month. Because the monetary base, in terms of nominal baht, hardly changed, the change in terms of dollar value was almost entirely a matter of exchange rates. The total value of the baht monetary base began around $17 billion, and then, due to the decline of the baht's value, shrank to a little under $10 billion.

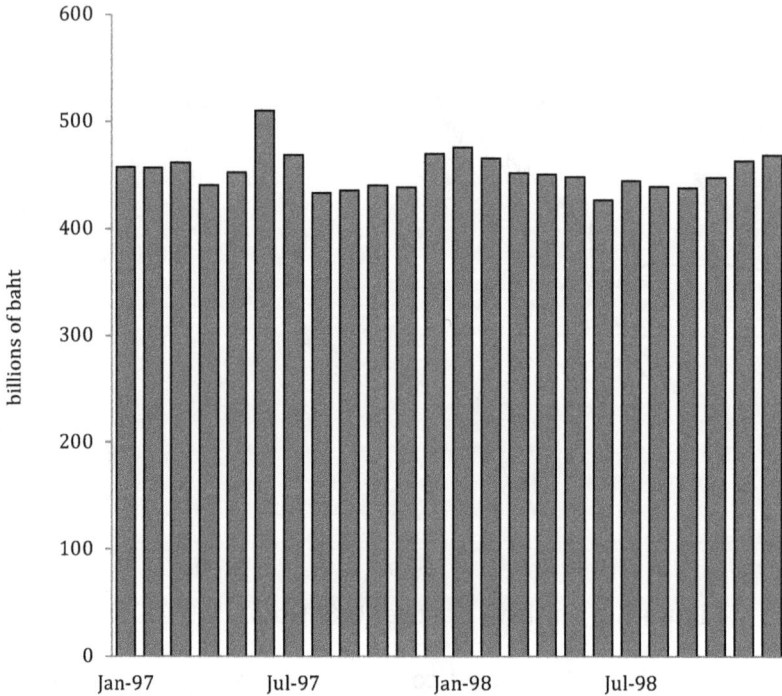

Figure 6.4: Thailand: Monetary Base, 1997-1998

Figure 6.6 shows Thailand's foreign exchange reserves, which dropped dramatically beginning in early 1997. The Bank of Thailand was "intervening" in the foreign exchange market, selling dollars and buying baht, to maintain the value of the baht compared to the dollar. In August 1997, the decline in foreign exchange reserves halts, because the Bank of Thailand ceased its intervention. This is when the market value of the baht began its collapse.

The operating technique of the Bank of Thailand was not a monetary base adjustment, in the manner of the Making Change system, but rather, simply "selling dollars" at a certain price. This is analogous to "selling gold" or "selling Mercedes S550 sedans" at a certain price in our prior examples. This selling of dollars did not result in any meaningful change in the baht monetary base. In other words, it was "sterilized." Not surprisingly, since the baht monetary base did not change, the problem of a baht value that was too low compared to its loose USD parity (supply in excess of demand) was not resolved. There was no adequate adjustment of supply. Although the Bank of Thailand did not run out of foreign exchange reserves completely, it halted its foreign exchange intervention when it saw that the pace of declines in its holdings would cause it to reach that point in short order.

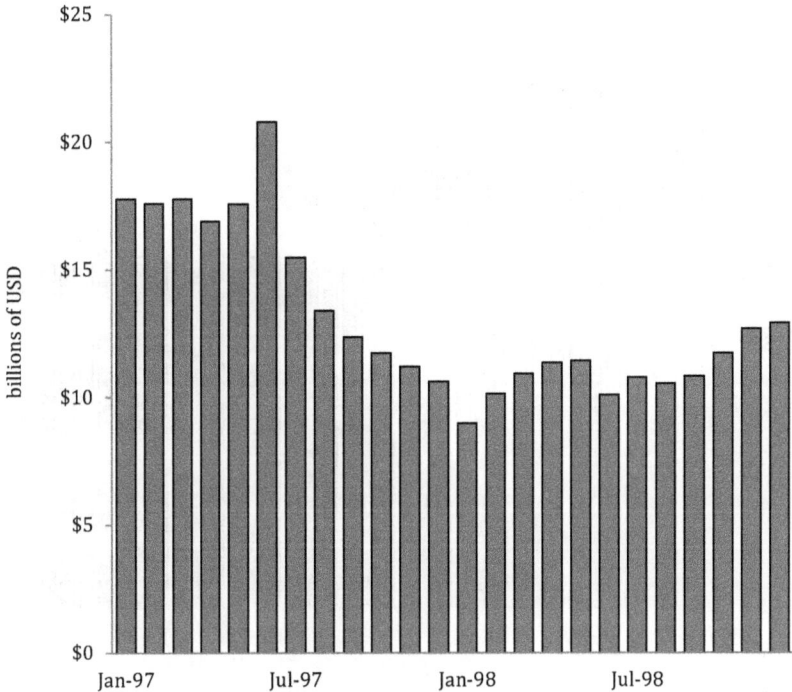

Figure 6.5: Thailand: Value of Monetary Base in U.S. Dollars, 1997-1998

From a peak of $39.9 billion in October 1996, foreign exchange reserves fell to a low of $25.9 billion in August 1997 – a drop of $14.0 billion.

The humorous thing here is that the total value of the entire baht monetary base, in January 1997, was $17.8 billion. If the Bank of Thailand had intervened in an "unsterilized" fashion, by reducing the baht monetary base by an equivalent amount for every dollar of foreign exchange reserves sold – in other words, taking the baht received in the sale of dollars and removing them from circulation, according to the operating mechanisms of the Making Change system

– the baht monetary base would have shrunk by $14.0 billion, or 79%! That is a very large drop indeed. In practice, such a large reduction in the monetary base would not have been necessary. Even in dramatic circumstances, a reduction of the monetary base by 20% is usually sufficient in supporting the value of the currency. That would have required the sale of only $3.6 billion of foreign exchange reserves.

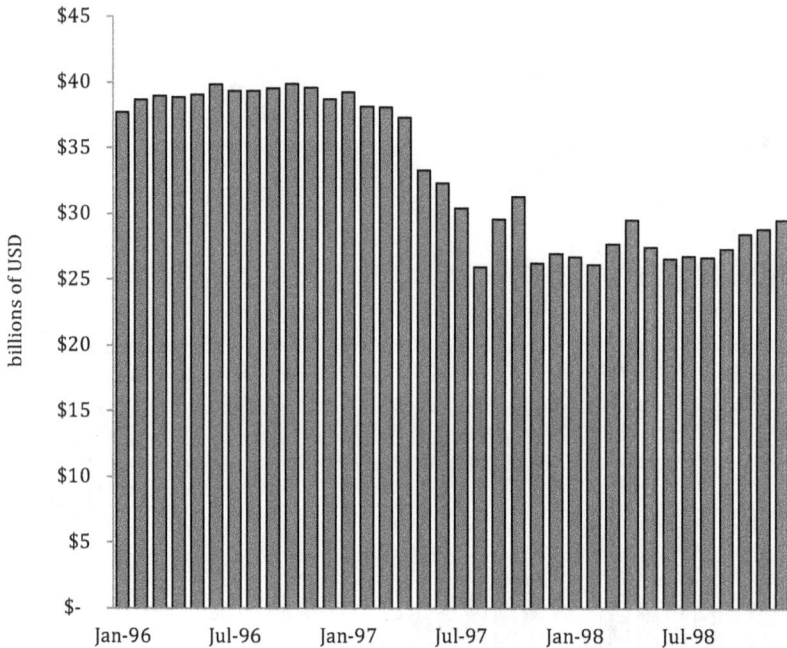

Figure 6.6: Thailand: Foreign Exchange Reserves, 1996-1998

The total amount of foreign exchange reserves at the start, of $39.9 billion, was vastly in excess of the value of the baht monetary base, of $17.8 billion. This was not a "100% reserve," it was a 224% reserve! The Bank of Thailand could have bought every baht in existence twice over, with more to spare. However, because the "foreign exchange interventions" were "sterilized," resulting in no meaningful change in the monetary base, the result was total failure.

Even after months of incompetence in the face of crisis, the Bank of Thailand, in August 1997, still had $25.9 billion of foreign exchange reserves. This was still enough to purchase every baht in existence, and certainly more than enough to purchase 20% of all the baht in existence, reducing the baht monetary base by 20%. This crisis was totally avoidable.

From this we can come to a few conclusions: first, the Bank of Thailand was tragically incompetent. Second, because the Bank of Thailand was closely advised by the International Monetary Fund throughout this episode, the IMF was also incompetent. We could extend this – correctly as it turns out – to the economics profession in general. This incompetence has rather dramatic and unfortunate consequences. During the crisis, the value of Thailand's SET stock market index fell by over 90% in U.S. dollar terms, and the Thai economy imploded.

Simply "selling gold at the parity price," in the context of an (attempted) gold standard system, will also fail in identical fashion, just as spectacularly, no matter how much gold the currency manager owns.

The idea that storing a bunch of gold, or foreign exchange reserves, in a vault will somehow manage a currency for you is absurd. The fact that the Thai baht was "backed" by foreign exchange reserves equivalent to 224% of the Thai base money supply was irrelevant. Similarly, a gold standard system that is "backed" by a lot of gold in a vault, even if it is equivalent to 200% or more of the base money supply, by itself is irrelevant if the currency is not managed properly. The notion of a currency "backed" by some quantity of dollar reserves or gold reserves is misleading. The real question is: does the currency manager know how to manage the supply of the currency appropriately?

* * *

Let's look at another example, quite similar to the Thailand example at the beginning, but which had a much happier ending.

The Russian ruble was stabilized against the U.S. dollar in 2000. For several years, it traded in a loose range between 25-30 rubles per dollar, even rising a bit beyond that in early 2008. Then, in the financial crises of 2008, the ruble began to lose value rapidly.

The basic cause of this was the same as for Thailand in 1997. In both cases, the U.S. dollar itself began to rise dramatically. Because there was no particular reason for the Thai baht or Russian ruble to rise alongside, these currencies tended to decline when compared to the rising dollar. However, it soon became clear, in both instances, that the currency managers (central banks) did not have the wherewithal to maintain the loose dollar parity that had been the apparent policy in the years leading up to the crisis. The result was that demand for both currencies dropped dramatically, and their market values fell further. The economic effects in both cases were catastrophic, in part because many businesses, having become accustomed to stable exchange rates, began to borrow extensively in foreign currencies. As the value of the ruble or baht collapsed, these borrowers' foreign currency debt burdens exploded.

Figure 6.7: Russia: Rubles per U.S. Dollar, 2008-2009

Just as was the case in Thailand, in the second half of 2008 the Russian central bank "intervened" in foreign exchange markets, selling foreign currency reserves and buying rubles. Again, these operations were "sterilized"; in other words, the rubles received in payment were not removed from circulation, which would have reduced the monetary base. The monetary base remained largely unchanged. Indeed, in January 2009, it even increased by a substantial amount. Although a year-end increase in the monetary base is a seasonal pattern in Russia, this increase in the monetary base in the midst of crisis probably reduced confidence in the central bank's management capacity still further, leading to an accelerated decline of the ruble. The ruble moved from 29.38 per dollar at the end of December 2008 to 35.41 at the end of January 2009, a decline in value of 17% in the space of a single month. This qualifies as a crash.

Figure 6.8: U.S.: U.S. Dollar Broad Trade-Weighted Index, 1995-2011

Due to this "foreign exchange intervention," the Russian government's international reserves fell from $596 billion in August 2008 to $427 billion in January 2009, a decline of $169 billion in the space of five months. However, the total value of the ruble monetary base, expressed in dollar terms, was only $219 billion in August 2008. The value of Russia's foreign reserves was 272% of the value of the monetary base in August 2008.

By January 2009, due to the decline in the ruble's value, the value of the monetary base in U.S. dollar terms was $117 billion. Russia's central bank had sold $169 billion of foreign currency, and bought rubles on the foreign exchange market. If these rubles had been removed from circulation, thus shrinking the monetary base by a comparable amount, the monetary base would have fallen from about $219 billion to $50 billion – a decline of 77%! Of course this didn't happen; the monetary base was unchanged, and the crisis continued.

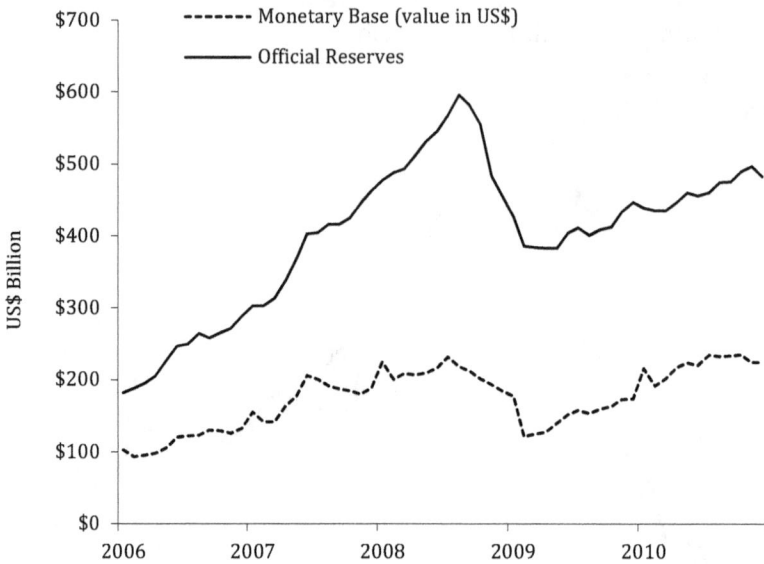

Figure 6.9: Russia: International Reserves and Monetary Base (Value in U.S. Dollars), 2006-2010

On November 24, 2008, in the midst of this crisis, an op-ed dealing with these issues appeared in *Pravda.ru*:

> On the surface, it appears that Russia's central bank is doing what it should to support the value of the ruble. Rubles are being purchased on the foreign exchange market, using foreign reserves. The central bank's interest rate targets have been raised, with the main overnight credit rate now at 12%.
>
> However, a closer inspection reveals that the central bank – like most central banks in these sorts of situations – is neglecting to address the most important factor, the number of rubles in circulation. The supply of rubles is largely unchanged. If the demand for rubles declines, and supply is unchanged, then a lower ruble value is the inevitable result. Indeed, once market participants notice that the central bank is not properly managing the supply of rubles, it is common for demand to fall even more.
>
> The "supply of rubles" is known as base money. As of November 10, the central bank reported that ruble base money was 4,416 billion rubles. At 27 rubles/dollar, that is worth about $163 billion. On September 1, the monetary base was 4,508 billion rubles. We see that, despite the apparent frantic efforts of the central bank, ruble base money has barely changed.

Example #1: The "Making Change" System

From August 29 to November 7, Russia's foreign reserves declined from $582 billion to $484 billion, a fall of $98 billion.

When the central bank sells dollars, it receives rubles in return. To support the value of the ruble, these rubles should disappear from circulation. In other words, base money should decline by an equivalent amount. If this had been done, base money would have declined by about 60%, or 2,646 billion rubles. Only 1,770 billion rubles would remain. If necessary, the central bank could buy every last remaining ruble in existence with an additional $66 billion.

A 60% decline in base money is very large. In practice, it would hardly take such a dramatic effort to support the currency's value, if the central bank is properly addressing the problem. A 20% reduction should be more than enough. That would require the use of about $33 billion of foreign reserves, a relatively small sum.

At least until the crisis passes, base money should not be allowed to expand via some other open-market operation, such as an interest-rate target. In technical terms, the ruble-buying operation should be "unsterilized."[1]

Whether this op-ed was ever read by anyone in Russia's government or central bank is unknown. What is known, however, is that the central bank did take exactly the course of action suggested in the piece: namely, to reduce the monetary base by about 20%, by selling the equivalent amount of foreign reserves.

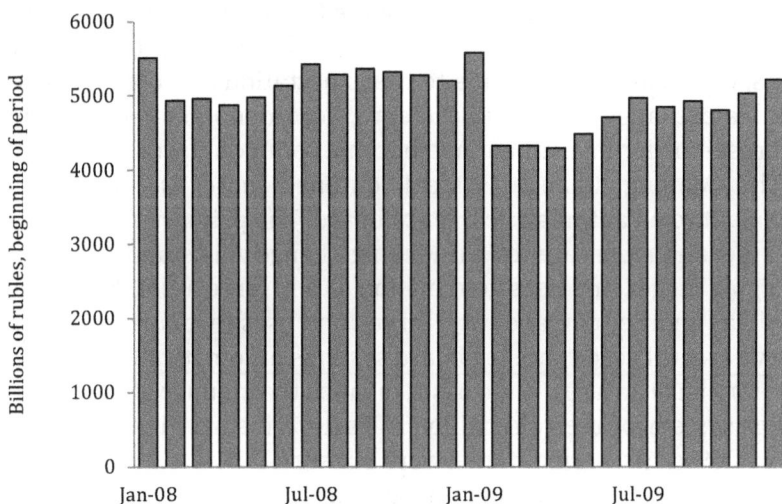

Figure 6.10: Russia: Monetary Base, 2008-2009

133

In February 2009, the monetary base shrank by 22% compared to a month earlier, and 12% compared to February 2008. The result? The ruble immediately stopped falling in value, and soon began to head higher, rising in value by 10% in March 2009 alone. During this one-month period in February 2009, the central bank continued to sell foreign exchange and buy rubles, selling about $41 billion dollars' worth during that time. However, unlike previous "foreign exchange interventions," this sale of foreign reserves had a corresponding reduction in the ruble monetary base. In that one-month period, the ruble monetary base shrank by 1,247 billion rubles, or about $39 billion. In effect, the central bank was taking the rubles received in the sale of foreign exchange, and removing them from circulation, thus reducing the monetary base by an equivalent amount. Afterwards, foreign exchange outflows immediately ceased, and inflows began again.

Many other countries in Eastern Europe had a similar experience during this crisis period. Ten of them had joined the European Union in 2003, with the plan to eventually begin using the euro. In the meantime, they were expected to stabilize their own currencies against the euro. However, most did not use a proper currency board arrangement to do this (an operating mechanism appropriate for the policy goal), but rather a loose, ad-hoc "peg" much like Thailand or Russia had used. Predictably, this did not work well. In the crisis of 2008-2009, the Hungarian forint fell 27% against the euro, before recovering; the Polish zloty fell 35%; the Czech koruna fell 24%. The Ukrainian hryvna eventually fell 43%. These were catastrophic moves, especially because, due to the expectation and recent history of stable exchange rates with the euro, euro-denominated financing and cross-border investment had become commonplace.

The Making Change system outlined here is functionally equivalent to an automatic currency board. The primary difference is the target and reserve asset: the Making Change gold standard system has a gold target, and uses gold bullion as a reserve asset. A currency board has another currency as a target, and uses that currency as the reserve asset. These currency board systems automatically adjust the monetary base on a real-time basis, in much the manner of the Making Change system, or the gold bullion ETFs described earlier. During the 2008-2009 crisis period, there were six euro-linked currency board systems in use: Estonia, Bulgaria, Lithuania, Latvia, the West African CFA franc and the Central African CFA franc. All six of these currency boards were entirely successful during the crisis, maintaining their exact euro parities throughout the crisis period. Estonia's currency board was implemented in 1992 and performed flawlessly for 19 years, until Estonia adopted the euro currency at the beginning of 2011.

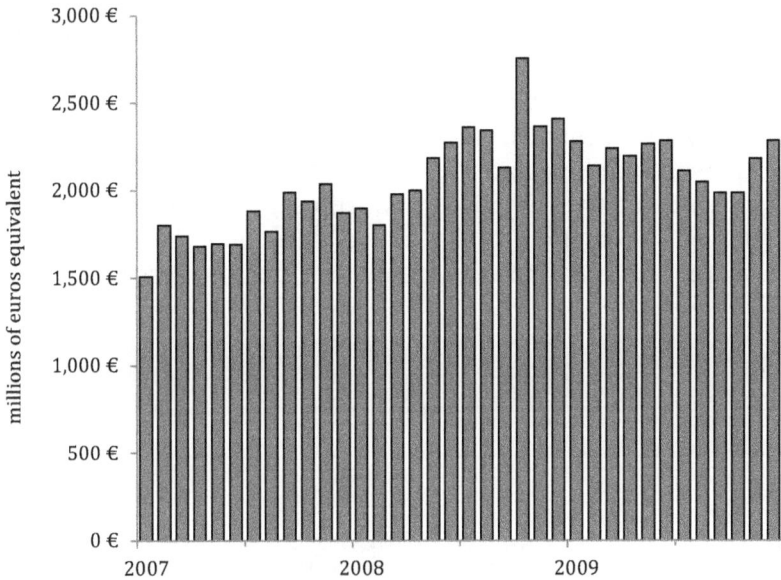

Figure 6.11: Estonia: Base Money, 2007-2009

Figure 6.11 shows the automatic operation of Estonia's currency board to adjust supply in response to changes in demand, a non-discretionary mechanism exactly equivalent to the way gold-based ETFs and the Making Change system work. Although this is monthly data, a currency board works on a daily basis much like ETFs.

＊ ＊ ＊

The Federal Reserve was created in 1913, just in time for World War I. It was soon pressured by the U.S. Treasury Department to take on a role for which it was never intended – in effect, to help the U.S. government finance its war effort by capping market interest rates. In practice, this required the purchase of U.S. government bonds, using expansion of the base money supply, or what amounted to the "printing press."

The U.S. entered the war in April 1917. The U.S. monetary base had already expanded rapidly since the war's outbreak in Europe in August 1914, most likely due to increasing use of U.S. dollars by Europeans. Their own currencies became floating fiat currencies at the war's outbreak, and their domestic bonds had a questionable future. The U.S. dollar, and dollar-denominated assets, represented a safe haven from the effects of European war. However, soon after the U.S. entry into the war, and resulting pressure upon the Fed to help finance the war effort with the printing press, gold reserves of the banking system began to decline, probably indicating that money creation was excessive and the value of the dollar was sinking. The U.S. government then imposed a wartime gold embargo, in effect suspending redemption of banknotes into gold bullion. This is represented as a flat line in U.S. bank system gold reserves (Figure 6.12).

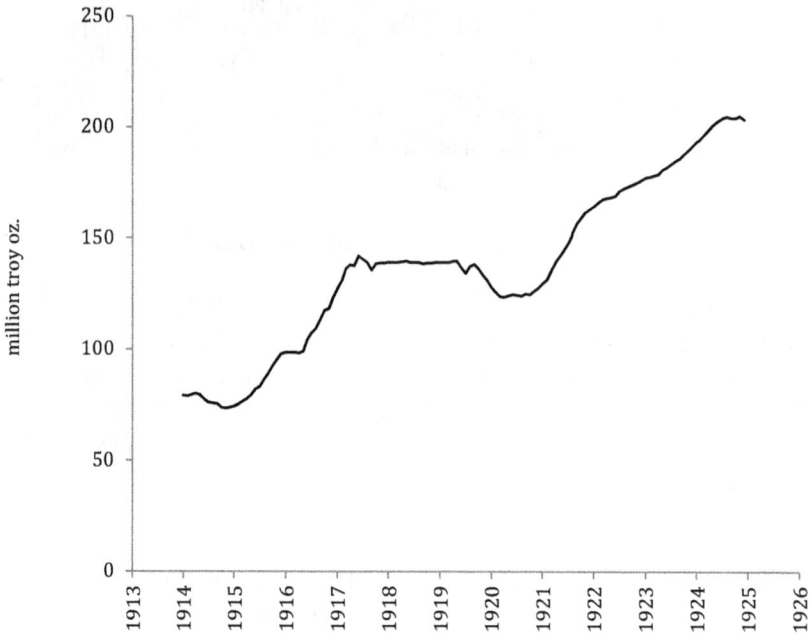

Figure 6.12: U.S.: Gold Reserves of the Banking System, 1914-1924

Despite the initial outflow of bullion, the U.S. monetary base continued to expand from 1917 to early 1920, as the Fed continued to be pressured to purchase U.S. Treasury bonds.

After the war ended, the gold embargo was lifted in 1919. Immediately, people rushed to dispose of excess base money, and receive gold bullion in return. For several months, into the first half of 1920, bullion outflows continued at a brisk pace. With the war's end, U.S. government expenditures dropped considerably. In fiscal 1919, the U.S. federal government spent $18,493 million, and had a deficit of $13,363 million. In 1920, the U.S. federal government spent $6,358 million and had a budget surplus of $291 million. The Treasury Department no longer needed to pressure the Fed to help with its bond issuance. The Federal Reserve was then free to react to the gold outflow with a substantial contraction in base money supply of 16.7% (Figure 6.13).

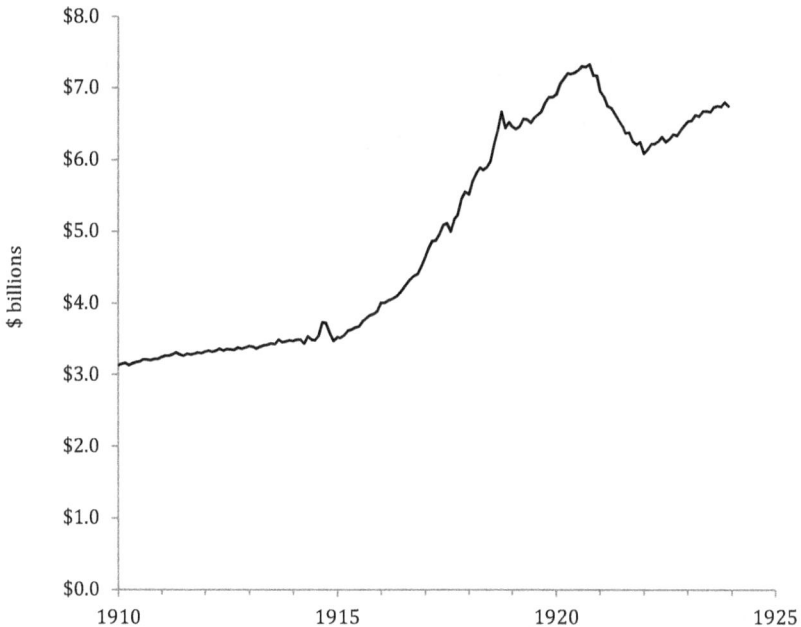

Figure 6.13: U.S.: Monetary Base, 1910-1923

Gold outflows ceased; the dollar's value was supported, the $20.67 per ounce of gold parity rate was preserved, and the U.S. gold standard system continued for another fifty years.

* * *

137

The outbreak of war in Europe in 1939 again led to a similar expansion of dollar base money, as capital sought a refuge from Europe's troubles. With the entry of the United States into the war, the Treasury, beginning in April 1942, once again began pressuring the Federal Reserve to assist in enabling the Treasury to fund its very large bond issuance. The Fed was asked to keep the interest rate on Treasury bills fixed at 0.375%. The limit on long-term government bonds was 2.5%. This policy resulted again in an excess of base money supply, and a resultant sag in the dollar's value vs. its gold parity at $35/oz. (Figure 6.14).

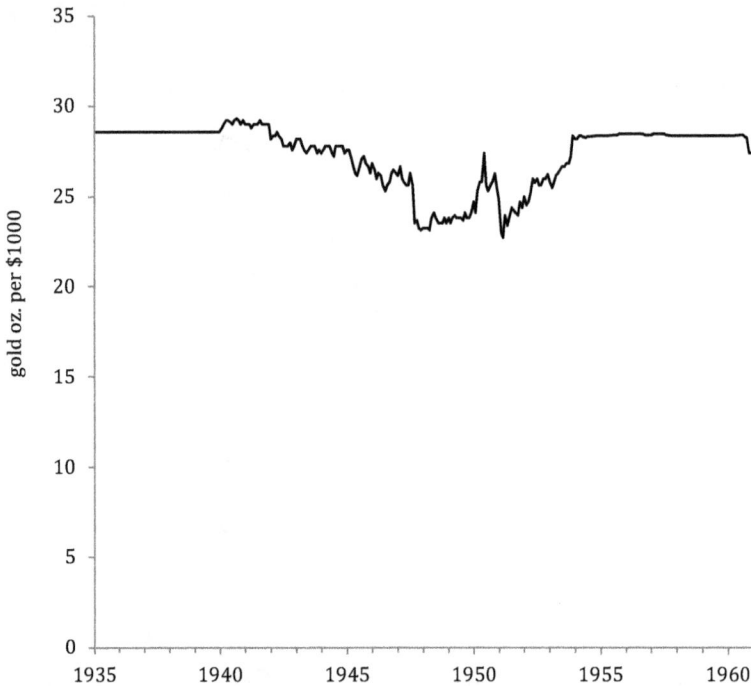

Figure 6.14: U.S.: Value of $1000 in Gold Oz., 1935-1960

The situation continued after the war. In 1947, the Fed raised its peg on the Treasury bill rate, but, at the Treasury's insistence, continued to put a ceiling on yields. Heated discussions between the Treasury and the Fed continued until, in March 1951, an accord was reached that lifted the requirement for the Fed to limit short-term and long-term Treasury yields.

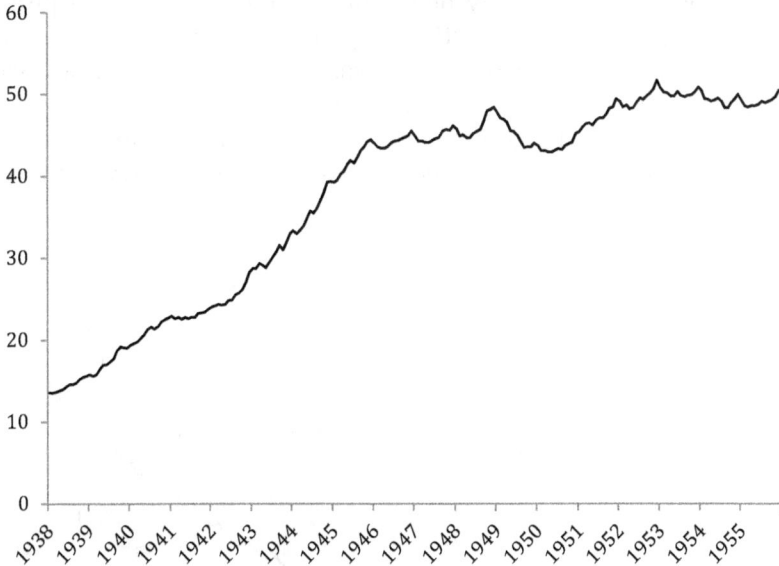

Figure 6.15: U.S.: Monetary Base, 1938-1955

In this case, the Federal Reserve did not contract the monetary base significantly, as it had in 1921. However, it did maintain the overall value at a stable level for an extended period, while demand for money grew alongside the economy as a whole (Figure 6.15). Currency holders were relieved that the Fed was no longer expected to directly monetize Treasury debt to limit interest rates. Both factors likely led to an increase in dollar demand. The result was that the value of the dollar slowly returned to the $35/oz. parity that had been promised since 1934. It reached that parity value around the beginning of 1954.

* * *

During the Bretton Woods period, 1944-1971, the U.S. dollar could not be redeemed for gold by U.S. citizens. However, European central banks could bring their excess dollars to the Federal Reserve and Treasury and have them converted into gold bullion. Beginning in the late 1950s, gold reserves began to flow out of the U.S. Treasury. This was generally a sign that the dollar was weak; in other words, the dollar's value was below its gold parity of $35/oz., or that base money supply was in excess of demand.

Base money had actually been quite stable for years, despite a growing economy. However, the sagging value of the dollar, and consequent gold reserve outflows, was evidence that supply was nevertheless in excess of demand. Demand may have shrank due to declining holdings of banknotes in the U.S. and worldwide, as people migrated toward the use of bank deposit accounts and bank checks for larger transactions.

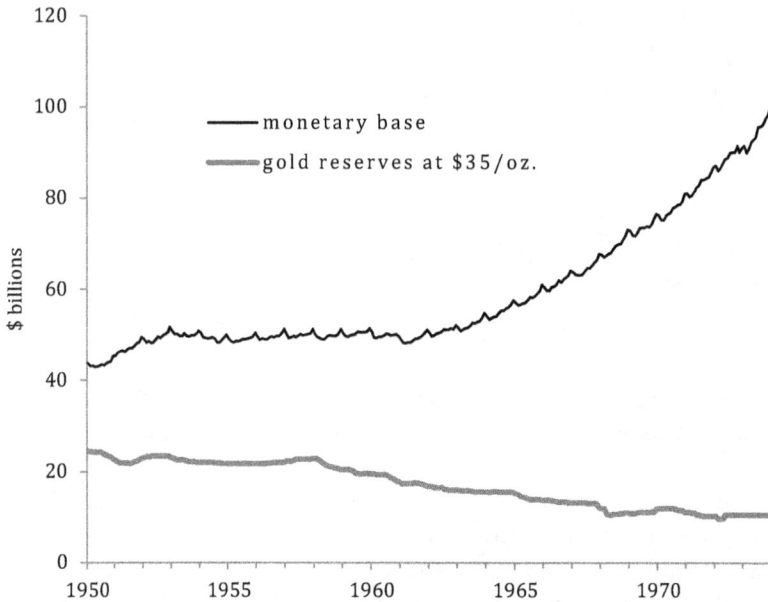

Figure 6.16: U.S.: Monetary Base and Gold Bullion Reserves, 1950-1973

The correct course of action here, to support the value of the dollar and halt gold outflows, was to reduce the size of the monetary base – ideally by way of the Making Change operating mechanism. Dollars received in the sale of gold are removed from circulation, thus shrinking the monetary base by the equivalent amount. This did not happen. Instead, beginning in the early 1960s, the monetary base began to grow by large amounts. Although the growing economy of the 1960s may well have led to greater demand for base money, nevertheless, the persistent gold outflows, and observations of the time, indicated that the value of the dollar was sagging below its gold parity. Supply was persistently in excess of demand, leading the European central banks to continuously dump their excess dollars on the Fed and take gold bullion in return.

Not only did the Federal Reserve fail to shrink the monetary base, as the gold outflows and weak dollar value indicated, the Fed actually increased it! This was exactly the wrong course of action.

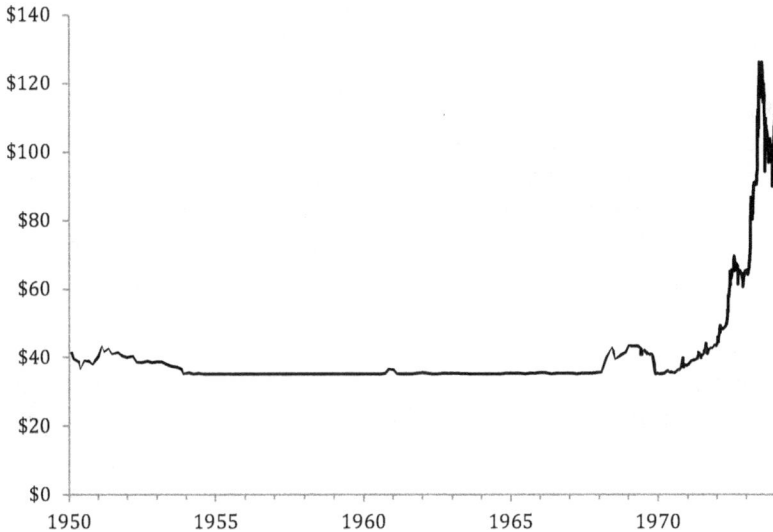

Figure 6.17: U.S.: Dollars per Ounce of Gold, 1950-1973

By this time, economists and bankers had, for the most part, forgotten how the gold standard system worked, and what it was for. They had become fascinated by various Keynesian theories, regarding interest rate manipulation, and also various Monetarist theories, by which credit and the economy as a whole could supposedly be managed by fooling around with the supply of money. These currency-manipulation theories are antithetical and incompatible with any automatic fixed-value system, such as a gold standard or currency board, but this was only hazily understood. The most fundamental principles of operation of a gold standard system – to increase or reduce the monetary base, as appropriate, to maintain the dollar's value at its gold parity – had been largely forgotten. They were so blind to their basic error that they persisted in it for a decade, for the most part without actually noticing the mistake they were making. These principles had been forgotten even by the gold standard advocates of the time. They mostly lamented that there was "not enough gold," as if piling an inert metal in a warehouse would somehow manage the supply of dollar base money for them. They too did not understand that the inflow and outflow of gold, with this

141

system, served primarily as an indicator to guide the management of the base money supply.

The end result of this incompetence, by all involved, was the end of the Bretton Woods gold standard system in 1971, and the beginning of the floating currency system that persists to this day. Indeed, the understanding of how gold standard systems operate hasn't improved much since 1971 – not even among gold standard advocates – which is one reason why governments have not returned to gold-based currencies despite their multi-century track record of success. If nobody knows how to do it (and the experience of 1971 proved without a doubt that they did not), then it is not a practical option. The end result would simply be another collapse of the system, not much different than the U.S. in 1971, or, for that matter, Thailand in 1997.

A full understanding of how the Making Change system operates is imperative, to serve as a foundation for understanding the more complex variants discussed henceforth.

* * *

The Making Change system is, ultimately, just one method to manage the supply of banknotes such that they match demand at the designated gold parity value. An even simpler version of this process occurs naturally in an economy that uses only gold and silver coins, as was more common before 1800.

How many gold coins exist in a country? It depends, obviously, on how many gold coins people want to hold and use (the demand). If anyone had more gold coins than they wished, they would trade a coin for some useful good or service (buy something). If someone did not have as many gold coins as they wished, they would trade some good or service for a gold coin (sell something), and, instead of trading that coin again, keep it in working inventory, thus adding to total holdings. The same applies to silver coins. Thus, people in a country that had no gold or silver mines, but who wished to use gold and silver coins for monetary purposes, would ultimately sell something and receive gold and silver in return. In a country that had ample gold and silver mines, whose production was well in excess of domestic demand for gold and silver, people would ultimately sell the excess gold and silver to foreigners, and receive goods and services in return. In this way, provided that trade in gold and silver bullion in unrestricted, supply naturally adjusts to meet demand in every situation. The quantities of gold and silver coins or bullion in a country varies up and down, on a daily basis, as demand itself fluctuates. In this way, gold is no different than any other manufactured good. People will also purchase copper or washing machines in exactly the amount that they desire (the demand), and no more.

Even in this simplest-possible case, the supply of currency (gold and silver coins) adjusts naturally on a daily basis to match demand. The Making Change system, using paper banknotes, is an extension of this natural process.

* * *

The Making Change system operates entirely by way of purchases and sales of gold bullion at the parity price. The sole determinant of action is whether private market participants wish to transact with the currency manager at that price, and in what quantity. Operationally, it is virtually identical to the gold-based exchange-traded funds described earlier.

As was also the case for the ETFs, a great multitude of factors, which have consumed the attention of many economists for decades, in fact do not matter. These include: interest rates; price indices; balance of payments conditions; trade surpluses or deficits; government fiscal surplus or deficits; gold mining production; imports or exports of gold bullion; unemployment; GDP growth rates; some imaginary "price-specie flow" mechanism; tax policy; and so forth. Any of these factors may prompt some private market participant to transact with the currency manager, thus changing the monetary base, but there is no need to single out any particular factor. It is probably impossible to do so, since even the private market participants themselves may not be able to explain exactly the reasons behind their decisions. This is why all analysis based on these premises tends to be vague and inconclusive.

Chapter 7:
Example #2: "Making Change" With Both Bond and Bullion Assets

In practice, the Example #1 "Making Change 100% bullion reserve" system is essentially unheard-of. The last such system, of prominence, was operated by the Bank of Amsterdam in the 17th century. Over the past three centuries, virtually all gold standard systems in the world have used a variety of reserve assets, including some form of loan or debt security denominated in a gold-based currency.

In other words, they were more like a "gold money market fund," holding gold-based debt assets, than a "gold ETF," holding exclusively bullion.

Historically, governments have generally not issued their own paper currencies. The practice was left mostly to the banking industry, including central banks. One problem with the Example #1 "100% bullion reserve" system is that it is inherently unprofitable. Any system has some overhead costs, for administration and management. Paper money wears out quickly and needs to be continually replaced. Also, currency managers soon learned that, in practice, there was hardly any need to hold so much gold bullion. Even the most dramatic events rarely required a contraction in the monetary base by more than 20%. A gold reserve holding equivalent to 20% of base money would be sufficient in those cases.

Today, an Example #1 system might be appropriate for a small country where the government wishes to issue its own currency – for example, New Zealand. Operationally and conceptually, it is the simplest and safest system possible, which are desirable traits for governments with no recent experience managing gold standard systems. Especially in the early stages, this improves confidence, as nobody wants a Thailand-style (or U.S.-style) implosion of their gold standard system. The currency manager would most likely be a government, because of the inherent unprofitability of the system.

In this variant of the Example #1 system, the currency manager is not required to hold only gold bullion as the reserve asset. The currency manager may, at its discretion, substitute some quantity of debt instruments (bonds or loans), denominated in gold or a gold-based currency, for gold bullion itself.

Some common debt instruments are: government bonds denominated in the domestic currency (the gold-based currency that the currency manager is managing); high-quality corporate bonds denominated in the domestic currency; high-quality mortgage-backed or other bonds denominated in the domestic currency; government bonds, high-quality corporate, or high-quality mortgage-backed bonds denominated in a gold-based foreign currency; direct loans to financial institutions, and direct loans to non-financial institutions, denominated in the domestic currency; direct loans denominated in a foreign gold-based currency.

This example again uses goldenbucks, with a gold parity of G$1,000 per ounce of gold. In its simplest form, using government bonds denominated in the domestic currency (goldenbucks), the balance sheet of the currency manager might look something like this:

Assets		Liabilities	
Government bonds	G$8.0m	Currency in circulation	G$7.0m
Gold bullion	2,000 oz.	Deposits of banks and the government	G$3.0m

In this case, the currency manager has decided to hold 20% of its reserves in the form of gold bullion, and the other 80% in the form of government bonds denominated in the domestic currency. The government bonds pay interest, which produces a profit for the currency manager. Profits that arise from the process of issuing and managing currency are known as "seignorage."

The operation of this system is identical to the Example #1 system. The currency manager takes no discretionary action. It merely offers to sell gold bullion (buy goldenbucks) in unlimited quantity at the parity price of G$1,000 (or slightly above), and buy gold bullion (sell goldenbucks) in unlimited quantity at the parity price of G$1,000 (or slightly below). When private market participants transact with the currency manager at these prices, the monetary base and reserve asset holdings automatically expand and contract by the equivalent amounts.

Perhaps, for whatever reason, people decide to trade their goldenbucks for gold bullion with the currency manager. The currency manager's balance sheet looks like this:

Assets		Liabilities	
Government bonds	G$8.0m	Currency	G$6.0m
Gold bullion	1,000 oz.	Deposits	G$3.0m

The monetary base has now contracted by 10%, a rather large amount, but people still wish to sell their goldenbucks.

Assets		Liabilities	
Government bonds	G$8.0m	Currency	G$6.0m
Gold bullion	500 oz.	Deposits	G$2.5m

The monetary base has now contracted by 15%. At this point, the currency manager becomes concerned that it will run out of gold bullion reserves. The currency manager then sells government bonds and, using the proceeds of the sale, purchases gold bullion. This transaction does not alter the monetary base.

Assets		Liabilities	
Government bonds	G$6.0m	Currency	G$6.0m
Gold bullion	2,500 oz.	Deposits	G$2.5m

The selling of goldenbucks continues.

Assets		Liabilities	
Government bonds	G$6.0m	Currency	G$5.0m
Gold bullion	1,000 oz.	Deposits	G$2.0m

The monetary base is now down to G$7.0 million, a contraction of 30% from its starting point of G$10.0 million. That is a large contraction, but still the selling continues.

Assets		Liabilities	
Government bonds	G$6.0m	Currency	G$4.5m
Gold bullion	500 oz.	Deposits	G$2.0m

At this point, the currency manager again sells government bonds, and uses the proceeds of the sale to purchase gold bullion.

Assets		Liabilities	
Government bonds	G$4.0m	Currency	G$4.5m
Gold bullion	2,500 oz.	Deposits	G$2.0m

Although gold bullion was only 20% of reserve assets at the beginning, the currency manager, by selling government bonds and purchasing additional gold bullion, is nevertheless capable of selling gold bullion until all goldenbucks in existence have been purchased, and base money outstanding is zero. The effect is the same as if the currency manager had held 100% of its reserve assets in the form of gold bullion. The currency manager, if it follows the proper operating procedures, will never "run out of gold."

The process can go the other way. As the goldenbucks monetary base expands – because people come to the currency issuer to sell gold and buy goldenbucks – the currency manager may adjust its holdings of government bond and gold bullion reserve assets.

Assets		Liabilities	
Government bonds	G$8.0m	Currency	G$7.0m
Gold bullion	2,000 oz.	Deposits	G$3.0m

Private market participants come to the central bank to sell gold and purchase goldenbucks.

Assets		Liabilities	
Government bonds	G$8.0m	Currency	G$8.0m
Gold bullion	4,000 oz.	Deposits	G$4.0m

This continues.

Assets		Liabilities	
Government bonds	G$8.0m	Currency	G$9.0m
Gold bullion	6,000 oz.	Deposits	G$5.0m

The currency manager decides that its holdings of gold bullion have become excessive, and that it would prefer to hold interest-bearing government securities instead. This would increase the profitability (seignorage income) of the currency issuer. The gold bullion is sold, and the proceeds of the sale are used to purchase government bonds. This transaction does not affect the monetary base.

Assets		Liabilities	
Government bonds	G$12.0m	Currency	G$9.0m
Gold bullion	2,000 oz.	Deposits	G$5.0m

We have used here an example of an approximate 80:20 ratio between debt and bullion reserve assets, but the currency manager could theoretically decide on any ratio it wishes. It could be 50:50 or 90:10. It could also change, for any reason or no reason at all.

For example, Italy, during the years 1861-1914, had a bullion reserve ratio that varied from a low of 6% to a high of 42% (Figure 7.1).

Despite this variability in reserve holdings, Italy nevertheless maintained an effective gold standard system throughout the period. The amount of gold in a vault supposedly "backing" banknotes in circulation is, in practice, almost irrelevant. Far more important is whether the currency manager understands the process of supply adjustment involved, and is willing to abide by it.

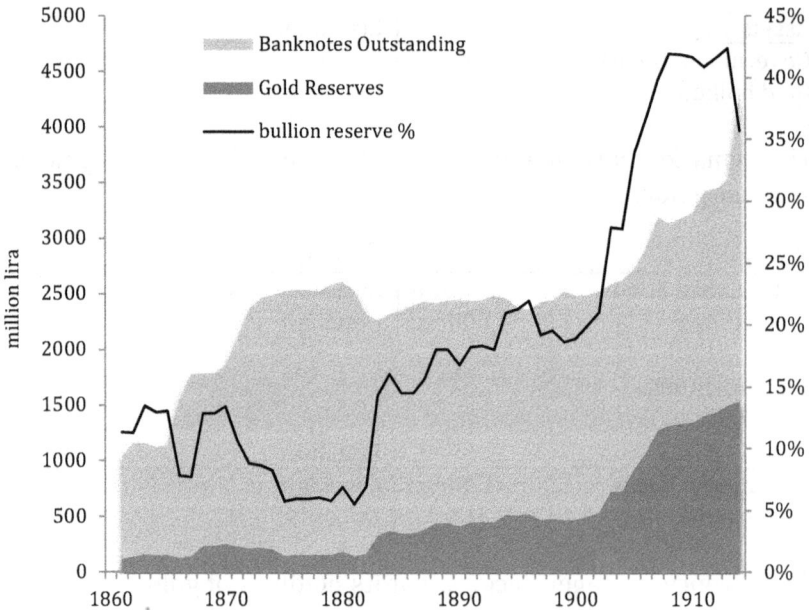

Figure 7.1: Italy: Banknotes Outstanding and Gold Bullion Reserves, 1861-1914

The gold holdings of the currency manager are not necessarily relevant in describing changes in the monetary base, or general monetary conditions. For example, the currency manager's gold reserve holdings may decline because market participants wish to sell goldenbucks and obtain bullion, in this way indicating that the value of the currency is below its gold parity, and that base money supply is in excess of demand. This would reduce the monetary base. However, gold bullion holdings may decline simply because the currency manager wishes to hold a greater portion of its reserve holdings in the form of debt securities. This would not alter the monetary base. In either case, the gold bullion holdings are a residual, the result either of the automatic operation of the Making Change system, or the discretion of the currency manager as to its reserve holdings. There is no process of causality by which the gold holdings increase or decrease (for some unidentified reason), and this then causes some change in the monetary base.

What if the currency manager did not use domestic government bonds as a reserve asset, but rather a foreign debt instrument of some sort, such as a government bond or perhaps a corporate bond, denominated in a foreign gold-based currency? The currency manager may prefer this arrangement because the domestic government is a poor credit risk, to sidestep any pressure by the domestic government to help finance its bond issuance, or perhaps because the domestic government is such a paragon of fiscal discipline that it has no debt outstanding. (This has been true of Hong Kong's government for several decades, and was true of the United States briefly in the 1830s.) In practice, whether the debt instrument is foreign or domestic, and whether it is denominated in the domestic gold-based currency or a foreign gold-based currency, is largely irrelevant. The operating mechanisms would be identical.

Variation #1: Targeting a Foreign Currency

A currency board uses the same automatic system as the Making Change-type gold standard system. The main difference is a difference in target: the target value is not a gold parity, it is a parity with another currency. Likewise, the reserve asset is not gold bullion and bonds denominated in gold-based currencies, but rather the targeted foreign currency and bonds denominated in that currency. The currency manager agrees to buy or sell the foreign currency and domestic currency at the parity price, in the process expanding or contracting the monetary base of the currency being managed.

Actual currency boards in operation generally do not hold, as a reserve asset, only base money of the target currency – banknotes and reserves (deposits) at the foreign central bank. In general, the largest portion of the reserve assets of currency board systems consists of high-quality bonds denominated in the foreign currency. This also generates income, in the form of interest paid on the debt.

The Bulgarian National Bank has used a currency board system since 1997, first targeting the German mark and then the euro. The parity value is 1.95583 lev=1 euro. At the end of 2011, the balance sheet of the Issue Department of the Bulgarian National Bank looked like this:

Assets (billions of BGN)		Liabilities (billions of BGN)	
Cash and foreign currency denominated deposits	6.722	Currency in circulation	8.728
Monetary gold and other monetary gold instruments	3.053	Liabilities to banks	6.177
Investments in securities	16.332	Liabilities to government and other government budget institutions	4.359
		Banking Department deposit	5.835

Most of the reserve assets of the BNB are in the form of euro-denominated debt securities (bonds). The BNB may hold euro-denominated deposits either at the European Central Bank or at highly-rated commercial banks. If the BNB holds deposits at the ECB, that would be a form of euro base money. If the deposits are held at a commercial bank, it would be a form of credit, in effect another type of debt instrument.

The Bulgarian National Bank is obliged to buy or sell euros at the parity price. If the BNB needs more euros to sell (euro base money), it sells some of its euro-denominated government bonds, and receives euros in return. If the BNB has more euro base money (or euro-denominated bank deposits) than it would like, it purchases more euro-denominated bonds. In this way, the BNB manages its mix of reserve assets.

An Example #2-type gold standard system is, in many ways, no more than a currency board that uses gold bullion as a policy target, rather than another currency. Thus, it is illustrative to see how currency boards work today, under normal conditions, and also under conditions of extraordinary duress.

In 1997-98, the value of the U.S. dollar rose considerably vs. gold, and also commodities and other foreign currencies (Figure 7.2).

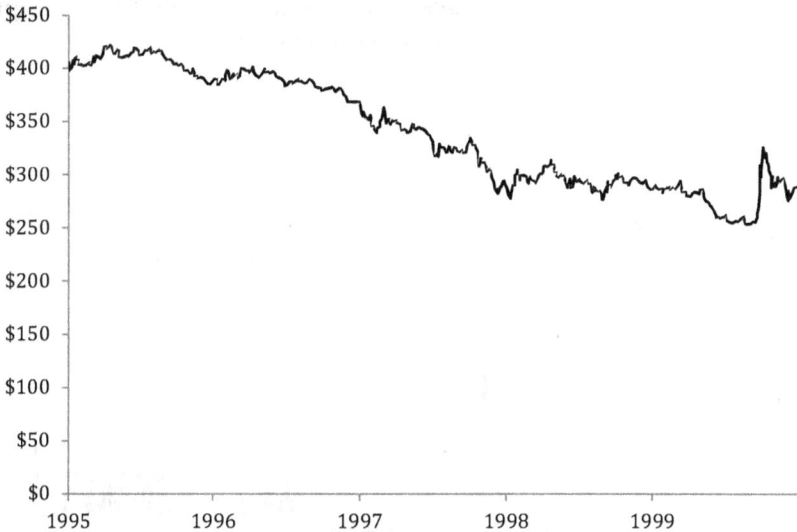

Figure 7.2: U.S.: Dollars Per Ounce of Gold, 1995-1999

This led to a series of failures of ad-hoc currency pegs (which did not have a proper currency board operating mechanism) around the world, especially in Asia. During this time, the Hong Kong Monetary Authority's currency board system was faced with a combination of two difficulties: first, it had to raise the value of the Hong Kong dollar to match the rise in the value of the U.S. dollar. Second, it had to fend off extraordinarily high levels of foreign exchange speculation based on the expectations that the Hong Kong dollar's value peg would fail in fashion similar to the recent failures in Thailand, Korea, the Philippines, Malaysia, Brazil, Russia and elsewhere at the time.

This was a more demanding situation than one would expect to arise in a proper gold standard environment, because the target (U.S. dollar) was unstable and rising, while gold would be stable in value. Also, the prevalence of ad-hoc pegs that did not have a proper currency board-type operating system, and their near-simultaneous failure worldwide, created an environment of extreme speculative action.

151

The Hong Kong currency board system automatically adjusted to this situation with a reduction in the monetary base. This reduced the amount of bank reserves, which in turn tended to drive overnight interbank lending rates to high levels (Figure 7.3). However, these increases in overnight rates were very brief, and within days, overnight lending rates fell back to levels comparable to overnight interbank rates for the U.S. dollar, the target currency.

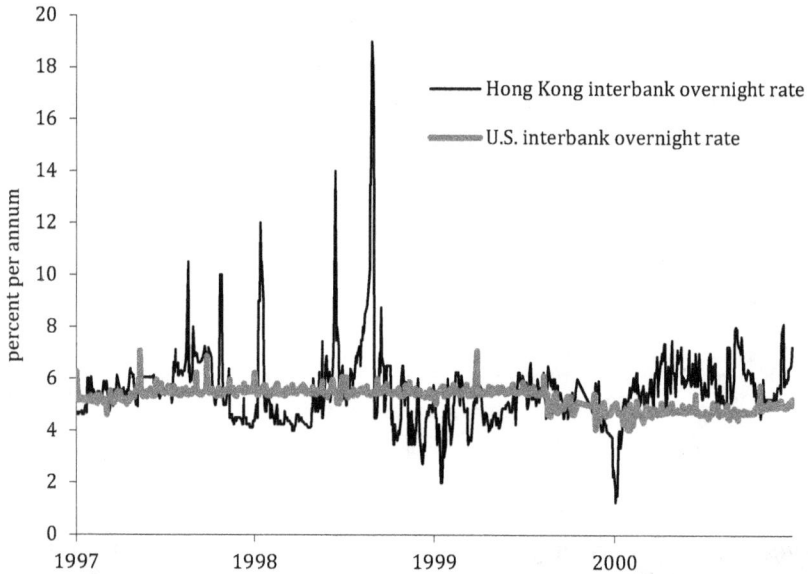

Figure 7.3: Hong Kong: Interbank Overnight Lending Rate, 1997-2000

In the end, the increases in overnight lending rates did not have much economic effect. Paying a 10%+ annualized rate for a day or two is not particularly significant. The crisis environment led to considerable selling of debt (rising yields) across the board – a result caused by market perceptions of risk, rather than overnight interest rates. As it became clear that the Hong Kong currency board would not fail, yields soon fell to normal levels.

Example #2 currency board-type systems, whether a link to another currency or directly with gold bullion, are extremely robust and do not create undue problems in their maintenance even in the most difficult circumstances imaginable.

Currency board operation, in an extreme environment, may lead to dramatic short-term increases in overnight lending rates. However, this is simply an outcome of the process of adjusting base money directly with sales and purchases of assets. There is no direct interest-rate policy. The currency board manager does not "raise or lower interest rates," in the fashion that central banks that use an overnight-rate target have in recent years.

Variation #2: Making Change with no gold bullion reserves

Because gold bullion does not pay interest, and government bonds do, the natural inclination of the currency manager (particularly if it is a private, profit-making institution) is to reduce bullion holdings and increase debt holdings. This could conceivably take the extreme case in which the currency manager holds no bullion reserves at all.

Assets		Liabilities	
Government bonds	G$10.0m	Currency	G$7.0m
Gold bullion	none	Deposits	G$3.0m

However, the operation of the system is identical to the Making Change system – in other words, the offer to purchase or sell gold bullion at the parity price.

If the currency manager has no bullion available, then how would it sell and deliver bullion? It would simply purchase the needed bullion, on the world bullion market, whenever it was obligated to sell bullion. The currency manager would sell government bonds, and use the proceeds to purchase bullion. This bullion would be delivered to the person who bought bullion from the currency manager, using goldenbucks. The goldenbucks base money received in trade would be removed from circulation, thus shrinking the monetary base. It would be exactly the same as shown previously, with a compressed timeframe.

After receiving G$1.0m in trade for 1,000 oz. of gold bullion, the currency manager would eliminate the G$1.0m received. Then, it would sell G$1.0m of government bonds, and with the G$1.0m of proceeds, purchase 1,000 oz. of gold bullion, for delivery to the original buyer. Afterwards, the balance sheet would look like this:

Assets		Liabilities	
Government bonds	G$9.0m	Currency	G$6.0m
Gold bullion	none	Deposits	G$3.0m

This system would rely upon a highly liquid market in both gold bullion and government securities. In other words, the amount of bullion that the currency manager might potentially want to buy or sell on short notice should be a small fraction of that typically available for sale or purchase on any given day on the world bullion market. This system would be impractical for a large international currency, with a monetary base counted in the tens or hundreds of billions of U.S. dollars. However, there are dozens of countries in the world whose currency systems are much smaller than this. The monetary base of the Nicaraguan cordoba was 23.605 billion cordobas at the end of 2011. This was worth US$1,588 million at the exchange rate of the time of 22.98 cordobas per dollar. Its value in gold was 1,037,908 ounces of gold.

A change in the monetary base by 1% in a day is fairly large. Over twenty working days – four weeks – the monetary base could expand or contract by up to 20% at this pace. A 1% change would be about $15.88 million, or 10,379 ounces of gold – about twenty-six 400 oz. institutional gold bars, each the size of a typical construction brick. These are relatively small numbers in relation to the daily turnover of the world bullion market as a whole.

Chapter 8:
Example #3: "No Gold" Systems

In Example #2, the currency manager might begin with a balance sheet that looked like this:

Assets		Liabilities	
Government bonds	G$8.0m	Currency in circulation	G$7.0m
Gold bullion	2,000 oz.	Deposits of banks and the government	G$3.0m

After the sale of 1,000 ounces of gold bullion, resulting in the shrinkage of the monetary base by G$1.0 million, the balance sheet looked like this:

Assets		Liabilities	
Government bonds	G$8.0m	Currency	G$6.0m
Gold bullion	1,000 oz.	Deposits	G$3.0m

The currency manager then decides to replenish its gold bullion holdings by selling G$1.0 million of government bonds, and using the proceeds to buy 1,000 oz. of bullion. The result is:

Assets		Liabilities	
Government bonds	G$7.0m	Currency	G$6.0m
Gold bullion	2,000 oz.	Deposits	G$3.0m

The net effect of these transactions is that the currency manager ends with as much gold bullion as it began. However, its holdings of government bonds have declined by G$1.0 million. Base money supply has also declined by G$1.0 million. Thus, the net transaction was G$1.0m of government bonds sold and G$1.0m of base money received, and removed from circulation.

The process of selling government bonds, using the proceeds to purchase bullion, and then delivering the gold bullion to the seller is somewhat cumbersome. Would it be possible to concatenate this process, so that we could simply sell G$1.0 million of government bonds, reduce the monetary base by the corresponding G$1.0 million received in payment, and not have to transact in gold bullion at all?

Of course it is possible, but it requires us to now depart from the basic operating mechanism of the Making Change system. The Making Change system is based upon purchases and sales of gold bullion at the parity price, initiated by a private market participant. This operating mechanism tells us when to either increase or decrease the monetary base, and by how much. If we do not use this operating mechanism, then we need another way to determine this essential information: When? And how much?

When there are more sellers than buyers at a given parity price – when, in other words, sellers come to the currency manager, to allow the market to clear at the parity price – this in effect means that the value of the currency is, at that moment, marginally below the parity price. If the currency manager didn't participate, the market would clear at a marginally lower price. This is even more obvious when the currency manager uses a trading band, and buys or sells at a point perhaps 1% away from the parity price.

Thus, the mechanism of increasing or decreasing the monetary base as a consequence of buying or selling gold bullion at the parity price – the operating mechanism of the Making Change system – is, in effect, a mechanism of increasing the monetary base when the value of the currency is marginally above its parity, and decreasing the monetary base when the value of the currency is marginally below its parity.

Instead of buying or selling gold, the currency manager could accomplish much the same thing by buying or selling its bond assets, using the market value of the currency vs. gold as an indicator of when to either increase or decrease the monetary base. Thus, if the currency was trading marginally above its gold parity value, the currency manager would purchase high-quality bonds on the open market, increasing the monetary base by an equivalent amount.

The currency manager's balance sheet would begin like this:

Example #3: "No Gold" Systems

Assets		Liabilities	
Government bonds	G$10.0m	Currency	G$7.0m
Gold bullion	none	Deposits	G$3.0m

The currency is trading a little above its gold parity, for example at G$990/oz. instead of the parity price of G$1,000/oz. (a 1% deviation). Thus, the currency manager acts to increase the supply of base money. After a purchase of G$100,000 of government bonds (1% of the monetary base of G$10.0 million), the balance sheet would look like this:

Assets		Liabilities	
Government bonds	G$10.1m	Currency	G$7.0m
Gold bullion	none	Deposits	G$3.1m

When the currency is trading below its parity value, at G$1,010/oz. perhaps, the opposite would occur. To begin:

Assets		Liabilities	
Government bonds	G$10.0m	Currency	G$7.0m
Gold bullion	none	Deposits	G$3.0m

The currency manager would sell G$100,000 of government bonds, take base money in payment, and remove it from circulation, thus shrinking the monetary base. Alternately, instead of a market sale, funds received due to interest payments or maturity of the bonds held as assets could be absorbed, thus reducing the monetary base by the same quantity.

Assets		Liabilities	
Government bonds	G$9.9m	Currency	G$7.0m
Gold bullion	none	Deposits	G$2.9m

Instead of buying or selling bonds, the currency manager could make direct loans. For example, to begin:

Assets		Liabilities	
Government bonds	G$10.0m	Currency	G$7.0m
Gold bullion	none	Deposits	G$3.0m

After a loan of G$100,000:

Assets		Liabilities	
Government bonds	G$10.0m	Currency	G$7.0m
Gold bullion	none	Deposits	G$3.1m
Loans	G$100,000		

Loans can be sold, or allowed to mature. In either case, the payments received are removed from circulation, shrinking the monetary base.

It does not particularly matter whether the reserve assets are denominated in goldenbucks (the domestic gold-based currency) or a foreign gold-based currency. Either way, the monetary base is adjusted via the purchase and sale of these assets, and the signaling mechanism is the value of the currency vs. gold in the free market.

The market value of the currency, compared to its gold parity, indicates when to act, but it does not indicate in what quantity. In practice, this is not much of a problem: the proper quantity is the one that returns the currency's market value to its gold parity value. This can be ascertained by trial and error. The currency manager acts in increasing size until the goal is achieved.

Although a "No Gold" system does not use purchases and sales of gold bullion as an operating mechanism, the currency manager can certainly hold gold bullion as a reserve asset if it wishes to.

Assets		Liabilities	
Government bonds	G$5.0m	Currency	G$7.0m
Gold bullion	5,000 oz.	Deposits	G$3.1m
Loans	G$100,000		

Rather opposite to the way in which Example #2 worked, in this case, if the holdings of government securities were depleted, the currency manager would sell gold bullion and, with the proceeds, buy government bonds.

* * *

The better Classical economists have long understood that it was not actually necessary to hold any gold bullion, transact in bullion, or require redeemability in bullion, to operate a gold standard system. The important thing was the management of the supply of base money, such that the currency's value would remain at the gold parity. David Ricardo wrote:

> *It is on this principle that paper money circulates: the whole charge*
> *for paper money may be considered seignorage. Though it has no*

intrinsic value, yet, by limiting its quantity, its value in exchange is as great as an equal denomination of [gold] coin, or of bullion in that coin ...

It will be seen that it is not necessary that paper money should be payable in specie to secure its value; it is only necessary that its quantity should be regulated [adjusted] according to the value of the metal which is declared to be the standard.
    –David Ricardo, *Principles of Political Economy and Taxation*, 1817.

John Stuart Mill described in detail the operation of a gold standard system without redeemability (also known as convertibility):

If, therefore, the issue of inconvertible paper were subjected to strict rules, one rule being that whenever bullion rose above the Mint price [gold parity], the issues should be contracted until the market price of bullion and the Mint price were again in accordance, such a currency would not be subject to any of the evils usually deemed inherent in an inconvertible paper.
    –John Stuart Mill, *Principles of Political Economy*, 1848

However, these same authors also found that the policy of redeemability – the obligation for the currency issuer to offer gold bullion on demand, in trade for base money – was a political necessity. Gold standard systems that did not have this element had a tendency to be short-lived, not because it was technically impossible to operate such a system, but rather that, without the redeemability element, the currency managers would soon begin to ignore their obligations and deviate from the principles of proper gold standard system management.

Experience ... shows that neither a state nor a bank ever have had the unrestricted power of issuing paper money without abusing that power; in all states, therefore, the issue of paper money ought to be under some check and control; and none seems so proper for that purpose as that of subjecting the issuers of paper money to the obligation of paying their notes either in gold coin or bullion.
    –David Ricardo, *Principles of Political Economy and Taxation*, 1817

But a still stronger consideration is the importance of adhering to a simple principle, intelligible to the most untaught capacity. Everybody can understand convertibility; every one sees that what can be at any

moment exchanged for five pounds [of gold], is worth five pounds. Regulation by the price of bullion is a more complex idea, and does not recommend itself through the same familiar associations. There would be nothing like the same confidence, by the public generally, in an inconvertible currency so regulated, as in a convertible one: and the most instructed person might reasonably doubt whether such a rule would be as likely to be inflexibly adhered to. The grounds of the rule not being so well understood by the public, opinion would probably not enforce it with as much rigidity, and, in any circumstances of difficulty, would be likely to turn against it, while to the government itself a suspension of convertibility would appear a much stronger and more extreme measure, and a relaxation of what might possibly be considered a somewhat artificial rule. There is, therefore, a great preponderance of reasons in favor of a convertible, in preference to even the best regulated inconvertible currency. The temptation to over-issue, in certain financial emergencies, is so strong, that nothing is admissible which can tend, in however slight a degree, to weaken the barriers that restrain it.
   –John Stuart Mill, *Principles of Political Economy*, 1848

Experience since these words were written shows that Ricardo and Mill's concerns were justified. When Britain suspended the redeemability of the British pound upon the outbreak of World War I, there was no overt policy of overissuance and currency depreciation. Yet, that is what happened – just as had happened when the redeemability of the British pound was suspended in 1797. The same thing happened when redeemability was suspended in the United States, upon entry into World War I, and again in World War II. When the outbreak of the War of 1812 led to the suspension of redeemability in Southern banks (but not Northern banks), the value of the Southern banks' banknotes soon fell below that of gold bullion and banknotes from Northern banks, although there was no overt policy of currency depreciation at the time.

In 1968, redeemability had not been available for U.S. citizens since 1933. Without gold coins and direct translation of paper into gold and vice versa, the general public's understanding of the monetary policies then in use indeed deteriorated as Mill suggested they would. However, the dollar was still redeemable for gold bullion among central banks. This was suspended in 1969, when the U.S. began offering only "special drawing rights," a basket of currencies consisting mostly of dollars, instead of gold bullion. It was called "paper gold" at the time, but the European central banks were not fooled. This was in no way intended to represent an end of the gold standard system; but soon after, the value of the dollar sagged vs. gold bullion, reaching $43.50 per ounce of gold on the open market. This was remedied in time by the hard work of Federal Reserve Chairman William McChesney Martin, who brought the value of the dollar back to its $35/oz. parity during 1969 – in effect using various transactions in debt as a way to manage base money supply, as there was no bullion redeemability in any form at that time. However, Martin was replaced in February 1970. The official suspension of gold bullion redemption on August 15, 1971 made *de jure* what had already been *de facto* since 1969: dollar redeemability was suspended. This was supposed to be a temporary measure. At no time did the Nixon administration officially abandon the gold standard policy. And yet, that is effectively what had happened.

Part of the problem with the Example #3 system is that it is typically dependent on discretionary self-directed action by the currency managers themselves. In Example #1 and Example #2, all action is prompted by private market participants, coming to the currency manager to transact in base money and bullion. Any hesitancy of the currency manager in responding to these requests would be immediately apparent. In Example #3, the currency managers are supposed to act when the value of the currency deviates from its gold parity. However, on any given day, they could decide: maybe tomorrow. The deviation is still small. If the deviation increases, they may say: now we should act, and in larger size, but that might affect interest rates or the prices of government bonds, or disturb some banking arrangement, or some other factor. It is all too easy to justify and rationalize some action other than the correct operation of the system. A discrete rules-based system may ameliorate some of these issues, but even then, the system would likely be understood by only a very few insiders with little support or attention from lawmakers or the general public. Do you have to follow rules when nobody cares if they are broken? Even discrete rules could be quietly superseded, and perhaps nobody would even be aware that this had happened.

For all of these reasons, the techniques inherent in the Example #3 system are perhaps best used as elements in a broader context. In practice, that is how these techniques were used historically, as part of hybrid systems described in Example #5. Redeemability – the obligation of the currency issuer to produce gold bullion on demand, at the parity exchange rate – seems to be a requirement for the political longevity of a gold standard system.

Variation #1: Non-Discretionary Mechanisms

Traditionally, the question of when to act, and in what quantity, was left to the discretion of the currency managers. With daily experience in the markets, they could be expected to develop a natural sense of appropriate action.

However, particularly over the past century, it is clear that the people tasked with managing currencies have repeatedly failed to act appropriately to achieve their policy goals. Leaving these matters to the operators' discretion didn't work. Thus, it could be worthwhile to formalize and automate the procedure.

A system of rules can be developed to determine when the currency manager will act, in what fashion, and in what quantity. For example, one potential rule could be: on a given day, if the currency's value is more than 1% from its parity value, the currency manager will increase/reduce the monetary base by 0.25%. If the currency's value continued to deviate from its parity for eight working days, the monetary base would be adjusted by a total of 2.0%.

A protocol of increasing action could be devised. If the currency's value is 1% or more from its parity value on a given day, the currency manager will adjust the monetary base by 0.25%. If the value is 1.5% or more from its parity value, the manager will adjust the monetary base by 0.5%. If the value is 2% or more from its parity value, the manager will adjust the monetary base by 1.0%. This would accelerate the pace of action such that, if the currency continued to deviate from its parity value by a large margin, the monetary base would be adjusted by up to 10% over ten working days.

The protocol could be based on time. For each consecutive day that the value of the currency deviates from its parity value by more than 1%, the degree of adjustment will increase by 0.25% to a maximum of 2.0%. Thus, on the eighth consecutive day of adjustment, the currency manager would be adjusting the monetary base by 2.0% per day, or a rate of 20% over ten working days.

A variety of such rule-based systems could be devised. In practice, such systems would always have, as an option, discretionary intervention if the operation of the automatic rule-based system was not giving adequate results.

Variation #2: Fine Art as a Reserve Asset

Example #3: "No Gold" Systems

High-quality debt denominated in a gold-based currency is normally used as a reserve asset because its value, upon sale or maturity, can be expected to be equivalent, or nearly so, to the corresponding quantity of gold bullion. G$10,000 of bonds can always be traded for 10 ounces of gold bullion, and vice versa. Plus, it pays interest income.

However, any asset could conceivably be used within the context of an Example #3 system. Instead of adjustments to the monetary base made via purchases and sales of bonds, the same adjustments could be made via purchases and sales of fine art.

Assets		Liabilities	
Fine art (estimated market value)	G$10.0m	Currency	G$7.0m
Gold bullion	none	Deposits	G$3.0m

The daily operation would be much the same. When, for example, the value of the currency deviated from its parity value by 1% or more on a given day, the currency manager may act to increase or decrease the monetary base via the purchase or sale of fine art. With a monetary base of G$10.0 million, a 1% adjustment would be G$100,000. Thus, if the currency was 1% above the parity value, the currency manager may purchase G$100,000 of fine art at auction, increasing the monetary base by G$100,000.

Likewise, if the currency manager wished to reduce the monetary base, it would sell perhaps G$100,000 of its fine art reserve holdings, reducing the monetary base in the process.

Of course, the market value of fine art would not be expected to maintain its equivalent value in gold bullion, as a high-quality bond would. The value of the reserve assets would vary from the value of the monetary base. (The difference between assets and liabilities is normally recorded as shareholders' equity or book value, here abbreviated as "capital.") Here, the market value of the fine art held as a reserve asset has increased by 50%:

Assets		Liabilities	
Fine art (estimated market value)	G$15.0m	Currency	G$7.0m
Gold bullion	none	Deposits	G$3.0m
		Capital	G$5.0m

This is not necessarily problematic. As long as the currency manager is able to adjust the monetary base appropriately, via the purchase and sale of fine art, the system will function properly. In practice, this is not much different than those countries today with floating currencies that hold foreign currency-denominated reserve assets, whose value in terms of the domestic currency varies on a daily basis.

A greater problem would arise if the value of the reserve asset fell by a large amount. Here, the market value of the fine art held as a reserve asset has fallen by 50%:

Assets		Liabilities	
Fine art (estimated market value)	G$5.0m	Currency	G$7.0m
Gold bullion	none	Deposits	G$3.0m
		Capital	(G$5.0m)

Although this would be a grave problem if the currency manager was a regular lending bank, in this case it would only be a problem if it was necessary to reduce the monetary base by more than the value of the reserve assets. For example, after the sale of the entire reserve holding of fine art, for a sale price of G$5.0m:

Assets		Liabilities	
Fine art (estimated market value)	none	Currency	G$3.0m
Gold bullion	none	Deposits	G$2.0m
		Capital	(G$5.0m)

At this point, the currency manager would no longer be able to reduce the monetary base via the sales of reserve assets. If demand for the currency fell further, and the currency manager was unable to act, the value of the currency would fall from its parity value. However, a 50% decline in a monetary base is quite large, so the currency manager may never encounter this problem.

A government could conceivably sell anything from its typically large collection of assets (an unused military base for example), absorbing the funds received in payment and thus reducing the monetary base. Even in the extreme case where that was not possible, a government could reduce the monetary base by taking tax revenue and, instead of spending it, removing it from circulation. This would be, in practice, just as effective as any other means of reducing the monetary base, such as the sale of gold bullion, the sale of high-quality bonds, the sale of fine art, military bases, or indeed any other asset. The government could do this even if is not the currency manager, since by increasing its holdings of base money (for example its deposit account at the currency manager), it is, in effect, reducing the amount of base money available for all other users.

Currency managers certainly have a wide range of powerful tools available to handle even the most dramatic situations. This is especially true if the currency manager is the government, or an entity closely associated with the government, as is normally the case today. In practice, a currency manager with mastery of these tools will rarely find itself in a crisis situation, although one may arise due to some external factor such as a foreign military invasion or domestic coup d'etat. Even in those extreme cases, there is no reason that a currency cannot be maintained at its proper parity value via the adjustment of base money supply.

Chapter 9:
Example #4: Linking to a Gold-Based
Reserve Currency

Instead of using gold bullion as a target, currency managers have often chosen to use a major international gold-based currency, such as the British pound or U.S. dollar, as their policy target. In effect, they have a currency board system (Example #2 Variation #1), such as that used today by Bulgaria. However, because the target is a gold-based currency instead of a floating fiat currency, the result is much the same as if the currency used gold bullion itself as a target. It accomplishes the goal of maintaining the value of the currency at a certain parity with gold bullion, and has an effective operating mechanism, so it is thus a type of gold standard system.

Because the currency manager then normally holds, as a reserve asset, base money and debt instruments of the foreign target currency, the target currency is referred to as a "reserve currency."

In practice, this system has been quite popular throughout history. Before World War II, much of the world consisted of the empires of the major European countries, and it is no surprise that the imperial governments would impose upon their colonies and territories a system dependent on the home country's currency. After World War II, virtually all countries used some form of this system (in principle) as part of the Bretton Woods arrangement, with the U.S. dollar as the target currency.

This method has some advantages: no gold bullion need be held, and no transactions in gold bullion need be performed. The reserve assets can consist entirely of base money and bonds denominated in the foreign currency, although in practice, currency managers often held gold bullion as a reserve asset as well.

However, the currency is then dependent upon the good management of the target currency. If the British pound was delinked from gold, the currency linked to the pound would also delink from gold (maintain its link with the now-devalued pound), unless some intervention occurred. Technically, it would be possible to switch to a direct gold link if the target currency began to float from its prior gold parity, allowing the former target currency to be devalued while remaining on a gold standard system. However, in practice, this has rarely occurred in an effective way, so the floating and devaluation of the target currency tends to lead also to the floating and devaluation of all currencies linked to it in this fashion.

This has been quite a problem historically, with the devaluation of the British pound in 1914 and again in 1931 leading to corresponding devaluations of many currencies worldwide. The same pattern appeared again in 1971, when the abandonment of the gold standard system by the United States resulted in all countries leaving the gold standard system – even those whose governments complained bitterly that the U.S.'s new floating currency policy would be disastrous.

The Example #4 system creates a somewhat artificial demand for debt denominated in the target currency – in practice, government debt – as a reserve asset. Purchases of the reserve asset take place due to the demand for the subsidiary currency, not for the investment merits of the reserve asset itself. This leads to some concern that the government of the target currency has a captive buyer for its debt, perhaps enabling the government of the target currency to run large budget deficits and engage in other forms of fiscal indiscipline.

In practice, this somewhat artificial demand for government debt has not led to problems. The U.S. Federal government did not run large deficits in the 1960s, when the U.S. dollar served as the reserve currency for the world. The average annual deficit for that decade was 0.8% of GDP, and the largest deficit was 2.8% of GDP in 1968. The Federal debt held by the public in 1969 (including foreign central banks) was equivalent to a modest 29.3% of GDP.

Before World War I, the Example #4 system (sometimes called a "gold exchange standard") was regularly used, although not as commonly as after the war. Among the countries which used some variant of this system were Austria-Hungary, Russia, Japan, Canada,

Australia, New Zealand, Argentina, the Philippines, South Africa and other British dominions, Egypt, the Netherlands, Scandinavia, India, Siam (Thailand), the Straits Settlements (Singapore), Eritrea, German East Africa, Italian Somaliland, and numerous other countries in Asia and Latin America.

During the 1920s, the world monetary system was rebuilt after the disasters of World War I. In 1929, at least fifty-four countries used a gold standard system. Of these, thirty-two were Example #4 systems; in other words, currency boards linked with other gold-based currencies. These included:

Austria	Finland	Philippines
Bolivia	Germany Greece	Poland
Brazil	Guatemala	Portugal
Bulgaria	Honduras	Romania
Canada	Hungary	Salvador
Chile	Italy	Siam [Thailand]
Costa Rica	Lithuania	Turkey
Czechoslovakia	New Zealand	Uruguay
Ecuador	Nicaragua	Yugoslavia
Egypt	Panama	
Estonia	Peru	

The Bretton Woods agreement of 1944 included 44 countries that agreed to use what amounted to a currency board system with the dollar. In other words, the dollar would be targeted to gold at $35/oz., and the other countries' currencies would be linked to the dollar. After World War II, a number of other countries joined the Bretton Woods system, including Germany, Japan, Italy, and, informally, China.

The Example #4 system has been quite common throughout the past two centuries.

The basic mechanism is identical to the Example #2 system, with the substitution of assets denominated in the gold-based reserve currency for gold bullion. Let's say the currency is the Singapore dollar, and it is linked to the British pound in a ratio of 4:1.

Assets		Liabilities	
British pound bonds	£8,000,000	Currency	S$32.0m
Deposits at commercial banks	£1,000,000	Deposits	S$8.0m
Deposits at the Bank of England	£1,000,000		

168

The currency issuer then offers to either receive Singapore dollars and give British pounds, or receive British pounds and give Singapore dollars, at the parity rate of four Singapore dollars per British pound. Note that the only base money held by the currency issuer is the deposit at the Bank of England. The rest of the assets, namely bonds and deposits at commercial banks, are forms of pound-denominated debt.

The currency issuer could, if it wished, hold some gold bullion as a reserve asset.

Assets		Liabilities	
British pound bonds	£4,000,000	Currency	S$32.0m
Gold bullion	£4,000,000	Deposits	S$8.0m
Deposits at commercial banks	£1,000,000		
Deposits at the Bank of England	£1,000,000		

For simplicity, the gold bullion holdings are indicated at their equivalent value in British pounds. At the longstanding gold parity of £3 17s 10.5d (£3.89375) per ounce of gold, which was maintained (in principle) for over two centuries until 1931, £4,000,000 of gold would be equivalent to 1,027,287.3 troy ounces. Note that, although the currency issuer holds gold bullion as a reserve asset, its operating mechanism remains limited to exchange of British pounds and Singapore dollars exclusively. Holders of Singapore dollars cannot redeem their Singapore dollar base money for gold bullion directly with the Singapore dollar currency manager, although they could purchase gold bullion on the open market for the same price.

Many gold standard advocates have been critical of this system. The main complaint seems to be related to the fact that currencies are not redeemable in gold, but rather in the currency of a foreign country. Although the target currency may, in turn, be redeemable in gold, actually redeeming banknotes for bullion may not be practical for the average citizen. Also, the reserve assets may have little or, indeed, no gold bullion at all. It appears that there is no gold "backing" the currency, but rather that the currency is "backed by debt" – namely the debt of the government of the target currency, held as a reserve asset. Supposedly, this is an insight of some momentous significance. In practice, it does not matter; the only thing that matters is if the currency maintains its promised gold parity, which it will, if the proper operating mechanisms are observed. Although these arguments tend toward superstition, nevertheless there is a core of truth to them. The quality of the currency is, in practice, highly dependent on the quality of the reserve asset. Gold bullion is more reliable than any foreign government's bonds.

Unfortunately, the vague distaste for the Example #4 system has also tended to lead to a wide range of inapplicable criticisms of the system, many centering on the so-called "balance of payments," which has long served as an all-purpose bogeyman (as far back as the 17th century Mercantilist era) because virtually nobody understands what it is. In practice, the "balance of payments" is irrelevant. The only thing that matters is whether people wish to offer British pounds and receive Singapore dollars, or vice versa – in other words, the proper operating mechanisms of the currency board system.

During both periods when the Example #4 system was in common use – the second half of the 1920s, and the Bretton Woods period after 1944 – various Mercantilist money manipulation ideas were gaining in popularity. The reserve currencies (primarily British pounds and U.S. dollars) were officially linked to gold, but they were not always managed with the proper operating mechanisms appropriate for this policy goal. The Federal Reserve, like many of its peers worldwide, became interested in the idea of fiddling with the economy by way of its influence upon the currency and credit conditions. This was rather minor during the 1920s, and did not lead to a significant deviation of the dollar's value from its gold parity, or significant effects upon the economy. However, it did introduce a small element of internal conflict within the management of the system, which was not present in the pre-1914 period. Throughout the twentieth century, the "balance of payments" was commonly blamed for problems which had to do with improper implementation of the gold standard systems then in use, or the natural reaction to threats that the government would soon attempt to implement some kind of Mercantilist "easy money" approach.

After 1944 in particular, the Bretton Woods system was compromised – by design – with the idea that the policy of maintaining the dollar's value at $35/oz., and other currencies' value in line with the dollar, would be combined with various forms of Mercantilist discretionary domestic monetary policy. This construct is completely contradictory, and led to continuous problems during the period. In particular, the dollar's value tended to sag beneath its $35/oz. parity, and the Federal Reserve did not address this condition in a way consistent with proper gold standard operating mechanisms: the sale of an asset to reduce the monetary base. The problem was thus never fixed. The deviation of the dollar's value from its gold parity became chronic and, in the mistaken interpretation common at the time, apparently insoluble. The self-contradictory arrangement of a gold standard policy combined with what amounted to an ad-hoc floating fiat currency operating mechanism could only be sustained by the application of considerable capital controls. Even so, the Federal Reserve and other central banks could not exercise very much in the way of a discretionary domestic monetary policy, lest the inherent contradictions overcome even the capital controls, as eventually happened in 1971.

Other governments were also experimenting with their own versions of a Mercantilist domestic monetary policy, which in turn came into conflict with their currency pegs with the dollar. The consequence was typically that the currency was devalued. This was the case for Britain, which devalued in 1949 and again in 1967. France devalued in 1948, 1957, 1959, and 1969. Spain devalued in 1958, 1959 and 1967. Mexico devalued in 1948, 1949, and 1954. The eventual devaluation of the dollar in 1971 mirrored common practice among governments worldwide at that time.

If the U.S. dollar had been managed according to proper gold standard operating mechanisms, the dollar's value would not have varied from its gold parity value, and the gold parity could have been sustained indefinitely. If other governments managed their currencies according to proper currency board operating mechanisms, their currencies would not have been devalued against the dollar. The Example #4 system works, but only if the proper operating mechanisms are observed.

Academic economists today represent this basic contradiction as a "currency trilemma." The "trilemma" is expressed as the idea that currency management is restricted to three basic conditions:

1) A fixed value policy, such as a link to gold or another currency; an automatic operating mechanism (like a currency board); no discretionary domestic monetary policy; no capital controls.

2) A floating fiat currency; discretionary domestic monetary policy; no capital controls.

3) A fixed value policy; a discretionary domestic monetary policy; capital controls.

In practice, option #3 is inherently unstable, and will eventually fail. The term "trilemma" suggests an insoluble problem. There is no inherent problem, but merely a choice, between a Classical approach to money, or a Mercantilist approach.

Oddly, among all the inappropriate criticism, the basic problem of the Example #4 system is often unmentioned. It is dependent upon the reliability of the target currency. When a major international currency, like the British pound, is devalued, the common result is a coincident devaluation of all currencies linked to the target currency. The system has a single point of failure. This not only has ramifications for the currencies directly involved, but for the world as a whole. Even countries which have gold standard systems independent of the devalued reserve currency face an environment where perhaps dozens of countries have devalued simultaneously. This creates great stress upon trading relationships, as the countries that have devalued often experience greater "competitiveness" due to the devaluation. Non-devaluing countries' exports become less competitive, and their domestic industries are faced with a flood of cheap imports. The devaluing countries may get an apparent boost in industrial activity, due to the increased trade "competitiveness" which is ultimately due to the fact that workers' wages and corporate debt liabilities have been devalued along with the currency.

The immediate result can be an economic downturn in the non-devaluing countries. This is sometimes termed "exporting deflation," because the effect of the new competitive trade pressures is both recession and a tendency toward lower prices (to compete with devalued imports). Within this context, political pressure emerges to return exchange rates to their pre-devaluation levels – in other words, to devalue the currency by the same amount as other countries' currencies have been devalued. People argue that the existing gold standard system is causing the country to "import deflation" (face new competitive pressures due to devalued foreign currencies). Thus, the pressures on trade and the political process lead more countries to devalue. This process is often known as a "currency war," "race to the bottom," or "beggar-thy-neighbor devaluation." This was the case for Japan, which devalued the yen in December 1931, after the British devaluation in September 1931.

The remaining non-devaluing countries were then faced with an increasing problem. Not only had the British pound been devalued (in 1931), along with many countries whose currencies were directly linked to the pound, but a few countries with currencies independent of the British pound (Japan) had also devalued due to trade pressures. This increased the trade pressures on the remaining non-devaluing countries still further, leading them too towards devaluation. This was the case for the United States, whose devaluation in 1933 brought dollar/pound exchange rates to roughly their pre-1931 levels, thus relieving trade-related pressures caused by exchange-rate variance. It was also the case in France, which became a lonely holdout amongst a sea of devalued currencies. France devalued in 1926, once again normalizing exchange rates.

This process was even more abbreviated when the U.S. dollar was devalued in 1971. Within the Bretton Woods system, virtually all countries had linked their currencies to the dollar, rather than to gold directly. The devaluation of 1971 thus led them all down the devaluation path.

With this historical record in mind, extensive use of currency boards linked to "reserve currencies" is not recommended. A better solution would be for countries to have currencies independently linked to gold (via an Example #2 or Example #5 system), as was more commonly the case before 1914. When currencies are independently linked to gold, they will naturally have a fixed exchange rate between each other.

Chapter 10:
Example #5: Hybrid Systems

Although the fully-automatic Making Change-type system was quite common in the past, it was common mostly in the form of Example #4 – a currency board linked to a major international gold-based currency, rather than some form of Example #1 or Example #2, in which the gold standard system targeted gold bullion directly. Those currency managers that maintained a direct link with gold bullion, instead of an indirect one via some other reserve currency, typically used some form of a hybrid between Example #2 and Example #3.

A currency manager would typically have a policy of redeemability; in other words, anyone could bring base money and receive gold bullion in return. The currency manager would not hold a 100% bullion reserve, but rather a mix of bullion and debt assets (Example #2).

However, the currency manager would also, at its discretion, buy or sell debt in the open market as a means to adjust the monetary base (Example #3). Since these currency managers were often commercial banks, they would also make loans, and allow existing loans to mature, accomplishing the same thing as buying or selling debt securities. Typically, some sort of operation in debt securities and direct lending was the first avenue of action. If the currency deviated by a slight amount from its parity, the monetary base would be adjusted by direct purchases and sales of bonds (Example #3). Ideally, these day-to-day adjustments would minimize the demand for redemption into bullion (Example #2), because the value of the currency would not deviate from its parity by an extent that would justify transactions in bullion, which have transportation and vaulting costs.

In the British example, these actions were performed by the Bank of England, which was both a currency issuer and profit-making commercial bank. In the United States, it was performed by a myriad of smaller commercial banks, which issued their own banknotes.

* * *

In 1844, the Bank of England came under new regulation, which split the institution into an Issue Department, which handled paper banknotes, and a Banking Department, which handled loans and deposits, and open-market operations in bonds. This turned out to be a rather confusing arrangement, as total base money was split between two divisions. In addition, the Bank was required to publish its balance sheet on a weekly basis, which provides excellent insight today into the daily operating mechanisms of the world's most important and influential central bank during the late-19th century "Classical Gold Standard" era.

The Issue Department operated on a simple Example #2 system, in which gold bullion and banknotes were traded at the parity value of £3 17s 10.5d (£3.89) per troy ounce of gold. The liabilities of the Issue Department consisted entirely of banknotes. The assets (or reserve) consisted of gold bullion, government debt (direct loans), and "other securities," essentially government bonds.

In a complicated bit of internal accounting, much of the banknotes issued by the Issue Department were held by the Banking Department, as a reserve against deposits. Thus, the currency in circulation consisted of the total issuance of the Issue Department, minus the holdings of the Banking Department.

All of the changes in currency in circulation are mirrored in holdings of gold bullion, indicating that the Issue Department was following an Example #2-type system in which currency and bullion are freely exchanged at the parity price. (Figure 10.1)

Roughly 40% of assets consisted of various forms of debt. Government Debt was unchanged during the period, expressed in the graph as a straight line. Other Securities had a stepwise pattern with stable plateaus. This indicates that the managers of the Issue Department would occasionally adjust the mix of reserve assets, reducing bullion holdings and increasing the holdings of government bonds, as described in Example #2. Silver bullion holdings were negligible at the start of the period, and soon disappeared.

175

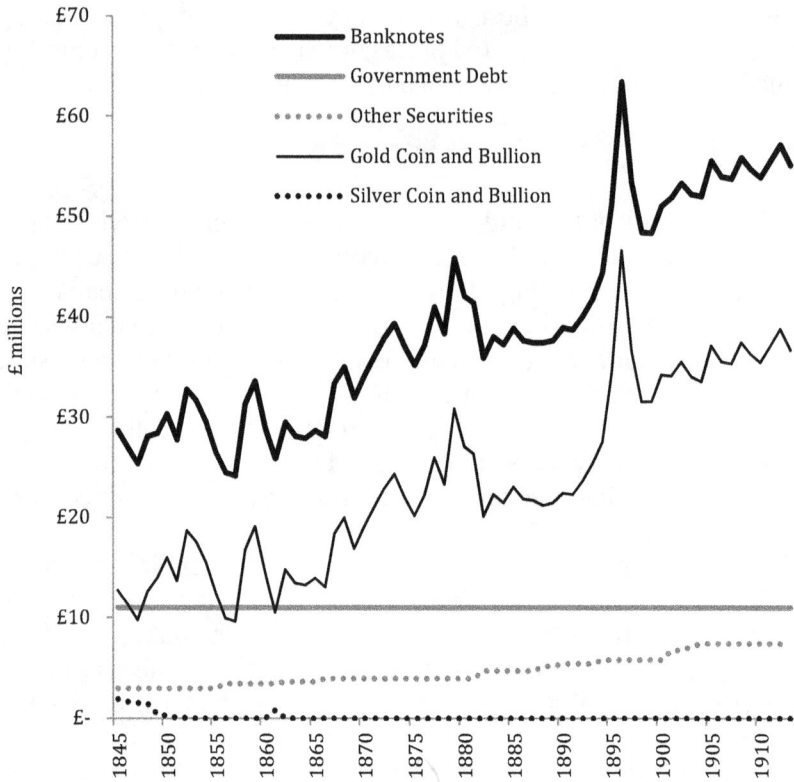

Figure 10.1: Britain: Bank of England, Issue Department, Banknotes Issued and Assets, 1845-1913

The operations of the Banking Department were considerably more complicated than the Issue Department. The liabilities side of its balance sheet consisted mostly of deposits, both public deposits (government deposits), and private deposits, mostly or entirely other banks (bank reserves). (Figure 10.2) The capital of the Banking Department (shareholders' equity or book value), according to the accounting conventions of the day, was split between "capital" – the original founding capital – and "rest," which was essentially retained earnings. "Capital," or original investment capital, was unchanged. The "rest" did not increase over time, as profits were regularly distributed as dividends. The Banking Department also borrowed a small amount of short-term funds from other institutions on the money market, indicated as "seven day and other bills."

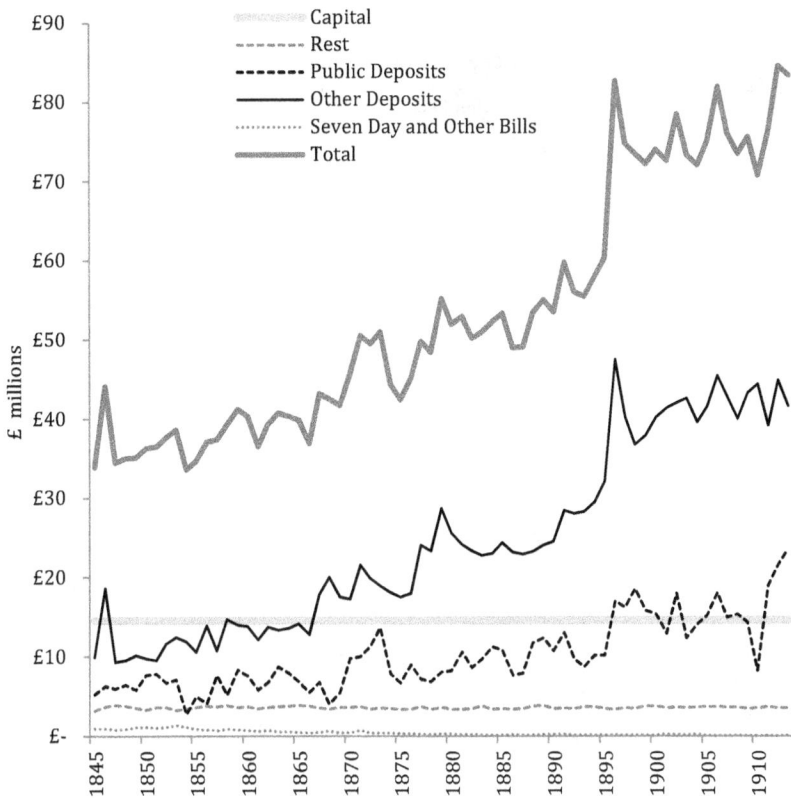

Figure 10.2: Britain: Bank of England, Banking Department, Liabilities and Capital, 1845-1913

The Banking Department held, as assets, a rather varied mix of government bonds, "other securities" (primarily discounted bills of trade, but also including direct lending), and banknotes of the Issue Department, which indirectly represented gold and government debt. (Figure 10.3). The Banking Department also held a little gold bullion, but this was negligible. Although central banks hold government bonds almost exclusively today, the Banking Department held much of its assets in the form of nongovernment debt, primarily discounted bills and direct lending.

177

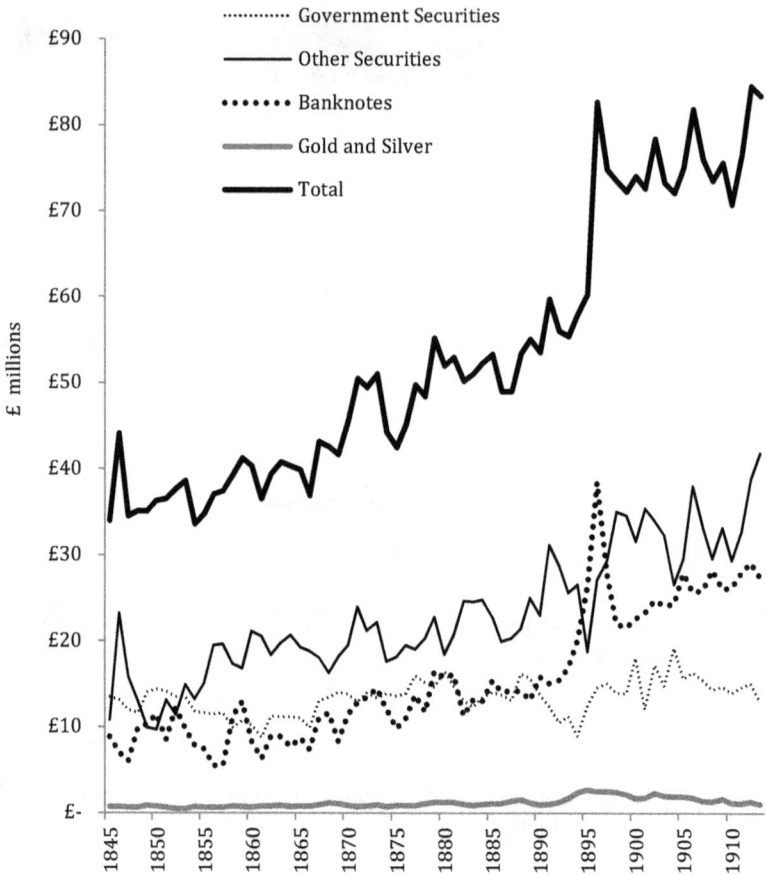

Figure 10.3: Britain: Bank of England, Banking Department, Assets, 1845-1913

On an aggregated basis (combining both the Issue and Banking departments), banknotes and deposits initially accounted for roughly half of total base money (Figure 10.4). After 1880, deposits became a larger component.

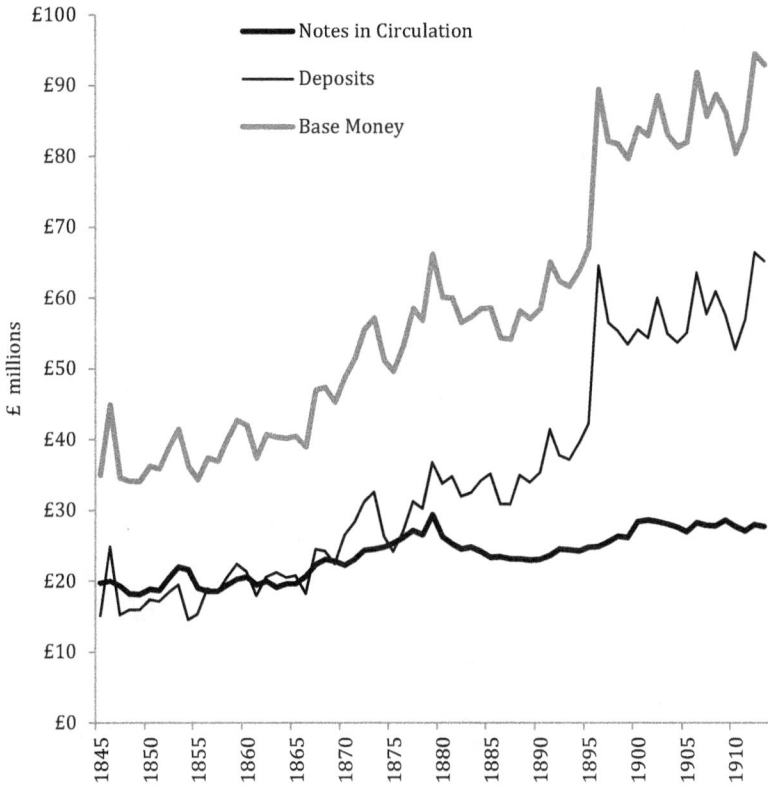

Figure 10.4: Britain: Bank of England, Aggregate Components of Base Money, 1845-1913

On an aggregated basis – comparable to central banks today – the Bank of England had a rather even mix of government bonds and debt, private-market discounting and lending ("other securities"), and gold bullion (Figure 10.5).

A look at weekly balance sheet data during 1904 and 1905 – a placid time – illustrates the Bank of England's day-to-day operating procedures in greater detail (Figure 10.6).

Figure 10.5: Britain: Bank of England, Aggregate Assets, 1845-1913

Total base money shows considerable weekly variation. On a net basis, aggregating the Issue and Banking departments, this variation took place almost entirely in deposits. Banknotes in circulation were steady, although there was a small degree of fluctuation.

Short-term changes in base money took place largely via the discounting and lending function. (Figure 10.7) "Discounting" was the purchase of third-party debts (usually commercial bills, i.e., third-party bills for payment of goods and services), with maturities typically around one to three months. "Lending" was a direct loan, often collateralized. Either one was subject to a short-term market interest rate. The "discount" referred to the purchase price. For example, a commercial bill for £1,000, payable in 90 days, would be purchased for £990, the "discount" reflecting the implicit rate of interest. Changes in government bonds and debt indicated open-market operations in government bonds.

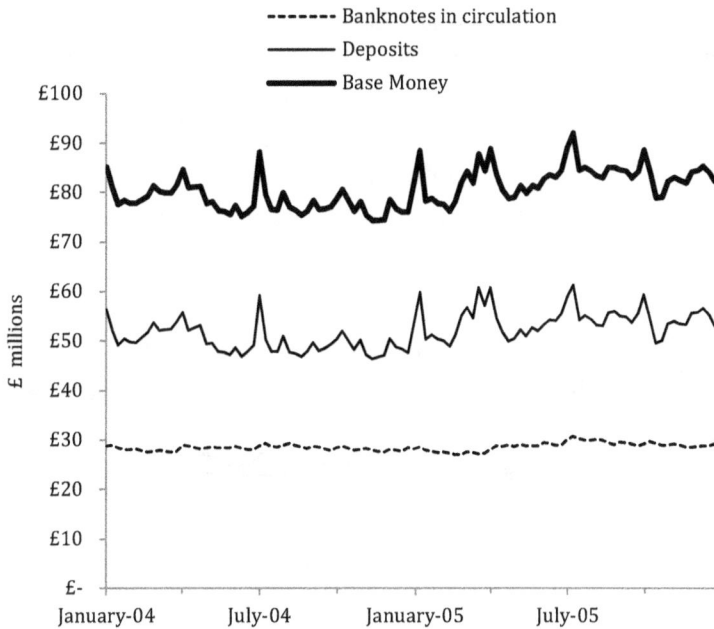

Figure 10.6: Britain: Bank of England, Composition of Base Money, 1904-1905

Gold bullion showed a surprisingly high amount of variation, basically moving opposite to debt assets, in the process cancelling out the changes in base money brought about debt operations (both discounting and lending, and open-market bond operations), as was necessary to maintain the value of the currency at its parity.

Because the Bank of England held a large part of its assets in the form of short-term discounted bills, its holdings of this short-term debt were highly dependent upon market rates of discount; in other words, short-term interest rates. If the Bank's rate was a little below the market rate (rate offered by other competing commercial banks), then the total volume of discounted bills would increase. If the Bank's rate was a little higher, then the volume of discounted bills would decrease. Because the market interest rate had some natural fluctuation, the Bank would have to change its own Discount Rate

181

from time to time, with the end result of influencing the Bank's total debt holdings. (Figure 10.8)

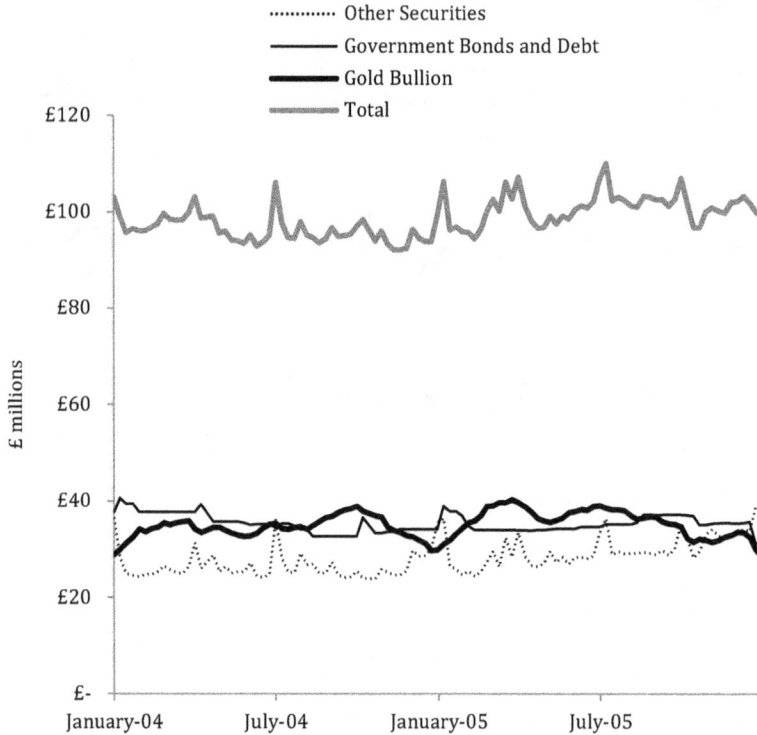

Figure 10.7: Britain: Bank of England, Aggregate Assets, 1904-1905

The interaction of market interest rates and the Bank's discount rate, resulting in changes in the total volume of discounting and lending; open-market operations in government bonds; and the operation of gold convertibility, all working simultaneously, resulted in an obscure and needlessly complicated daily operating methodology, subject to considerable management discretion. Yet, the basic principles were simple enough. If gold outflows from convertibility were deemed excessive, then holdings of debt would be reduced either with open-market sales of bonds, or by reducing the volume of discounting and lending, perhaps coinciding with a change in the discount rate. If gold inflows were ample, then debt holdings could be increased, which would maintain and increase profitability.

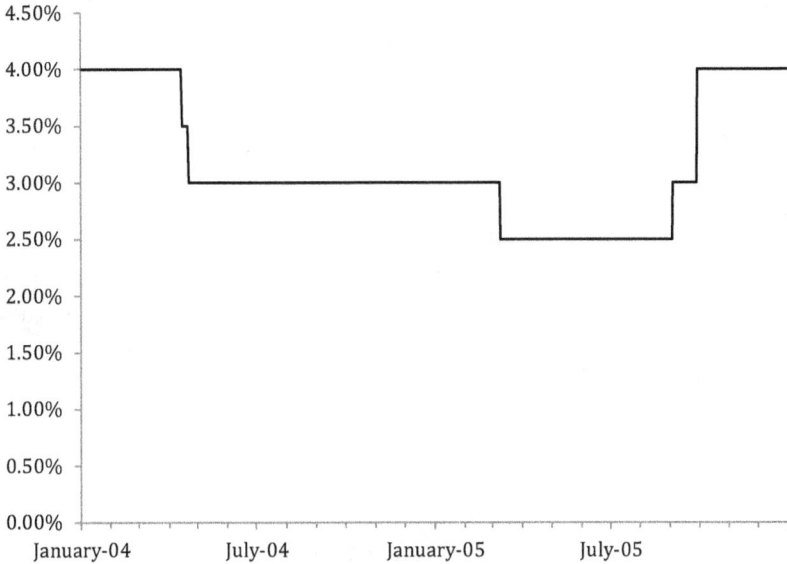

Figure 10.8: Britain: Bank of England, Banking Department, Discount Rate, 1904-1905

* * *

A hybrid-type system today might involve sales and purchases of debt securities (Example #3) to address minor, day-to-day variation in the value of the currency vs. its gold parity. This could be done either in a discretionary fashion, or an automatic, rules-based fashion. To this would be added the option of redemption or monetization (gold bullion transactions) at the parity price, or perhaps at trading-band points 1% from the parity price.

A currency manager wishes to maintain the value of goldenbucks at G\$1,000 per oz. of gold. The currency manager offers to trade gold for goldenbucks at G\$1,010/oz. and trade goldenbucks for gold at G\$990/oz. (Example #2). However, the currency manager also watches the open market value of goldenbucks on a daily basis, and when it deviates by a slight amount from its gold parity, engages in open-market debt transactions to adjust the monetary base. Thus, if the open-market value of goldenbucks was G\$1,005 on a given day, the currency manager (using discretion as to timing and size) would sell perhaps G\$1,000,000 in debt securities and take goldenbucks base money in payment, in this way reducing the goldenbucks monetary base by G\$1,000,000 (Example #3).

Alternately, gold bullion transactions could be given priority. For example, the currency manager offers to buy or sell goldenbucks at G$1,000/oz. of gold, using no trading band. (In practice, there would be a slight effective trading band due to transaction costs.) However, the currency manager may decide to add open-market transactions in debt securities when the size of transactions in bullion reaches high levels. For example, if redemptions of goldenbucks for bullion on a given day are unusually high, or if redemptions have been continuing at an elevated level for an extended period, the currency manager may increase the effective monetary base adjustment by also selling debt securities (using discretion as to timing and size), thus reducing the monetary base still further.

These hybrid systems could be considered a "belt and suspenders" approach, with two methods of operation, both of which would be sufficient by themselves.

Variation #1: Rules-based hybrid systems

Historically, these hybrid systems were run in a highly discretionary manner by the commercial banks and central banks that issued banknotes. Although the general principle of increasing and reducing base money supply according to changes in currency value was observed, the exact details of when to act, in what size, and also which asset to buy or sell, were left to the managers' good judgment (Example #3), often in parallel with an automatically-functioning system of gold bullion redeemability and monetization (Example #2). Due to the wide range of potential action, rules-based approaches can quickly become complicated.

In the first example, open-market transactions in debt securities are the preferred primary means of day-to-day adjustment. Bullion transactions are allowed with a 1% trading band from the parity price. In other words, the currency manager offers to trade bullion for goldenbucks at G$1,010/oz. and goldenbucks for bullion at G$990/oz. The open market operations will adjust the monetary base by 0.25% at a 0.25% deviation from the parity price (i.e. at $1,002.50/oz. and $997.50/oz.), by 0.50% at a 0.50% deviation from parity (at $1,005/oz. and $995/oz.), 0.75% at a 0.75% deviation from parity, and 1.00% at a 1.00% or greater deviation from parity. Ideally, these open-market operations will adjust the monetary base sufficiently, such that the value of the currency does not deviate from its parity to a degree that would motivate bullion transactions.

In the second example, bullion transactions are the preferred primary means of adjustment. The currency manager offers to transact in goldenbucks and bullion at the parity value of G$1,000/oz. If bullion transactions on a given day amount to more than 1% of the monetary base, an additional open-market operation in debt securities is performed that is equivalent in size to bullion transactions. Thus, bullion inflows or outflows equivalent to 2% of the monetary base would be mirrored by additional open-market operations of 2% of the monetary base.

In the third example, bullion transactions and open-market transactions are given proportional treatment. The currency manager offers to either buy or sell gold bullion, in unlimited quantity, at the parity value of G$1,000/oz. The currency manager holds reserve assets of consisting of 20% bullion and 80% debt securities, or a 1:4 ratio. When bullion transactions are done with the currency manager, the currency manager also performs open-market operations in a size four times larger than the bullion transaction. If G$1,000,000 of bullion is sold (goldenbucks redeemed) on a certain day, the currency manager then sells G$4,000,000 of debt securities. The combined operation would reduce the monetary base by a total of G$5,000,000. If G$1,000,000 of bullion is bought, the currency manager then buys G$4,000,000 of debt securities, increasing the monetary base by a total of G$5,000,000. In this way, the reserve assets are automatically maintained in a 20%:80% or 1:4 ratio between bullion and debt securities.

Chapter 11:
Example #6: Free Banking

We have been considering various situations in which it has been implied that a country would have a monopoly issuer of currency, such as a central bank or perhaps the government itself. This situation is near-universal today, but it has not been the situation in the past – particularly in the United States – and it may not be the situation in the future.

All of the operating principles and specific operating mechanisms illustrated so far could just as easily be applied to a small private institution, such as a local bank or other currency issuer. This was the rule, rather than the exception, in the United States until the introduction of the Federal Reserve beginning in 1913. That is why we have used the term "currency manager" rather than "central bank" or "government" thus far. A currency manager could be a small bank with a single storefront, serving a small town, and in the past it often was.

Until 1863, the United States had a policy of "free banking." Anyone could issue banknotes, which were considered a legal contract to deliver the equivalent gold upon demand. Except for their legal obligation to honor the terms of their contracts, banks were generally not regulated. After several bad experiences with state-issued banknotes during the Colonial era, and then the hyperinflated Continental Dollar, the United States was founded on the principle that Federal and state governments would not be involved in currency issuance except for the manufacture of full-weight bullion coins.

Currency issuers of the time (commercial banks) generally used some variant of Example #5, a hybrid system.

In 1791, the United States had four commercial banks, issuing their own banknotes. The currency consisted mostly of gold and silver coin, the majority of it of foreign origin. In 1800, the number of banks operating in the U.S. had reached 29. By 1810, the banking system had expanded to an estimated 102 chartered banks. In 1837, there were an estimated 788 banks in operation, most or all of them issuing their own banknotes.

The currency system of the "free banking" period prior to 1860 was something of a mess. Banknotes from hundreds of issuing banks were all, notionally, worth the same: a dollar banknote was theoretically worth 1/20.67th of an ounce of gold, and theoretically redeemable for that quantity of bullion at the issuing bank. However, in a country the size of the United States, banknotes could travel far beyond the locality of the issuing bank. The recipient of such a banknote, in trade, from a bank perhaps hundreds or even thousands of miles away, in a time before easy communication by telephone, would wonder what the financial condition of the issuing bank was, and indeed, if the issuing bank even existed. The banknote might not even be from the bank indicated, but rather a counterfeit – the counterfeiters relying on the fact that business regularly needed to be done with unfamiliar banknotes.

This state of affairs is represented by *Hodges Genuine Bank Notes of America, 1859*, a reference work on the desk of anyone engaged in commerce at the time. The book listed 9,916 legitimate banknotes issued by 1,356 banks. Even this comprehensive effort omitted hundreds of legitimate banknotes. In practice, banknotes traded "at a discount" depending on their perceived reliability. The dollar bill from an unfamiliar bank was not worth a dollar, but perhaps $0.90 in trade.

As the U.S. monetary and financial system matured, this arrangement became cumbersome. In 1863, Congress passed the National Currency Act (also known as the National Bank Act), thus establishing the National Bank system. Each National Bank was chartered by the Federal government, via the Office of the Comptroller of the Currency (which still exists). To assure financial reliability, National Banks were monitored and regulated, including reserve requirements (a required portion of assets that consisted of base money). All National Banks were also required to accept the banknotes of other National Banks at par (without a discount). This effectively made all dollar banknotes worth a dollar, standardizing the currency. In 1865, a tax was imposed on banknote issuance by banks that were not a part of the National Bank system, effectively eliminating banknote issuance by non-member banks.

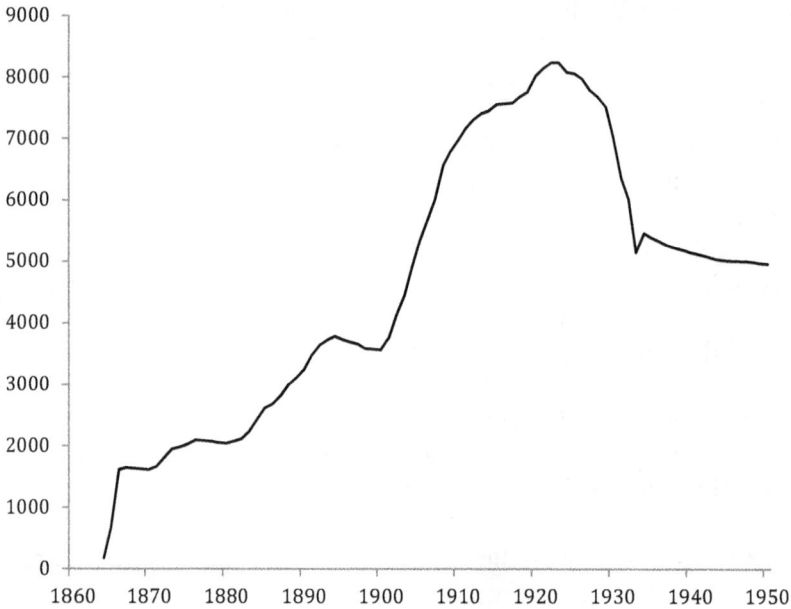

Figure 11.1: U.S.: Number of National Banks, 1864-1950

Proponents of decentralized currency issuance become more uncomfortable with some of the other elements of the National Bank system. Perhaps reflecting the wartime conditions in which the Act was passed in 1863, the system required that the reserve asset held against banknote issuance be U.S. Treasury bonds, thus creating a mandatory customer for the bonds. In 1900, National Banks held $299 million of U.S. Treasury bonds as a reserve asset against banknote issuance, compared to total U.S. Federal debt held by the public of $2,137 million.

Second, bullion assets held against banknote issuance were deposited with the U.S. Treasury. Thus, banks no longer held gold bullion individually as a reserve asset against redemption of banknotes, but rather held a deposit at the U.S. Treasury, where the gold bullion reserve assets of the banking system were aggregated.

People still used a bewildering array of banknotes. In 1930, 7,252 National Banks registered with the Office of the Comptroller of the Currency, of which 5,839 (80.5%) issued banknotes (Figure 11.1). However, the oversight provided by the National Bank system, and the requirement that all National Bank banknotes be accepted at par by other National Banks, made the currency system significantly more uniform and reliable.

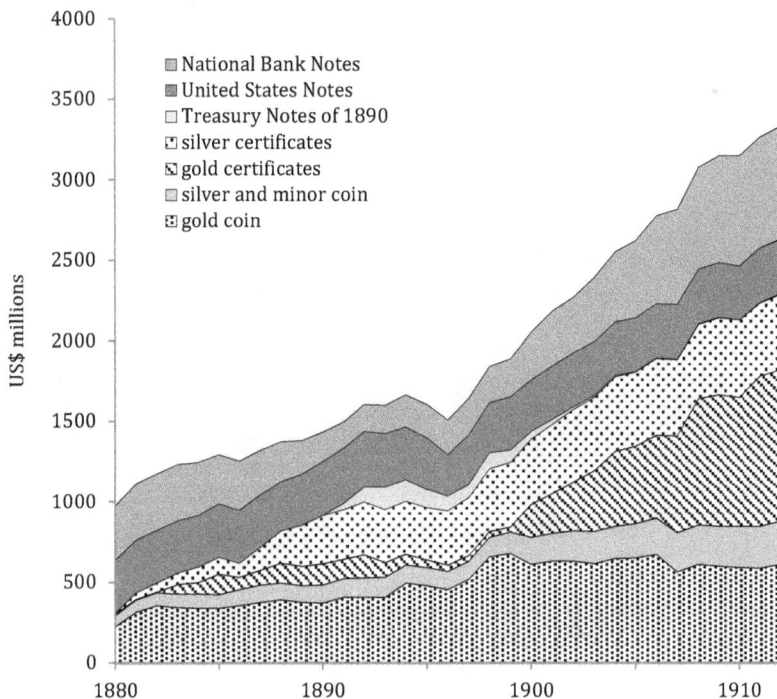

Figure 11.2: U.S.: Composition of Currency in Circulation, 1880-1912

The U.S. Treasury itself began, in 1882, to issue gold certificates, another type of banknote redeemable in bullion (Figure 11.2). Thus, a person wishing to redeem their National Bank banknote for bullion might receive, instead of bullion then held on deposit at the Treasury, a U.S. Treasury gold certificate instead. The Treasury gold certificates were likely perceived as even more uniform and reliable than the menagerie of National Bank Notes in circulation. Along with the similar U.S. Treasury silver certificates and remaining U.S. Treasury Notes ("greenback" banknotes) remaining from the Civil War, U.S. Federal government-issued banknotes became the most common form of banknotes by the eve of the First World War.

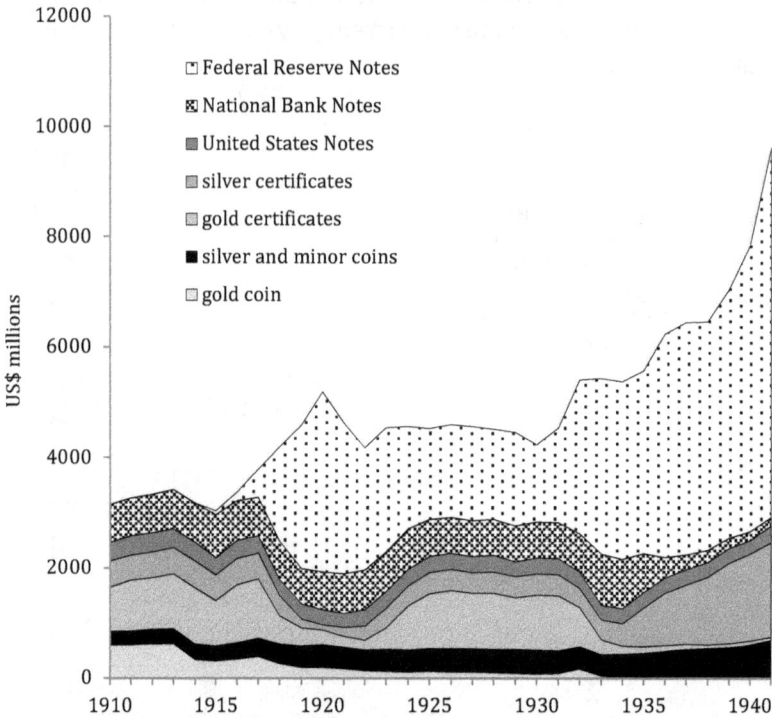

Figure 11.3: U.S.: Composition of Currency in Circulation, 1910-1941

The National Bank system was never allowed to become what the free-banking system was before 1860, the sole issuer of banknotes. However, the popularity of Federal government-issued notes after 1880 also shows that the extremely distributed nature of the National Bank system, with thousands of issuing banks, had also become burdensome. People preferred a uniform currency.

The introduction of the Federal Reserve in 1913 created a new, national scale, uniform issuer of currency. The Federal Reserve soon began to issue quite a lot of currency to help finance Treasury budget deficits during World War I (Figure 11.3). In 1933, both gold coin and gold certificates left the currency system as a result of a prohibition on ownership of gold. In the late 1930s, National Bank Notes largely disappeared.

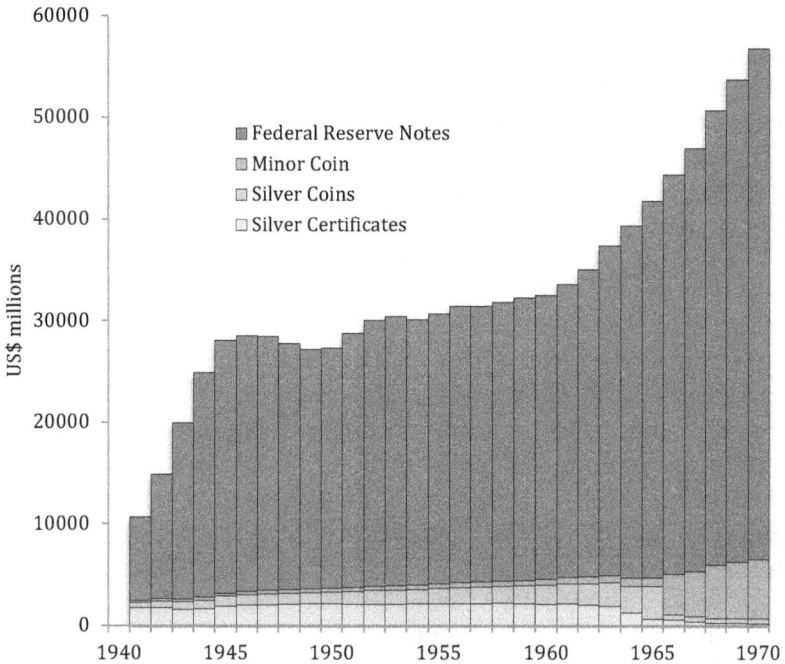

Figure 11.4: U.S.: Composition of Currency in Circulation, 1941-1970

During World War II, as was the case in World War I, the Federal Reserve was pressured by the Treasury to help finance large budget deficits. This led to increased issuance of Federal Reserve Notes, which became even more dominant in the currency system. After World War II, National Bank Notes, United States Notes, and gold certificates were no longer a significant part of the currency system (Figure 11.4). Silver certificates were still quite popular, and silver coins were used. This changed in 1965, when production of silver coins ceased, and all coins were then made of base metals ("minor coin"). This also spelled the end of the silver certificates. At this point, the U.S. currency system consisted entirely of Federal Reserve Notes and base metal coins, as remains the case today. The evolution from distributed "free banking" currency issuance, to Federal Reserve monopoly, took place over a century of incremental developments.

* * *

191

The free banking era, 1789-1860, represents a time when management of the U.S. currency system was not concentrated in either the U.S. Treasury or the Federal Reserve. When there are many, smaller issuers of currency, each using the principle of a dollar worth 1/20.67th ounce of gold, people could conceivably abandon any currency issuer which was not abiding by the proper operating principles of a gold standard system, and migrate towards one that was. Because currency issuance is profitable, due to seignorage income, a currency issuer would want its currency to be widely used. Thus, the natural process of competition would help ensure that all currency issuers abide closely to the proper operating mechanisms, and keep the value of their currencies at the specified parity rate. If a currency issuer failed for some reason, it would be a relatively minor event for the system as a whole, as no issuer would be "too big to fail." When a currency issuer has a monopoly position, such as the Federal Reserve today, the constant temptation exists to abandon proper gold standard system operating principles to achieve some other goal. People have no alternative currency to turn to.

A distributed "free banking" approach to currency systems has many advantages. However, in the U.S. case, the system also had a number of problems. It had become too distributed, with thousands of currency issuers, leading to a number of steps to introduce more uniformity and perceived reliability (through familiarity) to the system.

With this in mind, what could a contemporary version of a free banking system look like? The system still exists here and there, notably in the case of Hong Kong. Hong Kong uses a currency board system with the U.S. dollar as a target. Operationally, it is not much different than certain types of gold standard systems, but with another currency as the target and reserve asset instead of gold bullion. In Hong Kong, several banks issue competing banknotes, all of them linked to the U.S. dollar – just as in the United States of the 1850s, competing banks issued banknotes linked to a "dollar" (23.2 troy grains) of gold bullion.

In the Hong Kong system, three banks are chartered to issue banknotes: HSBC, Standard Chartered Bank, and the Hong Kong Bank of China. Also, the government of Hong Kong itself issues a HK$10 note. The banknotes from each issuer are different; thus, three different HK$20 banknotes are in circulation, one from each issuer.

For the United States, one could establish a limited number of chartered note-issuing banks: a number large enough to provide the advantages of a distributed system, in which no single issuer is "too big to fail," and without so many that the system becomes bewildering. This would perhaps be between ten and one hundred issuers. Issuing banks would be overseen by some central governing body, as was the case in the National Bank system. However, unlike that system, issuing banks would hold their gold reserves independently, in their own vaults, instead of as a deposit with the U.S. Treasury. Issuing banks could be allowed to hold high-quality commercial debt instead of U.S. Treasury bonds exclusively, as a debt reserve asset. As part of the regulatory structure for issuing banks, their monetary functions should be in a separate, bankruptcy-remote entity from all lending functions. In other words, their balance sheet should have only monetary liabilities (banknotes alone in this case, as deposits would not be base money in a distributed system), and U.S. government bonds or similarly high-quality and liquid corporate bonds as assets. (In effect, the balance sheets of issuing institutions would look much like that of the Federal Reserve.)

The desirability of uniformity and familiarity in a currency would perhaps lead to the dominance of one or perhaps three or four major issuers, thus eliminating many of the benefits of a distributed system. This was the case in the 1920s, when the Federal Reserve became the dominant issuer despite the existence of thousands of other banknote-issuing banks. In the 1817-1836 period as well, the Second Bank of the United States (a private commercial bank) became the most dominant currency issuer in the U.S., responsible for approximately 45% of all circulating banknotes in 1818. (Fear of the dominance of the Second Bank within the financial system led to the bank's dechartering in 1836.) Thus, a limit on issuance by a single entity could be established. For example, no issuer would be allowed to issue more than 10% of total base money outstanding.

A distributed system of currency issuance does not preclude a central clearinghouse for processing interbank transactions, one of the functions of central banks today. Also, a "lender of last resort" could be introduced. Indeed, one of the purposes of Peel's Act of 1844 was to separate the functions of the Bank of England into a note-issuing department (the Issue Department) and a banking department which served as a "central bank." This is a very old idea, and one that worked well for Britain in the latter half of the 19th century. Because this "lender of last resort" would not have the ability to issue currency itself, it would operate by holding a large reserve of perhaps 30% of base money outstanding – base money issued by a variety of other banks. The "lender of last resort" would then make loans using these reserve funds at appropriate times during crisis situations.

Banks themselves worked out various arrangements along these lines before the creation of the Federal Reserve. In 1908, the Aldritch-Vreeland Act was passed, which formally legalized and recognized nascent systems then in use. The decentralized clearinghouse system established by the Aldritch-Vreeland Act successfully averted a liquidity-shortage crisis upon the advent of World War I in 1914, before the Federal Reserve system was operational.

Although the era of "free banking" in the United States was a time when the financial system was considerably less sophisticated than today, the basic aspects of the system are fully compatible with today's financial system needs. A contemporary "free banking" monetary system could have a central payments clearinghouse and "lender of last resort" functions, and all other features of a contemporary financial system, as is the case in places like Hong Kong which use this system today.

Chapter 12:
Example #7: End the Fed

The U.S. banking system, and the gold standard system, existed before the Federal Reserve was created in 1913. Perhaps, as many argue today, the United States would be better off without the Federal Reserve. What might the U.S. monetary system look like in that case?

The Federal Reserve today serves several functions, many of which were never part of its intended purpose. The Fed acts as the sole manager of the currency; a clearinghouse for bank transactions; as a regulator for the banking industry; and as a "lender of last resort" entity. Other arrangements would have to be instituted to assume these functions now performed by the Federal Reserve.

Some system would be needed to manage the currency. This could be done, for example, by the U.S. Treasury itself, using one of the methodologies described previously. Indeed, the Treasury did just that for many years in the form of its gold certificates and silver certificates. During the 1890s, various forms of Treasury-issued banknotes (silver certificates, gold certificates, United States Notes and Treasury Notes of 1890) comprised over 80% of all paper banknotes in circulation. The Federal Reserve is not part of the Federal government, but is rather a private institution owned by the banking industry. Some people today argue that something as important as the management of the currency should be put in the hands of the Federal government, where it can be managed for the general good. The issuance of currency is a profitable business, and, arguably, the profits from currency issuance should flow to the state. Today, the Federal Reserve claims that it transfers its profits from currency issuance (the interest paid on the bonds held as reserve assets) to the Treasury, but some wonder whether this is in fact the case.

Unfortunately, leaving the management of a gold standard system to the U.S. Treasury is potentially even more problematic than leaving it to the Federal Reserve. After the disastrous hyperinflation of the government-issued Continental Dollar in the 1780s, the United States was founded on the principle that the Federal government would not be involved in currency issuance beyond minting full-weight bullion coins.

Alas, this principle was expressed in practice for only 23 years. With the outbreak of war with the British in 1812, the U.S. Treasury began issuing its own banknote, the United States Note, as a way to fund wartime expenditures. In other words, the Treasury printed money to pay military expenses. (Washington D.C. itself was burned by British forces in 1814.) Things were returned to normal after the war ended in 1815. With the outbreak of the Civil War in 1861, the Treasury again issued a large quantity of unredeemable United States Notes to help fund the military. The result was the effective end of the gold standard system until it was resumed in 1879, nearly two decades later. The Treasury did a similar thing again during World War I and World War II, as it pressured the Federal Reserve both times to help finance wartime deficits with interest-rate suppression techniques which involved excessive base money creation ("money-printing," in these cases literally true). Fortunately, during both of the World Wars, the situation did not get out of hand and was resolved soon after the end of hostilities. Nevertheless, the U.S. Treasury today has considerable history of abandoning gold standard principles whenever the needs of deficit financing become great enough.

If we wish to avoid both a monopoly private issuer (the Federal Reserve today) or a monopoly government issuer (the Treasury), this leaves some variant of the "free banking" system. The currency system would include multiple currency issuers, none of which is dominant, and any of which could be abandoned or replaced if they did not abide by proper gold standard system operating principles.

A multi-currency environment could be formally established, where any gold-based currency (or perhaps any currency of any type) could be used without favoring any single issuer. For example, if gold-based currencies were issued by the governments of China, Russia, and Germany, all three of these gold-based currencies would be formally recognized as acceptable within the United States in commerce. Even if these currencies were themselves issued by national governments, the overall effect would be much as if they were issued by private-sector issuers. They would compete with each other, and any currency manager that did not abide by proper gold standard operating principles would find that their currency would no longer be used. Foreign gold-based currencies, from either state or private issuers, could circulate alongside banknotes from U.S.-based private issuers, or indeed from the Treasury itself.

This scenario, as odd as it may seem today, is not far from the original monetary principles of the founding of the United States, which served until the 1860s. Foreign-made coins, from Spain, Portugal, Brazil, Britain and elsewhere, were used within the United States for much of the first half of the 19th century, and during the Colonial era. It would be a return to the libertarian values upon which the country was envisioned, before U.S. currency issuance became centralized and monopolized in a series of events spanning roughly a hundred and ten years from 1860 to 1970.

The Federal Reserve serves several other functions as well, which would need alternative institutions. A separate entity could be set up as a bank payment clearinghouse. In effect, it would hold base money (banknotes from other issuers) on deposit with a 100% reserve, allowing banks to make payments to each other without making transactions in banknotes. The balance sheet of this "clearinghouse bank" might look something like this:

Assets		Liabilities	
Banknotes of clearinghouse member banks	$10,000,000	Deposits of clearinghouse member banks	$18,000,000
Gold bullion	$10,000,000	Capital	$2,000,000

Regulation of banks should be done by some separate government entity, independent of the banking industry itself.

The last important function of the Federal Reserve is to serve as a "lender of last resort," in the 19th century meaning of the term. This was the original purpose of the Federal Reserve, although it is all but forgotten today.

The purpose of the "lender of last resort," in the 19th century meaning of the term, is to provide short-term "elasticity" of base money supply. We have seen that base money demand may vary for all number of factors. The normal operation of a gold standard system will naturally match this changing demand with appropriate changes in supply, producing a stable currency value. However, it was found during the 19th century that the financial system sometimes got into situations where these processes did not work smoothly, especially when short-term demand for base money underwent large changes. This was related to strong seasonal variation in the demand for base money, especially during harvest season in the autumn. Agricultural workers would often be paid for the entire summer's labor when farm production was sold in the fall. This payment was typically in the form of paper banknotes, thus generating a seasonal spike in base money demand.

This demand for banknotes was met when people withdrew cash from their bank accounts to pay workers. This cash (banknotes, "bank reserves," base money) came from banks' vaults. If a bank's holdings of banknotes were depleted, the bank would then borrow what it needed from another bank, in the "money market." However, if all banks were experiencing the same seasonal demand for base money, then all banks would have a deficiency and no bank would have a surplus available to lend. The result was that short-term interest rates, among solvent banks with no credit quality issues, would soar to very high levels, at times in excess of 100% per annum. This was a systemic liquidity shortage crisis: although banks were solvent (their asset quality was good), they could not borrow short-term for the simple reason that no lender existed.

This led to the idea of a "lender of last resort." The lender of last resort would be an entity that could make short-term loans to banks of high credit quality, when there was no other lender available due to systemic liquidity issues. This lending was normally done at a penalty interest rate, perhaps 10%, which would insure that the borrowing bank would seek other, lower cost alternatives (other banks with base money available to lend) if they were available. The lender of last resort would thus be active only during true systemwide liquidity shortage crises. These loans would naturally provide a short-term expansion in effective bank reserves and base money supply among the rest of the banking system. Because they bore high interest rates, banks would repay the loans as soon as possible, thus contracting the monetary base as soon as it was feasible. In this way, a seasonal contraction naturally followed the seasonal expansion. Supply of base money would match the changes in demand, exactly the purpose of any gold standard system.

In other words, the lender of last resort would make loans that any commercial banker would make: only to good quality borrowers, and at a profitable interest rate. In this way, the lender of last resort would avoid criticisms of favoritism, "bailouts," or other forms of government intervention in private commercial affairs.

This lender of last resort would not, in any way, be responsible for making loans to institutions of poor credit quality, and thus in danger of bankruptcy. Any bank in danger of insolvency eventually experiences a "liquidity crisis" as lenders refuse to loan the bank any more money, for fear of loss. In practice, it was easy to determine whether the banking system as a whole was experiencing a liquidity shortage crisis: if the interbank lending rate between banks of high credit quality was low, perhaps under 5%, then there was no systemwide shortage of liquidity. Any bank of high credit quality could borrow from other banks at a low rate. This was the case during the 1930s, for example. The Federal Reserve has often been accused of failing to act as a "lender of last resort" during banking system crises in the 1930-1933 period. However, the lending rate between banks of high credit quality was consistently low, indicating that borrowing was easy and cheap for solvent banks. The problem at that time was not a systemwide liquidity shortage, but rather systemwide bank insolvency. The money was available to borrow, but many banks didn't have the ability to pay it back. A freely-acting commercial bank would not make loans to these borrowers, and at the time, did not. The Federal Reserve did exactly what it was designed to do during that period. The Federal Reserve's own discount rate (the rate at which it would lend to solvent banks, serving as a lender of last resort) was 5.00% at the beginning of 1930, falling to 1.00% in 1942.

Today's Mercantilists will insist that "central banking" is not possible with a gold standard system. Of course this is nonsense. The "lender of last resort" is a 19th century invention, credited primarily to the Bank of England, which was also the world's most prominent example of long-term gold standard discipline. The problem today is not "19th century central banking," which worked alongside gold standard systems for many decades, but rather "20th century central banking."

Today's Mercantilists believe that the Federal Reserve should have made loans to insolvent banks during the 1930s, thus propping them up when no commercial lender would do so. This basic notion can be expanded to many other avenues; practically any financial problem can be resolved with a printing press, to create the needed money out of nothing. This sort of activity is wholly contrary to the operation of a gold standard system. If you are altering the base money supply according to one policy notion or another – rescuing insolvent banks – then you are not managing it in accordance to the gold parity target. Thus, the Mercantilists are correct that gold standard systems prevent their "20th century central banking." The solution is simply to abandon this practice of attempting to fix every sort of problem with money creation.

This does not mean that a government should stand idly by in the face of economic difficulties. It simply means that some other solution must be found instead of central bank money creation. Various forms of industrial support and other commercial interventions could be performed, but through Congress and the U.S. Treasury, using funds acquired by the issuance of government bonds. In the end, the bank insolvency crisis of the early 1930s was resolved with the "bank holiday" of 1933, when, with government oversight, many struggling banks were reorganized to restore their solvency. Also, a government deposit guarantee was introduced, which dramatically reduced weak banks' liquidity problems. While people debate even today whether these innovations were a good idea, nevertheless they did not involve Federal Reserve base money creation.

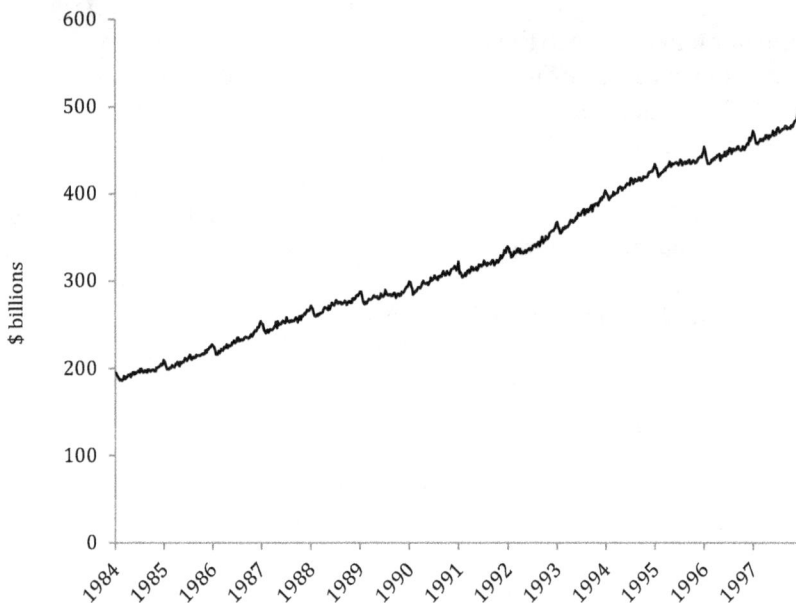

Figure 12.1: U.S.: Base Money, 1984-1997
not seasonally adjusted

Today, a separate entity could be formed whose sole purpose is to serve as a "lender of last resort," providing short-term base money supply (loans) to high quality credits when appropriate, at a penalty interest rate. Unlike the Federal Reserve, this entity would not have the ability to issue new base money. Thus, it would have to keep an inventory on hand, in other words a "reserve," originating from other base money issuers. This entity would hold perhaps 30% of total base money supply. Most of the time it would be inactive. When the occasional need arose, perhaps once every few years or even less than once a decade, it would be able to make these short-term loans to the banking system as appropriate, to good quality borrowers at a penalty interest rate.

An independent "lender of last resort" has been established in Bulgaria, as part of the euro-linked currency board system there. Bulgaria's Banking Department holds, as assets, a deposit with the Bulgarian National Bank (the currency manager) that consisted of 23% of total base money supply as of the end of 2011. This Banking Department could conceivably lend out these funds as necessary, thus serving as a "lender of last resort" in the 19th-century meaning of the term, although it appears that this has never actually taken place.

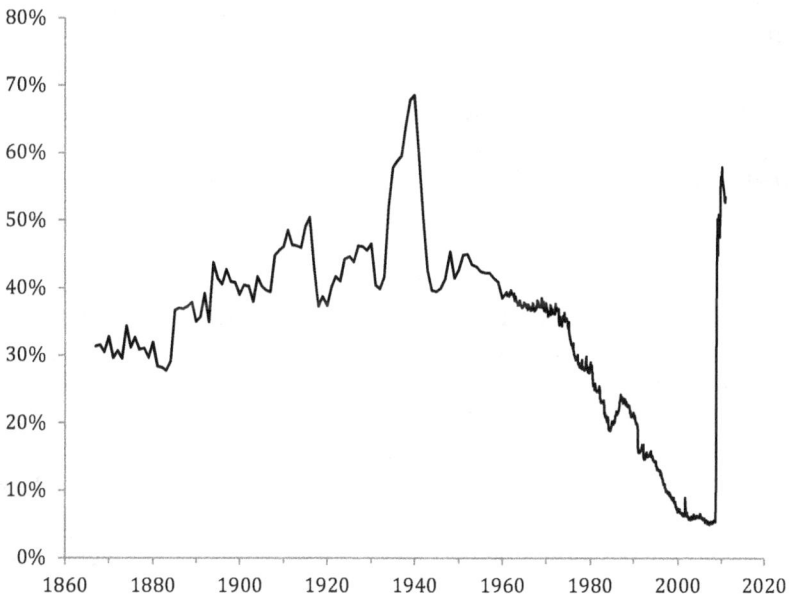

Figure 12.2: U.S.: Bank Reserves as a Percentage of Base Money, 1867-2010

The seasonality of base money use today is not as great as it was in the past, when agriculture had a primary role in the economy. In practice, there is still a small seasonal expansion of base money, of about 5%, around the end of the calendar year, which is withdrawn soon after (Figure 12.1). Thus, it may well be the case that, due to changes in the economy since the 19th century, a 19th-century style "lender of last resort" would not be needed at all in normal times, coming into use potentially only in the most dramatic circumstances of war or political upheaval.

In practice, banks could simply hold more reserves than they have in recent decades, when they have been able to borrow short-term from the Fed (via repurchase agreements) and each other on a daily basis. Larger bank reserves would allow banks to accommodate seasonal and other variation in base money demand without Federal Reserve participation – in other words, without the need for short-term borrowing from other entities, whether the Federal Reserve or other commercial banks. This would simply represent a return to the norms of past decades, before the Federal Reserve began operations, and before it became as active, on a day-to-day basis, as it is today (Figure 12.2). Banks' reserves don't earn income, which is why banks have a natural incentive to reduce their reserve holdings as much as possible. However, banks are perfectly capable of functioning profitably with much larger reserve holdings. The increase in reserve holdings after a crisis in 2008 (in reaction to the risk that borrowing from other banks and the Federal Reserve would not be possible) only brought the situation back to what had been the norm for most of U.S. history.

Thus, it is quite likely that a "lender of last resort" would not be necessary except perhaps in the most extreme circumstances. In the crisis year of 1932 when banks were failing every day, the aggregate demand for base money holdings did not increase by a particularly large amount. Even with the Federal Reserve eagerly serving as a "lender of last resort," base money increased by a modest 3.1% that year. While some form of a "lender of last resort" or "19th Century Central Banking" could be implemented as a form of insurance, unfortunately this introduces a new problem: that the institution, likely to be dormant for years on end when operating according to the principles of its establishment, could morph into some new form. Whether due to the typical process of bureaucratic expansion, or due to the intentions of people who would like to usurp the present monetary arrangements, this institution could begin activities that undermine the operating principles of the existing gold standard system. This, indeed, is a brief description of the Federal Reserve's own history since its inception in 1913.

Chapter 13:
Transitioning to a Gold Standard System

Today, a country might have a single national currency, which is operated as a floating fiat currency. The government wishes to transition this existing currency to a gold standard system. How would this be done?

This is quite easy to do. If the country was to adopt an Example #2-type system, then a gold bullion reserve would be established. If the bullion reserve was intended to be about 20% of reserve assets, and assuming the currency manager does not have any gold bullion to begin with, the currency manager would sell 20% of its reserve assets (likely government bonds), and with the proceeds of the sale purchase bullion on the world market. This transaction has no net cost. Afterwards, the currency manager would operate the system day-to-day as described in Example #2.

If the currency manager adopted an Example #3, Example #4 or Example #5 system, the transition is even easier, because the currency manager can then use transactions in bonds, foreign currencies, or other assets as an operating mechanism. Gold bullion can still be acquired as a reserve asset, but this can be done after the introduction of the system if desired. A transition to a gold standard system, from a floating currency system, could be accomplished in literally one day, and in fact a few hours or minutes if desired.

Throughout history, many countries have transitioned from floating fiat currencies to a gold standard system. In U.S. history, this took place in 1789 and 1879, with minor events also in 1818, 1920, 1934 and 1953. Britain transitioned to a gold standard in 1821, 1925 and 1944. France did so in 1926 and 1946. Germany did so in 1923 and 1949. Japan did so in 1871, 1897, 1930, and 1949. This is not a particularly mysterious or unfamiliar process.

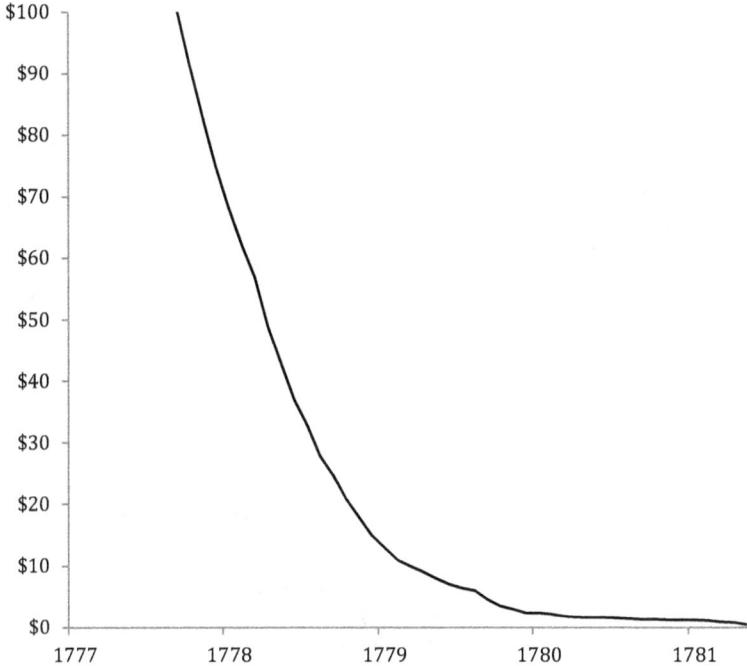

Figure 13.1: U.S.: Value of 100 Continental Dollars Vs. Bullion Coin, 1777-1781[1]

History shows three common patterns for a country that transitions from a floating fiat currency to a gold standard system:

Process #1: The old currency is abandoned, and a new currency is introduced. This is most common after a hyperinflation event. The Continental Dollar was abandoned, and replaced with the pre-Revolutionary War principle of a dollar worth 24.75 troy grains of gold, with banknotes issued by multiple commercial banks (Figure 13.1). Germany's devalued reichsmark was abandoned in 1923, and replaced by the rentenmark (Figure 13.2). Russia's depreciated ruble was replaced by the gold chervonets in 1921. Zimbabwe will likely introduce a new currency at some point, after the Zimbabwe dollar was hyperinflated into oblivion in 1999-2008.

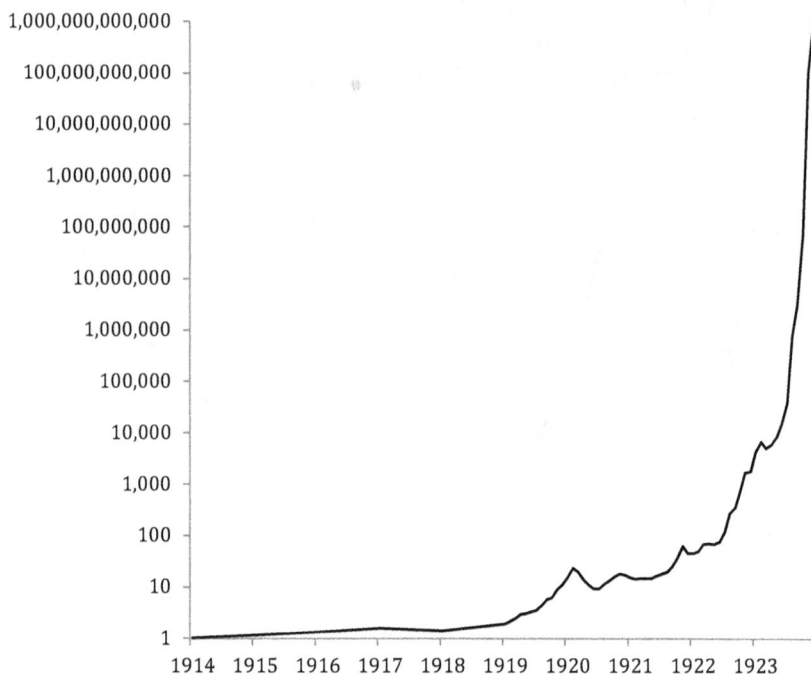

Figure 13.2: Germany: Value of Paper Mark Vs. Prewar Gold Mark, 1913-1923[2]
logarithmic scale

In this case, the gold parity value of the new currency can be anything, since there is no precedent. In practice, governments have tended to adopt a previous gold parity value. The new gold-based German mark, that was introduced to replace the hyperinflated paper mark, had a gold parity value equivalent to the prewar gold mark (86.85 marks per ounce of gold). It could have had a value of one gram of gold, or any other figure. Today, it is somewhat hard to imagine a U.S. New Gold Dollar with the pre-1933 value of 23.20 troy grains of gold ($20.67/ounce). The typical U.S. worker would have an income of about $1,000 per year. However, except for this mental adjustment (similar to what Italians experienced when they went from the lira, worth 2200 lira per dollar, to the euro in 2001), there is no particular problem with such a solution. Other prices would also reflect this higher dollar value, so that a month's rent on an apartment might be $20, and a barrel of crude oil might be about $1.60. In the 1920s, a Ford Model T automobile cost $260, or about 12.6 ounces of gold.

Figure 13.3: U.S.: Value of $1000 in Gold Oz., 1855-1885

A new currency can be introduced quite quickly, with little preparation. On September 26, 1923 – in the midst of hyperinflation – Gustav Stresemann, Chancellor of Germany, suspended seven articles of the Weimar constitution, effectively rendering Germany a military dictatorship. On October 15, the Rentenbank Ordinance was published. Hjalmar Schacht was appointed Germany's Commissioner for National Currency on November 13, 1923. On November 15, the first Rentenbank gold-based banknotes entered circulation, at a parity value equivalent to the prewar gold mark. The Rentenbank apparently held no gold bullion, and the rentenmark was not convertible into gold.

The Rentenbank's only assets were government loans secured by property (mortgages), in effect not much different than any other sort of government debt. It was a type of Example #3 system. Nevertheless, Schacht managed the supply of rentenmarks such that they held their parity value vs. gold. The new currency was widely adopted, and the hyperinflated paper mark was abandoned. The process took one week. Schacht oversaw the new currency from an office at the

Ministry of Finance that had been converted from a janitor's closet, and still smelled of cleaning supplies. His staff consisted of one secretary. While smoking his cigars, Schacht continually checked the market exchange rates of the rentenmark against gold and gold-based foreign currencies by telephone, managing the supply if necessary to maintain the rentenmark's gold parity. Aside from this, he did nothing.

Thus did Germany return again to gold-based money.

Figure 13.4: Britain: Value of British Pound in U.S. Dollars, 1913-1930

Process #2: The devalued currency is raised in value back to its previous gold parity. This is really only possible if the value of the currency hasn't fallen much, typically less than a factor of two (50% of its previous parity value) on a 12-month average basis. This was the case in the U.S. in 1860-1879, and to a lesser extent in 1920 and 1953 (Figure 13.3). In Britain, this was the case in 1821 and 1925, and in the Japanese case, 1930 – followed shortly thereafter by a Japanese devaluation in December 1931 (Figures 13.4 and 13.5). In all of these examples, the currency was floated at the onset of wartime. The process of raising the currency back to its prewar parity was spread over several years, and typically had a somewhat recessionary tendency.

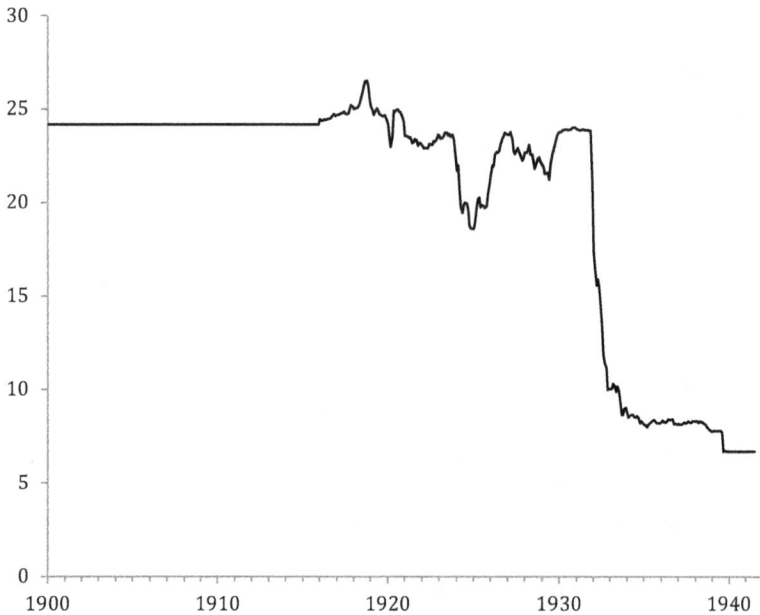

Figure 13.5: Japan: Value of 1000 Yen in Gold Oz., 1900-1941

The political success of this strategy can depend upon tax policy. A reduction in tax rates will counteract the recessionary tendency of the currency appreciation, producing a healthy economy. This was the case in Britain in 1821, which was preceded by the elimination of the income tax in 1816. During World War I, Britain's tax rates were raised dramatically to fund wartime expenditures. These tax rates were not reduced after the war, and the combination of very high tax rates and the recessionary tendency of currency appreciation produced a difficult economy in the mid-1920s. This result led to broad criticism of how the gold standard system was reinstated, an intellectual thread which led eventually to Britain's devaluation in 1931.

The United States also had a huge increase in income tax rates during World War I, but these were dramatically reduced during the 1920s. The result in the U.S. was a booming economy during that decade, compared to recession and high unemployment in Britain. Thus, a strategy that involves a revaluation of the currency to a previous gold parity should also include substantial tax rate reductions. A good solution today would be something like the Flat Tax systems implemented throughout Eastern Europe and elsewhere during the 2000-2010 decade.

A variant of this strategy could be to purposefully increase the value of one of today's floating currencies to correct and counteract previous currency depreciation. For example, the currency's new gold parity could be around the ten-year moving average vs. gold, which might involve an increase in value of as much as 100% (a doubling of value) from prevailing rates. In magnitude, this would be comparable to the revaluations of the U.S. after the Civil War and Britain after World War I. In this way, the negative effects of currency devaluation upon creditors and the real value of workers' wages would be somewhat counteracted. The degree of price adjustment required throughout the economy as a whole would be reduced. The disadvantages include the aforementioned recessionary tendency, and also the fact that this process would likely be spread over several years. Thus, the transition to a gold standard system could be delayed by five or even ten or fifteen years, a period when the economy would not be able to enjoy all the advantages of a gold standard system.

Process #3: Relink the currency to gold around prevailing rates.
When the extent of currency decline is too great to make returning to the previous parity feasible, the most common solution is to simply repeg the currency to gold around the present market value. This was done by France after World War I (Figure 13.6). The new gold value of the franc was about one-fifth of its prewar parity. A similar step was taken by Japan after World War II, when the yen was repegged to gold at ¥12,600/oz. in 1949, from roughly ¥150/oz. in 1940. The United States, arguably, did so in 1934, relinking the dollar to gold at $35/oz. after a period of floating and devaluation in 1933. Many countries did so in 1944, including Britain, as the world gold standard was re-established among the forty-four participants of the original Bretton Woods agreement (Figure 13.7).

Some advantages of this method are that any potential recessionary effects of purposefully raising the currency's value are avoided, and no protracted adjustment period stretched over years is necessary. A gold standard system can be implemented immediately. Disadvantages include the fact that this path would tend to maximize the total amount of currency devaluation, thus maximizing the devaluation's negative effects upon creditors or wages, and maximizing the amount of general price adjustment that would occur to reflect the new currency value.

Figure 13.6: France: Value of 1000 Francs in Gold Oz.,
1900-1940

At the time of this writing (2013), the general situation in the world is not one in which a wholly new currency, at a new parity, is the natural solution (with the exception of the introduction of a parallel currency, discussed later). There has not yet been the kind of hyperinflation or other currency abuse that tends to lead to the disappearance of the old currency altogether.

The time that has passed since the last gold parity (the $35/oz. of Bretton Woods) has been long enough, and the deviation from that parity large enough, that a return to that parity would be impossible except through a type of redenomination, such that, for example, $2,000 present dollars are redenominated as $35 new dollars.

Thus, of the three common historical avenues of action, the natural solution at the time of this writing, for the majority of countries worldwide, is to simply pick a parity value that is close to prevailing rates. As of the end of 2012, the dollar's immediate value was $1,664/oz. and the one-year average dollar/gold value was $1,670, which could be rounded to $1,700 per ounce of gold.

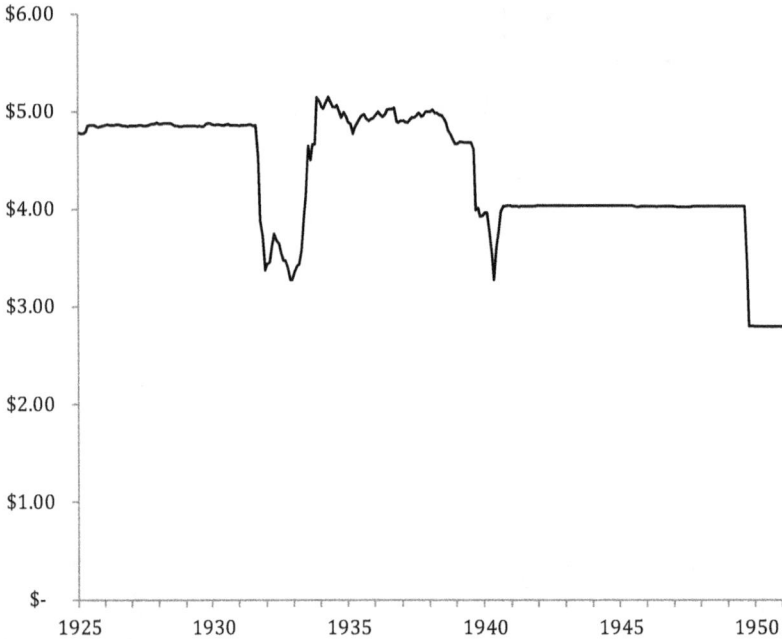

Figure 13.7: Britain: Value of British Pound in U.S. Dollars, 1925-1950

Some have argued that a figure around the ten-year moving average (about $870, which could be rounded to $900) would be more appropriate – in other words, the variant of Process #2 mentioned previously. That would involve a near-doubling ($900/oz. vs. $1,700/oz.) of dollar value compared to the Process #3 option. As noted, this doubling of currency value would help restore the value of creditors' assets, and potentially the real value of wages, while reducing the amount of price adjustment necessary throughout the economy. The negatives include a protracted adjustment period, substantial recessionary tendencies, and the need to coordinate tax policy to produce a favorable outcome.

Ultimately, the decision of which option to choose depends upon political consensus. If a consensus forms to undertake a protracted revaluation period that, for example, would return the dollar's value to perhaps $900/oz. (from $1700/oz.) over a period of five years, with a full understanding of all the advantages and challenges that path would entail, then that solution could certainly work. This was essentially the solution chosen by the U.S. Congress after the Civil War. It was what happened, largely by accident, in the early 1980s, when the dollar's value was raised from a momentary low around $850/oz. and a twelve-month average value of about $650/oz., to a band around $350/oz. in the 1980s and 1990s. This process was accompanied by a difficult recession in 1982, and, on the international level, widespread defaults on dollar-denominated debts by other sovereign governments. However, recessionary effects were also mitigated by major tax rate reductions during the Reagan administration.

Ideally, such a revaluation process would be enhanced by substantial growth-friendly tax reforms, which would counteract recessionary tendencies. In the U.S., after the Civil War, the wartime income tax was eliminated in 1872, in this way mimicking Britain's elimination of income taxes in 1816.

However, the political conviction needed for such a strategy is perhaps weaker today than it was in the days of Victorian propriety. Also, government policy, especially in a democracy, can be somewhat haphazard. Trying to coordinate tax policy at the same time could be problematic.

Currency depreciation tends to be a one-way street. What's done is done; often, trying to correct past error just introduces present and future complications, with little benefit. For the U.S., and most other countries, the simpler and potentially less problematic strategy is to use a variant of Process #3. Tax reform could still be implemented, with beneficial effects. A major advantage of this path is that no transition period is needed. A gold standard system can be implemented right away, with all of the economic advancement that tends to produce, instead of allowing the economy to wallow in a transition-period limbo. With the Magic Formula combination of Low Taxes and Stable Money, an economy can quickly recover from whatever hardships were caused by the previous years of currency depreciation and decline. This strategy was adopted by Japan and Germany after World War II, and, in a somewhat looser fashion, by Russia after 2000. The results, in all cases, were spectacular.

Chapter 14:
The Parallel Currency Option

We have assumed that a country has only one currency, which today is a floating fiat currency, and that currency would be relinked to gold in some sort of formalized manner. But, there is no rule that says a country can have only one currency. Most countries today have a variety of currencies in regular use. Typically, there is some sort of low-quality domestic currency, like the Peruvian nuevo sol, and a popular international currency, such as the dollar or euro. Both are used regularly in transactions and as the basis of contracts. Often, large corporations will regularly finance themselves with debt denominated in dollars or euros, instead of the domestic currency.

Even the national government itself will often issue debt denominated in international currencies. In 1995, roughly 73% of the government debt of Greece was denominated in foreign currencies. In 2009, even Germany's government issued a government bond denominated in dollars. A partial list of other governments that issue bonds denominated in non-domestic currencies includes: Hungary, Indonesia, Lithuania, Poland, South Africa, South Korea, Ukraine, United Arab Emirates, Venezuela, and Vietnam.

Some countries use foreign currencies exclusively. In 2012, several countries used the euro without being part of the official eurozone. This included: Andorra, Kosovo, Monaco, Montenegro, San Marino, and Vatican City. Several countries have been "dollarized," and use the U.S. dollar as their official currency, including: Ecuador, El Salvador, East Timor, the British Virgin Islands, the Caribbean Netherlands, the Marshall Islands, the Federated States of Micronesia, Palau, Panama, and the Turks and Caicos Islands. Some official members of the eurozone, Slovakia for example, have so little influence upon the European Central Bank that the euro is, for them, essentially a foreign currency. Even Germany and France, arguably, have little enough influence on the ECB that the euro is essentially beyond their ability to manage; effectively, the same as a foreign currency.

Some countries officially use the U.S. dollar alongside domestic currencies, including: the Bahamas, Belize, Uruguay, Nicaragua, Cambodia, Lebanon, Liberia, Zimbabwe, Haiti and Vietnam. Zimbabwe has an official "multi-currency" policy in which any foreign currency may be used in business as desired. In many other countries, usage of dollars or euros is informal. Even in the United States, there is no particular rule that says that people and corporations cannot undertake transactions or form contracts using euros, Mexican pesos, Canadian dollars, or any other currency; and this is often done.

Many countries use currency board systems, linked to the dollar or euro. This is, in effect, much like adopting the dollar or euro itself, although it does maintain a degree of separation. Countries with dollar-linked currency boards include: Hong Kong, Bermuda, Cayman Islands, Djibouti, and the East Caribbean dollar (Antigua and Barbuda, Dominica, Grenada, Saint Kitts and Nevis, Saint Lucia and Saint Vincent and the Grenadines), and Macau (indirectly). Twenty-six countries use currencies linked to the euro, mostly via currency boards, including Denmark, Lithuania, Morocco, Burkina Faso, Niger, Cameroon, and French Polynesia.

In practice, people throughout the world are quite accustomed to doing business in a variety of currencies. When the United States itself was founded, foreign gold and silver coins were used almost exclusively. The most popular was the Spanish silver dollar. The use of foreign coins in the United States was not officially forbidden until the Coinage Act of 1857; even so, U.S. citizens and businesses near the Canadian border regularly buy and sell using Canadian dollar notes and coins today, and nobody is particularly alarmed by this.

One option for the introduction of a gold-based currency system is not to transition the existing domestic floating fiat currency to a gold standard system, but rather to introduce a gold-based currency alongside the existing domestic fiat currency. People would be free to use this currency as they see fit, for transactions and as the unit of denomination of contracts, just as they use many foreign currencies in the same way today.

In the United States, this has some nice advantages. No discussion is needed regarding whether the Federal Reserve should transition the existing U.S. dollar to a gold standard system. No discussion is needed as to how this would be done, such as a new gold parity price or some form of transition period. The primary step is to formally legalize the introduction of a gold-based currency system, for example by private institutions such as banks. This would merely be a return, in many ways, to the monetary system of the "free banking" era or the National Bank system, in which many hundreds and eventually thousands of commercial banks indeed issued their own gold-based currencies.

There would be no formal "day of transition" from one system to another. Both currencies would coexist. Perhaps the gold-based currency would become more popular, and the floating fiat dollar less so. The gold-based currency would gradually replace the floating fiat dollar over a period of time, perhaps stretching over ten years or more.

This is, in fact, much the same situation as exists today. A U.S. citizen or corporation could, without undue inconvenience, use a variety of foreign currencies in trade and contracts, just as people do in other countries worldwide. The reason that people in the U.S. do business primarily in dollars is because the currencies of other countries are also floating fiat currencies, generally of lesser quality than the U.S. dollar. No particular advantage is gained, for the U.S. citizen or corporation, from doing business in South Korean won instead of dollars (unless, of course, they are doing business with South Koreans).

Each individual would choose to use one currency or another as best suits their interests. Thus, each individual would benefit from the option of currency choice. Nobody could complain that either the gold-based currency or existing fiat dollar doesn't suit their particular situation. They can use one or another as they wish. Politically, it is an easy policy to implement, because nobody suffers any particular discomfort or imposition. Economically, the introduction of parallel gold-based currencies would be smooth, easy, and trouble-free. If no one particular person or corporation suffers from the introduction of greater currency choice, and instead has a new option to engage in business in a currency of highest quality and reliability to their benefit, then the economy as a whole will not suffer either.

An additional benefit is organizational. Over the past century, the understanding of how to properly operate a gold standard system has deteriorated dramatically. The previous world gold standard system, the Bretton Woods system, crumbled in large part because those who were supposed to be responsible for the management of the system didn't know how to do it. They were never taught. Naturally, people would be nervous about any new gold standard system as well, particularly if the existing U.S. dollar is transitioned to a gold standard system. Does the Fed know how to operate this system properly? There is little evidence today that they do.

The introduction of gold-based parallel currencies in the United States, from a variety of private issuers, would allow experimentation and practice for those charged with managing these systems. Each issuer would be small enough that any mistakes would not have major economy-wide consequences. If mistakes are made, then other issuers could learn from these errors. Because there are many issuers, perhaps dozens and eventually hundreds, many thousands of people would be involved in managing these systems, and consequently would get the training, education and experience as to how to do so properly. A body of literature and study would develop. Over time, people would see that the managers of these systems had learned how to operate them properly, and had accumulated an extensive track record of doing so. People's fears of a disaster of currency mismanagement – fears that are fully justified today – would gradually abate. Consequently, the popularity of these gold-based currencies would increase, and perhaps eventually replace floating fiat currencies entirely in a gradual and trouble-free process.

In the United States today, this happy outcome is blocked primarily by a series of laws and policies, both *de jure* and *de facto*. The legal standing of parallel or alternative currencies, introduced by U.S. entities is hazy at best. A variety of "local currencies" have been introduced in the United States and around the world. At last count, there were sixteen in California alone, and another ten in Washington state, including Snohomish diamonds, Bainbridge Island bucks, Kettle River hours, and Skagit dollars. Mostly, these are linked to the existing U.S. dollar, or have some sort of creative basis such as "man-hours." Despite some attractions, they are generally of lower quality than the U.S. dollar and do not present a serious alternative for most forms of commerce.

Although the legal basis of a gold-based parallel currency in the United States does not seem to differ from these many other experiments, in practice the "local currencies" have been allowed to continue, while attempts to introduce gold-based currencies have been heavily suppressed. One entity in particular, Liberty Services (formerly the National Organization for the Repeal of the Federal Reserve and Internal Revenue Code) founded by Bernard von NotHaus, issued a gold- and silver-based Liberty Dollar from 1998-2009. The Liberty Dollar consisted of coins made of gold and silver bullion, and banknotes of several denominations redeemable in bullion. The banknotes bore no resemblance to Federal Reserve Notes, the regular circulating currency of the United States. Liberty Services claimed that Claudia Dickens, spokeswoman for the U.S. Treasury Department's Bureau of Engraving and Printing, had said that "there's nothing illegal about this," after the Treasury Department's legal team reviewed the currency. Nevertheless, Liberty Services' bullion depository was raided by the FBI in November 2007, and the bullion seized. Von NotHaus was later charged and convicted of several violations of laws preventing counterfeiting – in other words, imitating the existing Federal Reserve Notes and coins. The prosecutor reportedly claimed that the 90% silver Liberty Dollar coin was a counterfeit of the common 25-cent quarter-dollar coin. (The use of the counterfeiting ruse shows that actual statutes preventing the introduction of parallel currencies do not exist.) Von NotHaus faced up to 15 years of jail time. In 2011, von NotHaus was declared a domestic terrorist by the FBI.

The primary legal basis for preventing the widespread introduction of alternative currencies is apparently Section 5103 of Title 31 of the United States Code, which reads:

> United States coins and currency (including Federal reserve notes and circulating notes of Federal reserve banks and national banks) are legal tender for all debts, public charges, taxes, and dues. Foreign gold or silver coins are not legal tender for debts.

The term "legal tender" actually means that "United States coins and currency" are legally recognized to be considered repayment of dollar-based debt obligations. In other words, if you give a creditor a $20 Federal Reserve note, in repayment of a $20 debt, then that debt is legally recognized to have been repaid. Also, Federal Reserve notes are legally recognized as payment for public charges, taxes and dues – in other words, transactions with the government.

This Section does not contain any overt restriction against the use of parallel currencies, either of domestic origin, or foreign currencies, which are in fact used regularly. In 2007, a popular fashion model reportedly declared that she would henceforth be paid in euros rather than dollars. There was no particular restriction on U.S. entities (for example a fashion magazine) from indeed paying her in euros; in other words, using the euro in commerce. This is no different than if the model had insisted on being paid in gold coins, or a currency based on gold.

Thus, parallel currencies are in something of a legal limbo in the United States. Probably, an overt declaration would be needed that gold-based currencies are indeed legal. This could be broadened to a declaration that any sort of currencies are legal for use between consenting parties. Already, one of the most popular alternative currencies is Bitcoin, with a total money supply value of over $100 million U.S. dollars as of 2012. The supply and value of the currency is based in part on virtual "mining," in the form of computing power provided to solve difficult problems. While this exceedingly novel form of alternative currency proceeded mostly without molestation from U.S. authorities, currencies based on gold and silver, the most traditional of solutions, were aggressively suppressed.

Gold and silver coins produced by the U.S. Mint, such as the popular American Eagle series, are formally legal tender within the United States. However, use of these coins is, in practice, suppressed by various taxes on transactions in gold, which do not apply to transactions in euros or other foreign currencies. For example, if a house was purchased with 150 American Eagle 1 oz. gold coins, the transfer of the coins to the seller would likely be considered a "sale" for tax purposes, and thus subject to capital gains taxes. (The purchase of a house using euros would not be subject to taxes.) Capital gains tax rates for gold bullion, at present, follow a separate schedule for "collectibles" at a 28% rate, instead of the 15% rate that applies to capital gains from equities or bonds.

On top of that, many states charge sales taxes for "sales" of small quantities of gold. California charges sales taxes on bullion sales of less than $1,500. Thus, if a business owner wished to pay his employees using a ½ oz. American Eagle gold coin, the transfer of that coin (worth about $800 in 2012) to the employee may be subject to sales taxes.

With these factors in mind, Representative Ron Paul introduced H.R. 1098, the "Free Competition in Currency Act of 2011." The act would repeal Section 5103 of Title 31, United States Code, and provide that no Federal, State or local taxes would apply with respect to transactions in gold and silver, in coin or bullion form.

H.R. 1098 was not passed, but the State of Utah did pass a similar bill in March 2011 which formally declared that U.S. Mint gold and silver bullion coins would be considered legal tender, and that no taxes (at the State or local level) would apply to transactions in these coins. Unfortunately, Federal-level restrictions and taxes still apply in Utah, so the practical advantages of this step have not yet been fully realized. The Utah bill would not only legalize transactions of U.S. Mint bullion coins, but also various financial instruments based on these coins, such as various forms of debit cards, banking, checking, and so forth. Organization like GoldMoney already provide sophisticated banking and payment services based on gold bullion. Twelve other state legislatures had bills introduced to follow Utah's example.

* * *

In practice, the United States is not the most likely place for alternative gold-based currencies to be formally recognized and flourish. The natural tendency of the U.S. government will be to protect its present fiat dollar monopoly, especially as the U.S. dollar is already the world's premier international currency. When you are already on top of the monetary world, there is no need to be innovative. This intrinsic fear of competition was expressed by Anne Tompkins, the attorney for the Western District of North Carolina and the prosecutor in the case against Bernard von NotHaus and the Liberty Dollar. Tompkins stated that the gold-based Liberty Dollar was "a unique form of domestic terrorism" that was trying "to undermine the legitimate currency of this country." A later press release quoted her as saying: "While these forms of anti-government activities do not involve violence, they are every bit as insidious and represent a clear and present danger to the economic stability of this country."

Other countries' governments, however, may find that it is in their interest to have a high-quality alternative to the mismanaged fiat dollar. Alternative gold-based currencies could be introduced by Switzerland, Hong Kong, the United Arab Emirates, Brazil, or any other country that considers the present U.S. fiat dollar hegemony worldwide to be problematic. These gold-based alternative currencies would not replace existing domestic currencies, at least initially. They could be issued either by private institutions, such as large banks, or by the government itself. Alongside notes and coins, a full range of banking services could be introduced, including deposit accounts, payment services, credit and debit cards, wire transfers, lending and so forth, all denominated in this new gold-based alternative currency.

This process has already begun in places like China, where large banks provide "gold savings accounts." These accounts apparently do not yet have payment services, so that one account holder can pay another, but that could be easily introduced. In principle, it is no different than payment services from an account denominated in any other currency. Even before the introduction of notes and coins, bank accounts denominated in gold can provide many (perhaps most) of the benefits of a fully realized gold-based monetary and financial system. These bank accounts may be "redeemable" in some form. For example, the withdrawal of 1000 goldenbucks from a bank account may be paid by the bank in the form of a one-ounce gold bullion coin.

These alternative gold-based currencies would not only be useful domestically, but could become quite popular worldwide. If banks in Hong Kong issued gold-based banknotes, in addition to the dollar-based banknotes they already issue today, these banknotes may find favor throughout the region and the world as a medium of transactions, just as U.S. dollar banknotes are found serving as money throughout the world. In other words, this new Hong Kong goldenbuck would become a premier international currency. It might even become popular in the United States itself, where, despite restrictions on domestic issuers of gold-based money, there does not seem to be any restriction on the use of foreign currency. Thus, the U.S.'s gold-based alternative currency may originate from Hong Kong. In the United States, there would be the low-quality domestic fiat currency, and also a high-quality international currency, both in regular use – the situation that exists already in most countries in the world.

In 2002, the prime minister of Malaysia, Mahathir Mohamad, proposed the introduction of a gold dinar currency for use throughout the Islamic world – in effect, an international parallel currency. Unfortunately, that effort stalled when Mahathir retired in 2003, but the Malaysian state of Kelantan nevertheless began issuing, in 2006, a gold coin in the traditional Islamic dinar weight of 4.25 grams of gold.

In 2011, the parliament of Switzerland began discussion on the creation of a gold franc, which would be issued by the Swiss national government and circulate in parallel with the existing Swiss franc. The initiative is part of the "Healthy Currency" campaign sponsored by the conservative Swiss People's Party.

In 2011, the Dubai Multi Commodities Center introduced a gold coin, called the khalifa, which was intended to serve as currency throughout the Gulf States area.

In 2009, at a G8 meeting in Italy, Russian President Dmitry Medvedev presented a 1/2 oz. gold bullion coin, calling it an example of "a future unified world currency."

Historically, parallel gold-based currencies have sometimes been issued by governments to replace existing currencies that were rapidly becoming unusable. This was done in Germany in 1923, when the gold-based rentenmark circulated shortly alongside the devalued "papiermark." The introduction of a new gold-based reichsmark in 1924, equivalent in value to the rentenmark, rendered the rentenmark superfluous. Nevertheless, the rentenmark circulated alongside the reichsmark until 1948.

A similar step was taken by Russia in 1922, when the gold-based chervonets currency was introduced to circulate alongside the existing ruble, which had become a floating currency at the onset of World War I. The two circulated side-by-side until 1947, when the chervonets was retired in favor of the ruble, which had by then also been linked to gold.

* * *

Parallel gold-based currencies can serve a special role today, as many governments worldwide search for a way to replace the existing fiat dollar-centric monetary system. A major difficulty that the Chinese government faces, when considering whether to fix the yuan's value to gold bullion, is that such a step would produce radical exchange-rate fluctuations compared to the floating fiat dollar, floating fiat euro, and other fiat currencies worldwide. Due to the effects on trade and business, this exchange rate volatility would quickly become intolerable.

For this reason, most countries in the world today either have a formal link to a major international currency, or an informal one, in which a currency officially floats freely but in practice is managed such that it remains in a recognized trading range with major international currencies. The Chinese yuan has a formal link to the dollar, although one that changes over time, in a "crawling peg" arrangement.

For China to transition to a gold-based currency, one strategy would be to introduce a parallel gold-based currency as described.

Chinese people could use either the existing, dollar-linked yuan or the new goldenyuan, as they see fit, for transactions and as a denominational basis for contracts.

People would use one or the other depending on which is perceived to provide the most benefit. In a situation where the dollar is rapidly losing value vs. gold (the "dollar price of gold" is rising), some businessmen may perceive that it would not be a good idea to sell their products priced in goldenyuan, because they may quickly become uncompetitive due to exchange rate issues. However, at some point, the same businessman may conclude, like the aforementioned fashion model, that getting paid in a currency that is rapidly losing value is not a good business proposition, and insist that only goldenyuan be accepted in payment for valuable goods and services.

The businessman would probably like to pay his workers and suppliers in dollars and dollar-linked yuan, as the value of both declined. However, workers and suppliers may insist on being paid in goldenyuan. At this point, the businessman would probably be forced to also accept goldenyuan in payment.

As more and more individuals begin to use goldenyuan instead of existing dollar-linked yuan, the disadvantages to using goldenyuan diminish and the attractions increase. Other countries may follow a similar two-currency strategy, such that, although no one country has formally adopted a gold standard policy, and use of existing floating fiat currencies could still be quite high, an international gold-currency-using community would form. Thus, not only would Chinese be able to transact with other Chinese using a gold-based currency, but also with other entities worldwide who also wish to use gold-based currencies as their monetary basis for business. The Chinese company could transact with the German company, on a gold-based basis without the problems of currency exchange rate fluctuations – even as the same companies did business with others in fiat dollars, euros and yuan, according to their immediate interests.

Eventually, when it best serves the needs of all Chinese businesses and workers, the goldenyuan alone would perhaps be used within China. The transition away from the floating fiat yuan, and consequently the floating fiat dollar, would be complete. Other countries pursuing a similar two-currency strategy would follow alongside. There would be no formal agreement, like the Bretton Woods conference of 1944, establishing a new monetary order. It would emerge organically, throughout the world, due to the individual decisions and preferences of people everywhere. The transition period might take several years, even a decade or more. No exact "time of transition" would be easily identified. Because each individual, and business, makes the transition wholly or partially when it best suits their individual interests, the transition would be smooth and painless.

This strategy provides great advantages, with hardly any identifiable problems. It is, perhaps, the best way to establish a new gold-based monetary system worldwide today.

Chapter 15:
Dealing with Bank Insolvency

Due to their leveraged nature, banks often become insolvent. Broad changes in the economy as a whole affecting all banks, and the copycat nature of most banks' management, may cause much of the entire banking industry to become insolvent simultaneously. The prospect of a chaotic series of defaults and bankruptcies across the entire financial system looms. This seems to happen every ten to twenty years.

Increasing pressure is placed on the government to solve the problem of bank insolvency one way or another. This generally takes the form of either a "bank bailout" using large amounts of public funds, or some sort of money-printing activity by the central bank, in excess of its responsibility as a "lender of last resort" in the 19th-century meaning of the term. Both are wholly unnecessary.

Banks, the beneficiaries of these "bailouts," are generally able to get away with this form of taxpayer thievery due to a series of threats about impending economic catastrophe if their demands are not met. This situation is compounded by general ignorance of how banks operate, among politicians and other non-bankers, which would lead to an understanding of better means of action.

Bank insolvency, in practice, can become a major avenue by which a gold-based monetary system could be undermined. Or, a floating fiat currency system may be justified by the argument: "what would we do in the case of widespread bank insolvency?"

A commercial bank is a simple business. It borrows money at one rate of interest, and then lends the money at a higher rate of interest.

The difference between the interest payments received (on money lent) and interest paid (on money borrowed) is the bank's profit.

	As of the year end ($ millions)
Assets	
Cash and short-term investments	3
Securities	10
Loans	100
Total Assets	113
Liabilities	
Deposits	95
Borrowings	3
Bonds	2
Total Liabilities	100
Shareholders' Equity	13
Total liabilities and shareholders' equity	113

Table 15.1: Generic Bank Balance Sheet

In the generic form, a bank's balance sheet might look like Table 15.1. This bank has borrowed $100 million, mostly in the form of deposits. These are bank checking accounts, bank savings accounts, Certificates of Deposit, and other means of direct loans to the bank. The bank has also borrowed a little bit of money from non-depositors, perhaps from another bank on the "money market." Lastly, the bank has issued a small number of bonds, which constitute another form of borrowing.

The bank has taken this $100 million, plus the equity capital of the bank ($13 million), and has loaned it out. The banks' loans are its assets. "Cash and short-term investments" includes forms of base money (banknotes and deposits at the Federal Reserve), and also short-term loans to other banks, such as an overnight loan.

"Securities" refer primarily to publicly-traded bonds, such as U.S. Treasury bonds and corporate bonds. These are a securitized form of loan.

"Loans" are bank loans of various types, such as mortgages, commercial loans, credit-card lending, auto loans, and so forth.

The difference between the assets and liabilities is the "Shareholders' Equity" of the bank, also known as capital or book value. When the liabilities are in excess of the assets, the bank is insolvent. The leverage of the bank can be calculated in numerous ways, but the simplest is the ratio of assets ($113m) to equity ($13m), to produce a capital ratio of 11.5%, or the reciprocal, leverage of 8.7 times. If the value of the assets falls by only 11.5%, then the shareholders' equity will be zero and the bank will be formally insolvent.

	As of the year end ($ millions)
Assets	
Cash and short-term investments	3
Securities	10
Loans	94
Total Assets	107
Liabilities	
Deposits	95
Borrowings	3
Bonds	2
Total Liabilities	100
Shareholders' Equity	7
Total liabilities and shareholders' equity	107

Table 15.2: Bank Balance Sheet After Asset Writedown

The value of assets declines when the borrower is judged to be at risk of not paying back the full interest and principal of the loan. For example, if a borrower is judged to have a 50% risk of default, and the bank expects a $0.50 recovery in the case of default, then the value of the loan might be (50%*$0.50)+(50%*$1.00)=$0.75 on the dollar. In other words, the loan's value has fallen by 25%. Note that the borrower does not actually have to default for the loan to be considered an impaired loan.

Liabilities generally do not decline in value; the bank has to pay all the money back.

Perhaps this bank has made all of its loans to commercial real estate developers, who used them to build shopping malls. In time, it is found that far too many shopping malls have been built. The rental revenue from the half-vacant malls is insufficient to pay the interest and principal of the debt. These loans are mortgages; when the developer defaults, the bank becomes the owner of the shopping mall. The value of the shopping mall is rather low in this situation, below the value of the debt outstanding. The bank calculates that perhaps

20% of its loans to developers will default; and that the average loss borne by the bank on defaulted loans will be 30%. The value of the loans is thus the original $100 million lent (as noted on the balance sheet), minus losses of (20%*$100m*30%=) $6 million, leaving $94 million. The value of the loans are adjusted on the bank's balance sheet (Table 15.2).

	As of the year end ($ millions)
Assets	
Cash and short-term investments	8
Securities	10
Loans	94
Total Assets	112
Liabilities	
Deposits	95
Borrowings	3
Bonds	2
Total Liabilities	100
Shareholders' Equity	12
Total liabilities and shareholders' equity	112

Table 15.3: Bank Balance Sheet After Recapitalization
Via Equity Issuance

The shareholder's equity is still positive. The bank has not yet become formally insolvent, by this measure. However, the risk of insolvency has increased, as has leverage. The bank now has $107 million of assets and $7 million of capital, a leverage ratio of 15:1. A 6.5% decline in asset value would wipe out all equity. This bank is "undercapitalized." What could happen at this point is that the bank would sell new equity, thus raising new funds from investors. If the bank raised $5 million, the balance sheet would look like Table 15.3.

Cash has increased by $5 million, the amount paid to the bank by those that purchased the newly-issued equity. This increases overall assets to $112 million, leaving shareholders' equity of $12 million. Leverage decreases to 9:1, and the capital ratio is 10.7%.

Perhaps the bank's estimates of losses have been too conservative. Fully 50% of all of its loans enter default, and the average loss on defaulted loans is 50%. Thus, the total loss is

228

(50%*$100 million*50%=) $25 million, which reduces the value of the loans to $75 million (Table 15.4).

	As of the year end ($ millions)
Assets	
Cash and short-term investments	3
Securities	10
Loans	75
Total Assets	88
Liabilities	
Deposits	95
Borrowings	3
Bonds	2
Total Liabilities	100
Shareholders' Equity	(12)
Total liabilities and shareholders' equity	88

Table 15.4: Bank Balance Sheet After Large Asset Writedowns

The bank now has liabilities in excess of its assets, represented as negative shareholders' equity. It is formally insolvent.

The bank's liabilities are generally short-term in nature. Lenders (depositors) can receive their funds on demand, or after a short period to maturity. If the bank's existing lenders do not continue to lend to the bank, the bank must find other lenders. These other lenders are also not likely to want to extend loans to the bank. Commonly, banks will take every possible step to present their condition in the best possible light. If the bank's official condition is weakened, lenders know that the bank's true condition is likely to be much worse.

In a situation where the bank's lenders are requesting the return of their funds, and no other entities are willing to make loans to the bank, then the bank would have to sell assets. It is quite likely that, under this condition of forced selling, the bank would not receive as much as the claimed asset value, and perhaps not as much as the true economic value. Thus, the effective value of the assets declines, and the bank becomes effectively insolvent.

As depositors and other creditors rush to have their debts repaid, the bank runs out of cash to do so. The bank thus declares bankruptcy. Bankruptcy is a legal condition, which temporarily relieves the bank from meeting its obligations. From there, it can proceed in many different directions.

The bank could be liquidated, with all of its assets sold to the highest bidder, and the proceeds used to pay creditors. In this case, the assets would be sold for $88 million. The proceeds from the sale would be distributed among the creditors, who collectively have claims of $100 million. Thus, the creditors would get $88 million/$100 million or $0.88 on the dollar for their claims, on average. This would be in the form of a cash payout. In practice, there is a hierarchy of creditor seniority. Junior creditors would take all the losses, while senior creditors would get a full 100% recovery.

Bank liquidation is actually uncommon. The Federal Deposit Insurance Corporation is a bank regulator and the guarantor of deposit liabilities in the United States, so insolvent banks typically fall into FDIC receivership. This happened to 25 U.S. banks in 2008; 140 banks in 2009; 157 banks in 2010; and 91 banks in 2011. Bank insolvency and restructuring (a form of bankruptcy) is quite common, and need not cause any great crisis, or disruption to small bank depositors.

"Receivership" means that the FDIC is responsible for the future of the bank, including its assets and liabilities, which is to say, its creditors. The bank is typically sold to another bank, which merges it into its existing operations. Insured depositors of the insolvent bank become depositors in the acquiring bank. Their accounts are transferred seamlessly. Uninsured creditors may suffer partial or total losses. For example, an uninsured account with a balance of $1 million may become an account worth $500,000 in the acquiring bank.

Assets of the insolvent bank are typically transferred to the acquiring bank, without being sold on the open market. For example, a portfolio of auto loans will be acquired and managed by the acquiring bank, with no change in conditions for borrowers. Existing bank branches remain open, quickly rebadged with the acquiring bank's names and logos.

We have been looking at a simplified, generic balance sheet. However, the same principles apply to real-world banks. As an example of a typical regional bank, we will look at the annual report of People's United Bank for the year 2011 (Table 15.5). People's United Bank was a premier regional bank in the U.S. Northeast, with 416 branches at the time in Connecticut, New York, Massachusetts, Vermont, New Hampshire and Maine.

	December 31, 2011
Assets	($ millions)
Cash and due from banks	370.2
Short-term investments	410.7
Total cash and cash equivalents	780.9
Securities purchased under agreements to resell	–
Securities	
Trading account securities, fair value	71.8
Securities available for sale, at fair value	2,725.5
Securities held to maturity, at amortized cost	56.4
Federal Home Loan Bank stock, at cost	77.7
Total securities	2,931.4
Loans held for sale	101.9
Loans	
Commercial	7,382.0
Commercial real estate	7,712.2
Residential Mortgage	3,628.4
Consumer	2,217.4
Total loans	20,400.0
Less allowance for loan losses	(182.9)
Total loans, net	20,217.1
Goodwill	1,951.4
Other acquisition-related intangibles	222.8
Premises and equipment	339.6
Bank-owned life insurance	332.7
Other assets	690.1
Total assets	27,567.9
Liabilities	
Deposits	
Non-interest-bearing	4,506.2
Savings, interest-bearing checking and money market accounts	10,970.4
Time	5,339.2
Total deposits	20,815.8
Borrowings	
Retail repurchase agreements	497.2
Federal Home Loan Bank advances	332.4
Federal funds purchased and other borrowings	27.1
Total borrowings	856.7
Subordinated notes and debentures	159.6
Other liabilities	510.8
Total liabilities	22,342.9
Stockholders' Equity	5,225.0
Total liabilities and stockholders' equity	27,567.9

Table 15.5: U.S.: People's United Bank, Balance Sheet, 2011

It is somewhat more complicated than our simplified example, but the basic features are the same. Out of total assets of $27,567.9 million, People's United Bank held $780.9 million of cash and short-term investments (2.8%), securities of $2,931 million (10.6%), and loans of $20,217.4 million (73.3%). The remainder is odds and ends such as the banks' buildings and office equipment. ("Goodwill" is an accounting artifact related to the past acquisition of another bank, and can be ignored for our purposes.)

Against this, People's United Bank had $22,342.9 million in liabilities. These included deposits of $20,815.8 million (93.2%), borrowings of $856.7 million (3.8%), and bonds ("subordinated notes and debentures") of $159.6 million (0.7%).

The difference between the assets and the liabilities is the stockholders' equity, of $5,225.0 million. Note that the total assets ($27,567.9 million) and total liabilities and stockholders' equity ($27,567.9 million) are the same. In other words, they balance, which is why this is known as a "balance sheet."

* * *

FDIC receivership, restructuring and sale has been the normal process for small banks that become insolvent in the United States. However, this process has generally not been applied to large banks. If a large bank becomes insolvent, a similar process to what happens to smaller banks can be implemented. The essence of the process is what is known as a "debt/equity swap." This is actually easier for a large bank than a smaller one, because larger banks typically have a greater portion of their liabilities in the form of bonds and bank debt, rather than deposits (Table 15.6).

	As of the year end ($ millions)
Assets	
Cash and short-term investments	3
Securities	20
Loans	110
Total Assets	133
Liabilities	
Deposits	70
Borrowings	20
Bonds	30
Total Liabilities	120
Shareholders' Equity	13
Total liabilities and shareholders' equity	133

Table 15.6: Generic Large Bank Balance Sheet

This bank also finds that 50% of its loans default, with a 50% loss rate. Thus, the value of its loans is $110m minus losses of (50%*$110m*50%=) $27.5m, leaving $82.5m (Table 15.7).

The bank is insolvent. At this point, the bank would enter a restructuring of liabilities. In such a case, there is an established order of seniority, established over centuries of corporate law. The more junior creditors suffer losses before senior creditors. The existing equity holders get nothing. The junior bondholders are converted to equity. Direct lenders are more senior than bondholders, and here are unaffected. The most-senior depositors are unaffected. (We will assume that deposits are senior, in bankruptcy, to bonds.) Investors that own the bonds of the bank no longer own bonds, but rather, equity. They become the new owners of the bank. After the restructuring of liabilities, the bank's balance sheet looks like Table 15.8.

	As of the year end *($ millions)*
Assets	
Cash and short-term investments	3
Securities	20
Loans	82.5
Total Assets	100.5
Liabilities	
Deposits	70
Borrowings	20
Bonds	30
Total Liabilities	120
Shareholders' Equity	(19.5)
Total liabilities and shareholders' equity	100.5

Table 15.7: Large Bank Balance Sheet After Asset Writedown

Because the bonds were converted to equity, the total liabilities shrink. Liabilities are again less than assets, and the bank is again solvent.

The bondholders began with bonds with principal of $30 million. Afterwards, they own the equity of the bank, which eventually trades upon the stock exchange. What is this equity worth? The bank's book value (shareholders' equity) is $10.5 million. However, a healthy bank typically trades at a premium to book value, of perhaps 50% although it could be larger than that. At 1.5x book value, the bank's equity would have a total market capitalization of $15.75 million on the stock market. Thus, the bondholders traded $30 million of bonds for $15.75 million of equity. This represents a loss of course, but it is a relatively manageable loss in the scheme of things. The bank's direct lenders and depositors suffer no losses at all.

	As of the year end ($ millions)
Assets	
Cash and short-term investments	3
Securities	20
Loans	82.5
Total Assets	100.5
Liabilities	
Deposits	70
Borrowings	20
Bonds	(none)
Total Liabilities	90
Shareholders' Equity	10.5
Total liabilities and shareholders' equity	100.5

Table 15.8: Large Bank Balance Sheet After Debt/Equity Swap

After the restructuring process, the bank's assets have been properly adjusted to a reasonable estimate of their true economic value. Liabilities have been reduced, and shareholders' equity increased, so that the bank is now solvent again, with an ample capital base. The bank, and its assets, were never liquidated. The bank continues its existence as an ongoing concern, not much differently than it had before. No employees were fired. No offices and branches were closed. The only thing that took place was a ledger adjustment to the liabilities side of the balance sheet. Depositors suffered no losses. No public money was necessary. This is what is supposed to happen in the event of larger bank insolvency.

Citigroup's balance sheet is somewhat more complicated due to the addition of broker/dealer operations to regular bank operations, but the basic pattern is the same (Table 15.9).

	Dec. 31, 2011 ($ millions)
Assets	
Cash and due from banks	28,701
Deposits with banks	155,784
Federal funds sold and securities borrowed or purchased under agreements to resell	275,849
Brokerage receivables	27,777
Trading account assets	291,734
Investments	293,413
Loans, net of unearned income	
Consumer	423,731
Corporate	223,511
Allowance for loan losses	(30,115)
Total loans, net	617,127
Goodwill	25,413
Intangible Assets (other than MSRs)	6,600
Mortgage Servicing Rights (MSRs)	2,569
Other assets	148,911
Total assets	1,873,878
Liabilities	
Non-interest-bearing deposits in U.S. offices	119,437
Interest-bearing deposits in U.S. offices	223,851
Non-interest-bearing deposits in offices outside the U.S.	57,357
Interest-bearing deposits in offices outside the U.S.	465,291
Brokerage payables	56,696
Trading account liabilities	126,082
Short-term borrowings	54,441
Long-term debt	323,505
Other liabilities	69,272
Total liabilities	1,694,305
Stockholders' equity	179,573
Total liabilities and equity	1,873,878

Table 15.9: U.S.: Citigroup, Consolidated Balance Sheet, 2011

Let's assume that the total value of Citigroup's assets fell by 20%, leaving a total asset value of $1,499,102 million. This would be less than total liabilities of $1,694,305 million, rendering the bank insolvent.

The exact details of a restructuring plan would depend on the specifics of bankruptcy law and terms of contracts with counterparties. However, we can make a rough example. The existing shareholder's equity would be cancelled. This leaves the bank's creditors. The least senior creditor would likely be the bank's bondholders, listed as "short-term borrowings" and "long-term debt," and totaling $377,946 million.

In this example, the entirety of this debt is converted to equity. (Other solutions, such as a partial conversion to equity, are possible.) The bondholders become shareholders.

Total assets	1,499,102
Liabilities	
Non-interest-bearing deposits in U.S. offices	119,437
Interest-bearing deposits in U.S. offices	223,851
Non-interest-bearing deposits in offices outside the U.S.	57,357
Interest-bearing deposits in offices outside the U.S.	465,291
Brokerage payables	56,696
Trading account liabilities	126,082
Short-term borrowings	(none)
Long-term debt	(none)
Other liabilities	69,272
Total liabilities	1,316,359
Stockholders' equity	182,743
Total liabilities and equity	1,499,102

Table 15.10: Citigroup Balance Sheet After Debt/Equity Swap

For example, one new share of equity could be exchanged for each $50 of debt principal owed. (This ratio is arbitrary, chosen simply to produce an appropriate share value). The $377,946 million of debt becomes ($377,946 million/$50=) 7,558.92 million shares, issued to the former bondholders (Table 15.10).

The bank now has a capital ratio (equity/assets) of 12%, a relatively healthy level. The equity would probably trade at a premium to book value (stockholders' equity), of perhaps 1.5x. Thus, the equity market capitalization of the bank would be around $274,115 million, and each share would have a value of $36.26. In the end, the bondholders traded $50 of debt principal for $36.26 of equity, which is not a particularly disastrous outcome. Depositors, in this case senior to bondholders, did not suffer any losses at all. The bank continues as a business, with no employees terminated, offices closed, or assets liquidated. The process is simply a modification of contracts.

Most important, however, is that the bank, which was insolvent, is now financially healthy, because its liabilities have been reduced and its assets have been written down to a reasonable estimate of their true economic value. The problem of bank insolvency has been resolved, without the need for taxpayer funds. Nor was there any need for a central bank to prop up the insolvent bank by loaning it large sums of money.

* * *

Unfortunately, this is not always the way it works out. Banks' managements have a strong aversion to a balance sheet restructuring of this sort, as do banks' creditors. The bank's managers could lose their jobs, and all the perks of power that come with them. Perhaps more significant, however, is that large banks often have many obligations to other large banks, not only in the form of simple borrowing, but also in the form of derivatives, repurchase agreements, and many other situations which are not necessarily apparent on the balance sheet. Also, money market funds are often creditors to large banks to a significant degree. Other banks and money market funds could in turn be forced into financial turmoil by the bankruptcy and restructuring of a large bank, to a much larger degree than for smaller local or regional banks, which are funded overwhelmingly by depositors. In the United States, large banks have also adopted substantial broker-dealer operations following the repeal of the Glass-Steagall Act in 1999, which prevented such operations prior to that point.

These elements have led governments to subsidize weak banks with taxpayer funds on a regular basis, particularly as the financial industry became more complex after about 1970. This subsidy can take many forms, including various forms of "bailouts."

Many subsidy strategies involve either selling the government something at a price that is much higher than could be obtained in the private market, or buying something for a price that is much lower than could be obtained. The government may be persuaded to recapitalize the bank through the purchase of various forms of equity capital, at a very bad price, or to make loans to the bank at extraordinarily lenient terms. Commonly, the government will set up some sort of "bad bank," "super SIV," or other such entity, which purchases distressed assets from banks at an artificially high price that allows the banks to avoid losses. Another common strategy is for the government to bail out some entity which threatens to go bankrupt, which in turn eliminates the losses suffered by creditors if that entity indeed entered bankruptcy without government assistance. This was the case for American International Group in 2008, and arguably for General Motors in 2009 as well. Often, the entity enters some sort of bankruptcy anyway, but due to government involvement, creditors' losses are substantially mitigated.

The government may also sell banks some sort of asset at a price that produces a radical advantage to the buyer, in this way transferring an economic advantage to the purchasing bank and thus helping to recapitalize the purchasing bank. This is commonly the case when a smaller bank enters FDIC restructuring and is sold to some larger bank. Many hundreds of failed smaller banks have been sold by the FDIC to larger ones, often with substantial guarantees and other advantages that can practically guarantee a large profit – and corresponding loss to the seller (and guarantor), in this case the government. This has also included some very large banks, such as the sale of Wachovia to Wells Fargo in 2008, and the sale of Washington Mutual to JP Morgan, also in 2008. Assets sold in the liquidation of banks and other institutions by the government, such as loan books or property, may be offered to insiders at extremely advantageous prices, as was common in the savings and loan liquidations of the early 1990s. Large banks may enjoy curious advantages in bankruptcy court, such as JP Morgan's seniority to other creditors in the bankruptcy of Lehman Brothers in 2008.

Often, the government of a smaller country can be persuaded to, in effect, guarantee the investments of foreign banks. This happened to Ireland beginning in 2008, with the result that the Irish government's debt, as a percentage of GDP, increased from 25% in 2007 to 118% in 2012 (Figure 15.11).

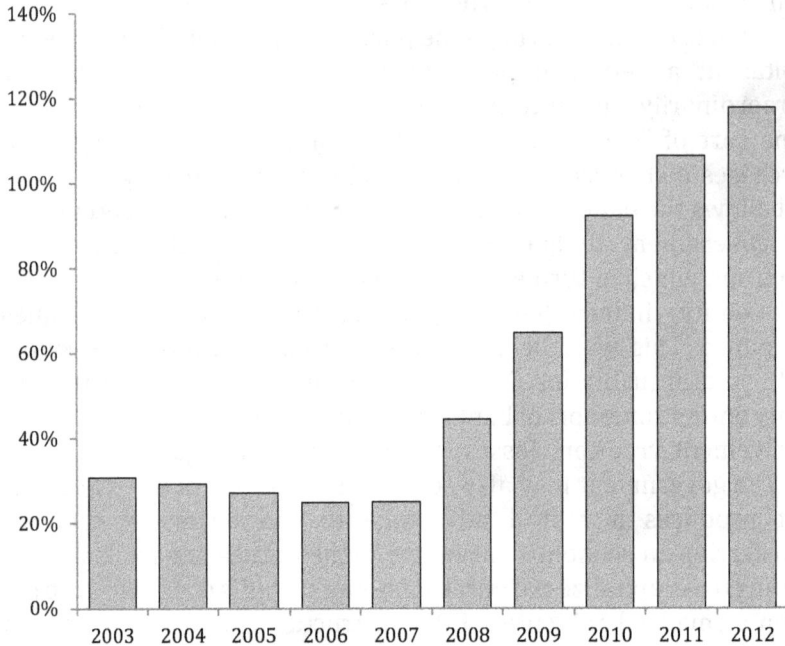

Figure 15.11: Ireland: Government Debt as a Percentage of
Gross Domestic Product, 2003-2012

This additional government debt incurred was wholly unnecessary;
the country's insolvent banks could have been restructured, as
illustrated previously, with no cost to the government at all. However,
that would have caused foreign private creditors to take a loss. The
foreign private creditors decided that they would much rather have
the Irish government absorb the loss, and managed to find a way to
do so. The money raised by the issuance of new government debt did
nothing for the people of Ireland, who must nevertheless pay it back.
The money went directly to foreign banks. (Figure 15.12)

This pattern has repeated many times over the past several
decades, notably during the Asian Crisis of 1997-98, in which Asian
governments assumed large quantities of debt to bail out foreign
creditors (primarily banks), and during the Latin American debt crisis
of the 1980s, when many Latin American governments did the same
to, again, cover the losses faced by many large U.S. banks.

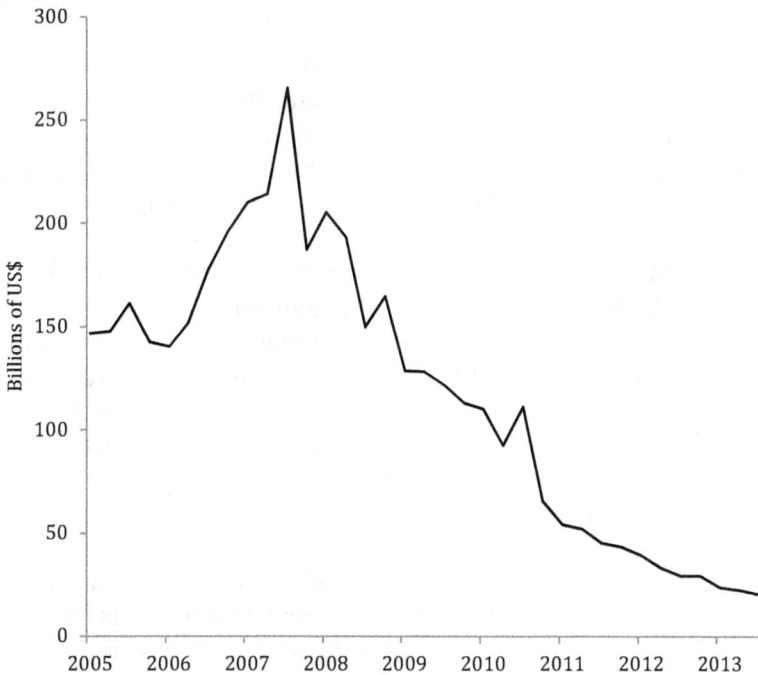

Figure 15.12: Ireland: Foreign Liabilities of Banks, 2005-2013[1]

None of these "bailouts," at public expense, are necessary. Default, insolvency and business failure are regular features of capitalism, and the courts are well equipped for such eventualities.

* * *

Another unfortunate variant of the "bail-out" is the "bail-in," which, at first glance, looks very similar to the proper capitalistic process of recapitalization via a debt/equity swap as described previously. The main difference is a change in the effective seniority of creditors. Certain crony entities, such as other financial institutions, enjoy super-senior status, and thus may avoid all losses, while other creditors (such as general non-interest-bearing deposits) which would normally enjoy seniority are thus pushed into a junior position, where they may take large losses.

This was the case in Cyprus in 2013. The government officially allowed private financial institutions and the government to claim super-senior status, which pushed the losses of the bank upon the non-crony creditors.

Once this fundamental crime is achieved, the tendency is for many other essentially criminal acts to be committed which increase the losses of non-crony creditors (such as general depositors), and decrease the losses or indeed, create profits for crony entities. Some strategies that may take place alongside a "bail-in" include:

1) Dumping low-value assets on the defunct bank. The bank is sold a large amount of assets at a high price, just before the "bail-in". The bank may borrow money from the central bank to enable the purchase. After the "bail-in" restructuring, the central bank claims super-senior status and gets a 100% recovery of its loans to the bank. The assets are revealed to have low values, and the losses are borne by non-crony creditors.

2) Asset write-downs. Crony entities have their loans written down before the "bail-in" restructuring. In effect, this is loan forgiveness – the crony entities do not have to pay back the money they owe to the bank. The non-crony creditors suffer additional losses.

3) Liquidation of assets at very low prices. Instead of holding the assets on the books, after the "bail-in" restructuring, assets are sold to cronies for prices well below their economic value. For example, an asset, such as a nonperforming loan, with an economic value of $0.50 on the dollar is sold for $0.05. The additional $0.45 loss is borne by non-crony creditors.

4) Assignment of assets at very high prices. This might be done in the form of a "bad bank," which is separated from a "good bank" in some way. Creditors associated with the "bad bank" could take huge losses, while they may have been senior (and thus unaffected) if the bank had not been split in this fashion. There is no need for a "good bank/bad bank restructuring."

Due to its leveraged nature, the assets of a bank do not have to decline very much for the bank to become insolvent. If a bank has $10 of assets, $1 of equity capital and $9 of liabilities, and the value of the assets declines to $8, the bank is insolvent. However, $8 of assets remains to satisfy the $9 of creditors' claims. In this case, creditors should recover $8/$9 or $0.88 on the dollar, in the form of debt or equity book value. Junior creditors would have the bulk of adjustments, and senior creditors would likely have no losses at all.

During November and December of 1931, the first great wave of U.S. bank failure during the Great Depression, six hundred and eight U.S. banks failed. The largest was the Bank of the United States, a commercial bank that suffered losses primarily on real estate-related loans. The banks' assets were liquidated in bankruptcy into one of the worst markets of the 20th century. Despite this, creditors eventually recovered $0.835 on the dollar. Senior creditors likely had no losses.

The "bail-in" situation, where normally senior non-crony creditors (general depositors) suffer losses of 50% or more, while crony creditors have no losses and often large profits, is a criminal corruption of proper capitalistic and legal processes. The most senior creditors, normally non-interest-bearing deposits, should not suffer any losses at all.

* * *

The default and bankruptcy of one large institution could lead directly to the failure of many other institutions as well, threatening to produce a chaotic pattern of financial collapse. This is known as "systemic risk."

Fear of such an outcome, combined with broad ignorance of alternative strategies, leads governments to acquiesce to banks' demands to cover their private losses via public assistance, or engage in many forms of fraud and favoritism contrary to the principles of capitalism and legal process.

Instead of "bailouts," governments may have an important role to play in orchestrating the balance sheet restructuring of many institutions simultaneously, in a quick and effective fashion. This is commonly known as a "bank holiday," because, in essence, the entire financial system enters a state of restructuring simultaneously. During this "bank holiday," the financial standing of banks can be examined, and those that need a balance sheet restructuring (for example, a debt/equity swap as previously described) can undertake that as needed. This need not cost the public anything.

One such "bank holiday" took place in 1933. On March 9, 1933 a "bank holiday" began in which all banks' financial condition were reviewed, and their liabilities restructured as appropriate. The plan was budgeted at $2.0 million, a paltry figure even then, to cover administrative expenses. Banks reopened on March 13, 1933. The 1933 "bank holiday" removed most worries about the state of the financial system and its future, as banks were returned to financial health system-wide. On March 15, 1933, the first day of stock market trading after the bank holiday, the Dow Jones Industrial Average rose 15.34%, its largest one-day gain in history.

Chapter 16:
Dealing with Sovereign Default

Sometimes, governments borrow more than they should; indeed, they borrow more than they are willing or able to repay. Perhaps, as Adam Smith suggested, all governments reach this point eventually.

> *The practice of funding* [financing budget deficits with debt issuance] *has gradually enfeebled every state which has adopted it. The Italian republics seem to have begun it. Genoa and Venice, the only two remaining which can pretend to an independent existence, have both been enfeebled by it. Spain ... was deeply in debt before the end of the sixteenth century, about a hundred years before England owed a shilling ...*
>
> *When national debts have once been accumulated to a certain degree, there is scarce, I believe, a single instance of their having been fairly and completely paid. The liberation of the public revenue, if it has ever been brought about at all, has always been brought about by a bankruptcy; sometimes by an avowed one, but always by a real one, though frequently by a pretend payment.*
> –Adam Smith, *The Wealth of Nations*, 1776

"Bankruptcy" is a word little understood. In the layperson's mind, it is loosely associated with total commercial disaster. But, its only meaning is that the debtor does not make a contracted payment at the contracted time. This is known as a "default." The term "bankruptcy" itself is rather vague; it means the process that follows a default, whatever that may be in the applicable jurisdiction. In the case of sovereign default, often, in practice, no specific rules apply, and the process can be somewhat open-ended. Creditors have means of applying pressure even to sovereign borrowers, however, such as international sanctions or seizure of assets held in foreign jurisdictions.

The typical outcome of a sovereign default is that some agreement is reached between the government borrower and its creditors – the owners of the government's bonds. This typically takes the form of a reduction in principal due, for example by 50%, or a change in the terms of payment, for example a lengthening of maturity or a change in the interest rate paid. Often, both occur. This is known as a "debt restructuring."

Once the debt restructuring agreement is reached, life continues on. The government enjoys a lighter debt load according to the terms of the restructuring agreement. The creditors accept their losses, and perhaps learn not to make excessive loans to governments that cannot pay them back. At least, a higher interest rate may be required to account for the risk of default. What effect on an economy might this have? It need not have much effect at all. The effect on the government can be quite welcome, as the government's debt service payments can be radically reduced. Creditors suffer losses, but this does not necessarily affect daily commerce. Investment losses are a fact of reality in any healthy economy. Presumably, the investor has diversified their holdings sufficiently to prevent a catastrophic outcome; if not, they will learn to do so in the future. Usually, a sovereign default is no great surprise, but preceded by years if not decades of ample warning for anyone willing to pay sufficient attention. By the time of the default itself, many of the creditors are short-term speculators. The risk-averse investor divested their holdings long previous.

Any one country might have a sovereign default only about once a century, if even that. It may seem so rare as to be inconceivable. However, across the globe as a whole, it is drearily familiar (Table 16.1).

Austria	1938, 1940
Germany	1932, 1939
Greece	1932
Hungary	1932, 1941
Poland	1936, 1940, 1981
Romania	1933, 1981, 1986
Russia	1918, 1991, 1998
Turkey	1915, 1931, 1940, 1978, 1982
Argentina	1951, 1956, 1982, 1989, 2001
Bolivia	1931, 1980, 1986, 1989
Brazil	1902, 1914, 1931, 1937, 1961, 1964, 1983
Chile	1931, 1961, 1963, 1966, 1972, 1974, 1983
Colombia	1900, 1932, 1935
Costa Rica	1901, 1932, 1962, 1981, 1983, 1984
Dominican Republic	1931, 1982, 2005
Ecuador	1906, 1909, 1914, 1929, 1982, 1999, 2008
El Salvador	1921, 1932, 1938
Guatemala	1933, 1986, 1989
Honduras	1981
Mexico	1914, 1928, 1982
Nicaragua	1911, 1915, 1932, 1983, 1987
Panama	1932, 1983, 1987
Paraguay	1920, 1932, 1986, 2003
Peru	1931, 1969, 1976, 1978, 1980, 1984
Uruguay	1915, 1933, 1983, 1987, 1990, 2003
Venezuela	1983, 1990, 1995, 2004
Algeria	1991
Angola	1985
Central African Republic	1981, 1983
Cote d'Ivoire	1983, 2000
Egypt	1984
Kenya	1994, 2000
Morocco	1903, 1983, 1986
Nigeria	1982, 1986, 1992, 2001, 2004
South Africa	1985, 1989, 1993
Zambia	1983
Zimbabwe	1965, 2000
China	1921, 1939
Japan	1942
India	1958, 1969, 1972
Indonesia	1966, 1998, 2000, 2002
Myanmar	1966, 1998, 2000, 2002
Philippines	1983
Sri Lanka	1980, 1982

Table 16.1: Major Defaults of Sovereign Borrowers, 1900-2010[1]

The tally is all the more impressive when considering that many countries listed in Table 16.1 did not even exist until after World War II.

Sovereign default is quite common, and need not be particularly mysterious.

Table 16.1 describes what Adam Smith called an "avowed" default; it does not include real default by a "pretend payment." Smith describes what he means by that term:

> *The raising of the denomination of the coin has been the most usual expedient by which a real public bankruptcy has been disguised under the appearance of a pretended payment. ... A national debt of about a hundred and twenty-eight millions, nearly the capital of the funded and unfunded debt of Great Britain, might in this manner be paid with about sixty-four millions of our present money. ...*
>
> *A pretended payment of this kind ... aggravates in most cases the loss of the creditors of the public; and without any advantage to the public, extends the calamity to a great number of other innocent people. It occasions a general and most pernicious subversion of fortunes of private people; enriching in most cases the idle and profuse debtor at the expense of the industrious and frugal creditor, and transporting a great part of the national capital from the hands which were likely to increase and improve it, to those which are likely to dissipate and destroy it. When it becomes necessary for a state to declare itself bankrupt, in the same manner as when it becomes necessary for an individual to do so, a fair, open, and avowed bankruptcy is always the measure which is least dishonourable to the debtor, and least hurtful to the creditor. The honour of the state is surely very poorly provided for, when, in order to cover the disgrace of real bankruptcy, it has recourse to a juggling trick of this kind, so easily seen through, and at the same time so extremely pernicious.*

Smith is talking about default via currency devaluation. "Raising the denomination of the coin" means taking, for example, a one-ounce gold coin, worth $20, and declaring that it is now worth $35 or $100. All countries today have engaged in some variation of this strategy. The U.S. dollar, at the end of 2011, was worth about an eightieth of its value in 1920, in terms of equivalent ounces of gold bullion. Most other currencies in the world lost even more value than that during the same time period.

After the devaluation of 1933, when the U.S. dollar's value fell from 1/20.67th of an ounce of gold to 1/35th, bondholders sued to collect their interest and principal according to pre-devaluation rates. Ever since the Civil War devaluation of the 1860s, this had been formalized in bonds and lending contracts as a "gold clause." One such clause, from an actual contract of the time, read that payment of principal and interest "will be made ... in gold coin of the United States of America of or equal to the standard of weight and fineness existing on February 1, 1930." In 1934 the Supreme Court, in a 5-4 decision, rendered these gold clauses invalid.

"Currency devaluation" can be an expressed policy goal, as it was in 1933. However, a government may also rely increasingly upon the central bank, on a day-to-day ad-hoc basis, to help smooth its increasingly difficult debt financing, and finally, to become the sole buyer of its bonds. This was the case in the U.S. during World War I and World War II. The result of either path is a tendency towards a decline in currency value, contrary to the goals of a gold standard system.

Is currency devaluation a superior form of sovereign default? The effects on the defaulting government's creditors are much the same as an avowed default: whether they get paid back $0.50 on the dollar via a debt restructuring, in an unchanging currency, or they get paid back 100% in the form of dollars worth only 50% of their prior value, the outcome is similar.

The problem lies with all the other relationships in the economy. A restructuring of the government's debt affects only the government and its creditors. A currency devaluation affects all economic relationships with negative overall effects, as Smith describes.

Thus, the preferred path for a government facing default, as Adam Smith stated over two centuries ago, is to have an avowed default and debt restructuring, while maintaining a stable currency value – ideally a gold standard system. Alas, despite the very long history and experience with such defaults, governments seem to have trouble with this today. Smith's discussions of "honour" seem quaint in our cynical times; and yet, the reason that governments avoid doing what is best for themselves and the nation as a whole – to have a formal default no different than a default by a corporation or household – seems to be wrapped up in notions of "honor," or at least, appearances. These considerations should be discarded, in favor of the method that, besides being far more honorable, will also produce the best outcome for all involved.

* * *

Sovereign default is normally associated with all sorts of economic disaster. There is good reason for this, and ample precedent, but this certainly does not need to be the case. Sometimes, a sovereign default can be the start of a very productive period in a country's history.

Russia's government defaulted on its debt on August 17, 1998, in the midst of a financial crisis that was engulfing much of Asia and also Brazil. The value of the ruble soon collapsed, from around 5.3/dollar in 1997 to 25/dollar in 2000. As a result of the currency collapse, measured price inflation reached 84% per annum in 1998. The defaulted debt was restructured in 2000, with the net present value of the $39 billion of total debt affected reduced by 44% via a combination of principal reduction and changes in the lending terms. As an example of one such restructuring (there were many, corresponding to different types of bonds and different groups of creditors), the face value (principal) of $18.3 billion of London Club debt, representing more than 600 Western banks, was reduced to $10.5 billion.

In Russia's case, the currency was indeed devalued, by 80%. However, this did little to reduce the government's debt load, for the simple reason that it was mostly denominated in foreign currencies. Most national governments today issue debt in international currencies specifically to avoid the risk of default via devaluation. Creditors simply would not buy a bond denominated in a local currency perceived to be of low quality. In this case, the result of a currency devaluation is disastrous: the government's tax revenue is in the form of local currency, but its debt is denominated in an international currency. The effect of the devaluation is to reduce the government's income dramatically, in terms of the international currency. Thus, default via currency devaluation is really only an option for those countries whose currencies inspire sufficient confidence that creditors are willing to own domestic-currency bonds.

As a result of the devaluation and general economic disaster, Russians' per-capita income fell to an abysmal $1,326 in 1999. Promising a productive era of high economic growth, Vladimir Putin won the presidential election of March 2000, and was inaugurated in May 2000. In July 2000, Russia's parliament passed a law that replaced Russia's existing income tax with a flat-tax system that featured a 13% rate. The new tax system went into effect at the beginning of 2001.

The VAT rate was reduced to 20% from 23% in 1999. In 2002, the corporate tax rate was reduced to 24% from 35%. In 2004, the VAT rate was reduced to 18% from 20%. In 2005, inheritance and gift taxes were eliminated. In 2008, the tax rate on dividend income was reduced to 9% from 15%. In 2009, the corporate tax rate was reduced to 20% from 24%.

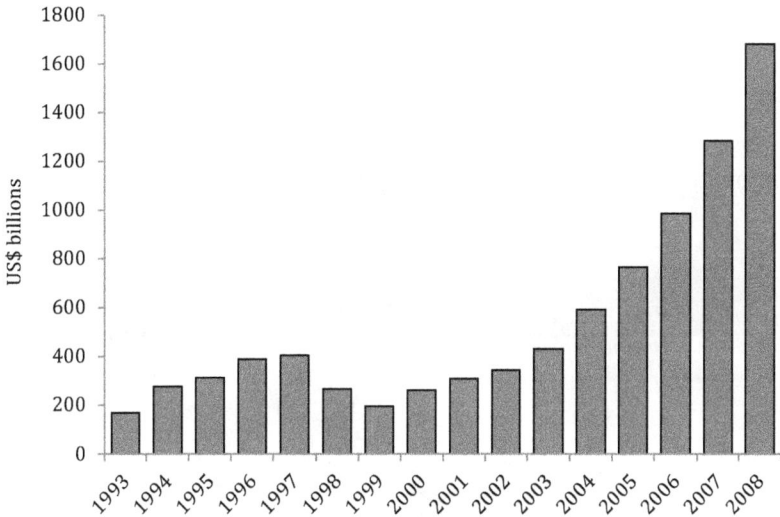

Figure 16.1: Russia: Gross Domestic Product in U.S. Dollars, 1993-2008

Tax revenues from all levels of the Russian government were 31.4% of GDP in 2000, the last year before the implementation of the 13% flat tax. In 2008, the tax revenue/GDP ratio was 31.6%. The value of the ruble was held steady around 27/dollar from 2000.

Russia's version of the Magic Formula – Low Taxes and Stable Money – resulted in incredible economic expansion. Between 1999 and 2007, the official nominal GDP of the Russian economy increased by 757% in dollar terms, a compounded growth rate of 31% per annum (Figure 16.1). In 2008, Russia's GDP (in dollars) was four times larger than it was in 1997, before the crisis. All of this happened while the population of Russia actually fell, from 147 million in 1999 to 142 million in 2010. In 2011, the Russian government's debt/GDP ratio was estimated at 8.7%.

It may seem easy to ascribe this rise entirely to a rise in the price of natural resources, of which Russia produces ample quantities. Yet, in 2010, all mining and quarrying (including extraction of energy commodities) accounted for only 9.8% of GDP. Unlike countries

251

whose economies are dominated by resource extraction, Russia's economic expansion benefited all classes. The average monthly employee wage rose 783% between 2000 and 2010.

The decade following Russia's default was one of spectacular success. Russia's experience contrasts with those who assume that a sovereign default must cause decades of hardship. It depends on what the government does after the default. In Russia's case, the political environment created by the default allowed a change of leadership, which in turn allowed the implementation of economy-friendly policies – namely the Magic Formula combination of low tax rates and a stable currency.

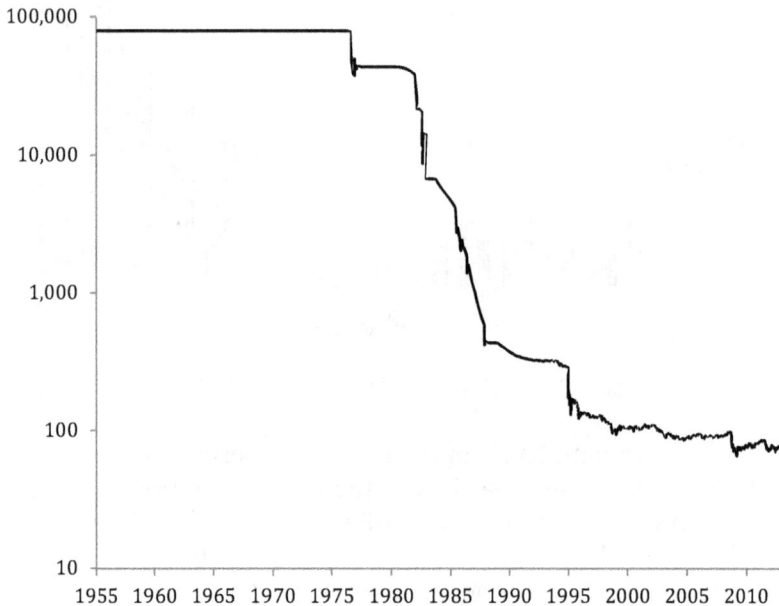

Figure 16.2: Mexico: Value of 1000 Pesos (1 Million pre-1993 Pesos) in U.S. Dollars, 1955-2012
logarithmic scale

A less-happy outcome was experienced by many governments in Latin America that defaulted in the early 1980s. In these cases, economic policy after the default was guided largely by the IMF, and followed a basic pattern: higher taxes (to pay creditors), and continuous currency depreciation leading to hyperinflation throughout the continent. The Mexican peso, to take one of many examples, fell in value from 26/dollar in the middle of 1982 to nearly 2,300/dollar in 1988, when the hyperinflation ended (Figure 16.2).

The combination of soaring tax rates and hyperinflation, the exact opposite of the Magic Formula, led to a "lost decade" throughout Latin America.

During the hyperinflation period, 1982-1987, Mexico's GDP in U.S. dollar terms shrank. In 1986, Mexico's nominal GDP, in U.S. dollar terms, was only about half that of 1981, five years previous (Figure 16.3).

As one would expect from this degree of currency devaluation, the official Consumer Price Index soared by triple digits (Figure 16.4).

Another devaluation in 1995 (Figure 16.5) had much the same effect. Fortunately, that was a one-off episode, not the beginning of another "lost decade."

Over the longer term, Mexico's GDP, measured in U.S. dollars, had its greatest advances during times of currency stability. The 1995 devaluation caused another major setback. It took five more years for Mexico's nominal GDP, in U.S. dollar terms, to regain pre-devaluation levels (Figure 16.6).

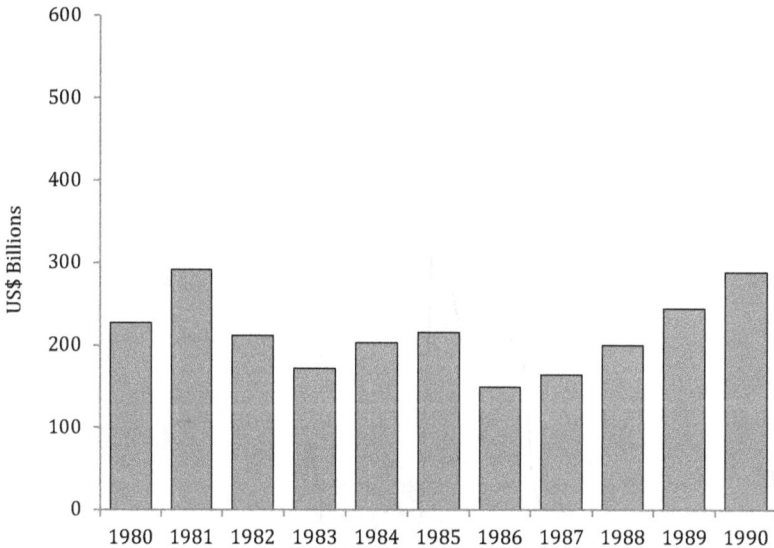

Figure 16.3: Mexico: Nominal Gross Domestic Product in U.S. Dollars, 1980-1990

Russia enjoyed a decade of extraordinary prosperity after its default in 1998. Mexico had years of hyperinflationary catastrophe following its default in 1982. Is there an example of a country that undergoes a sovereign default with little effect on the economy as a whole? Indeed there is: Ecuador's government defaulted on $3.6 billion of debt in December 2008, part of a strategy of renegotiating (restructuring) $10.2 billion of external debt, roughly 25% of GDP at the time. President Rafael Correa declared the debt to be "odious debt," a term in international law that refers to national debt incurred by a regime (in Ecuador's case a prior military regime) that does not serve the best interests of the nation. The default had no effect on Ecuador's currency. The country is "dollarized," and U.S. dollars are the official currency. (This is equivalent to countries in the eurozone, which share the euro.) The default had no particular effects on gross domestic product. GDP growth was 0.36% in 2009 and 3.58% in 2010, in line with countries around the world. (2009 was a crisis year for most countries worldwide, with the world GDP growth rate estimated at a negative -0.8%.) The debt default was popular among Ecuadorians. In April 2009, only four months after the default, Correa won a presidential election in the first round with 51.9% of the vote. It was the first time in thirty years that a president had been re-elected in the first round.

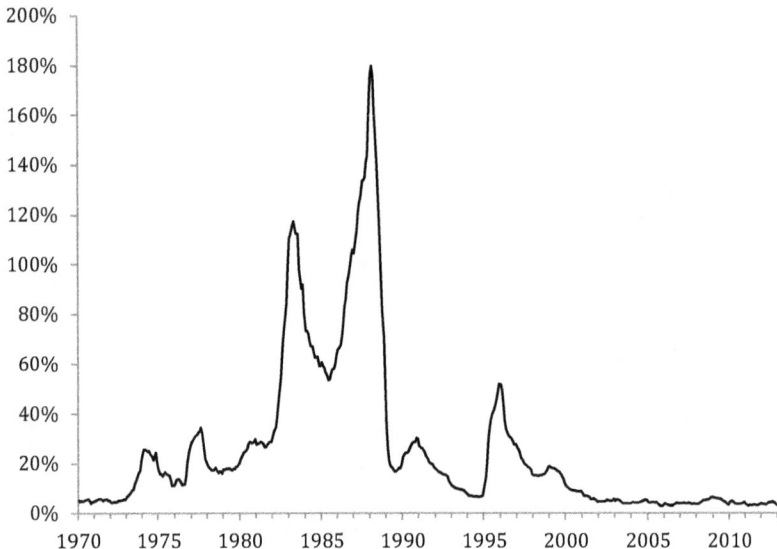

Figure 16.4: Mexico: Consumer Price Index, Year-on-Year Percentage Change, 1970-2012

Correa was a western-trained economist, with a Master of Arts in Economics from the Universite Catholique de Louvain in Belgium, and a Master of Science and PhD in Economics from the University of Illinois. Before becoming president, he was Ecuador's Minister of Finance.

* * *

The problem of sovereign indebtedness includes not only what happens after the default, but what happens before. Typically, the government raises tax rates in a panicky fashion, in a failed "austerity" strategy. Usually, economic policy, especially tax policy, is quite poor to begin with. This can be a fundamental reason for the default; a country with rapidly rising GDP and tax revenues, such as Russia after 2000 as it enjoyed the effects of its Magic Formula policy mix, rarely has debt problems.

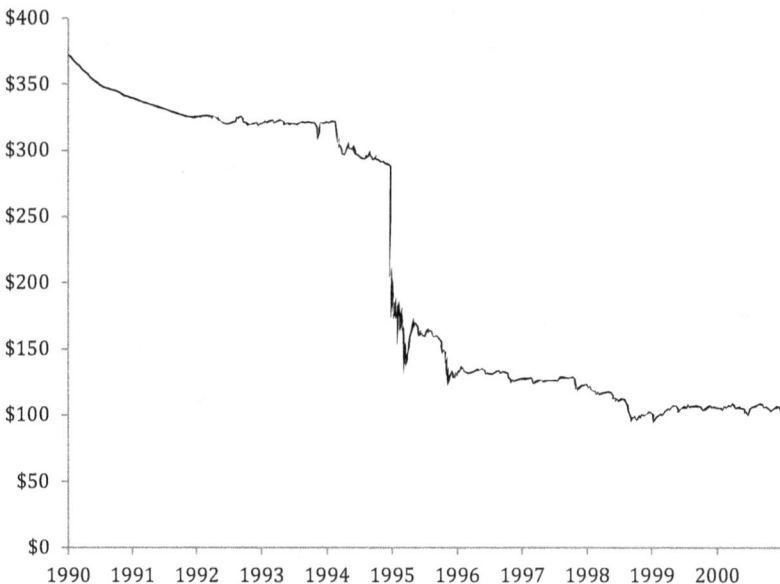

Figure 16.5: Mexico: Value of 1000 Pesos in U.S. Dollars, 1990-2000

The increase in taxes just makes a bad situation worse. Tax revenue as a percent of GDP rarely rises, and may even fall. GDP, however, may stagnate or even shrink dramatically, and the result is lower nominal tax revenue. The government is faced with deteriorating revenues and also greater calls for economic assistance, such as welfare-related payments. In the midst of a contracting private economy, government spending proves to be difficult to reduce, as all those dependent on government largesse refuse to leave what they perceive to be a safe haven in an environment of deterioration and struggle. The government becomes increasingly unpopular, and politicians and bureaucrats do not want to undermine their power base further by cutting off payments to corporate cronies and government employees. Important, high-profile but financially meaningless government services are terminated. Public libraries and national parks close, disappointing many but making little change in budget realities. Tax evasion, likely entrenched already due to excessively high tax rates to begin with, becomes even more common. Budget deficits do not shrink as hoped; they often get larger. This process continues for a few more rounds. Tax rates rise still further. The private economy contracts. Tax revenue disappoints. Demands on the government increase. Budget deficits continue and often grow larger. Default looms ever closer, especially as it has become apparent that the government's policy strategy is not effective in resolving the issue.

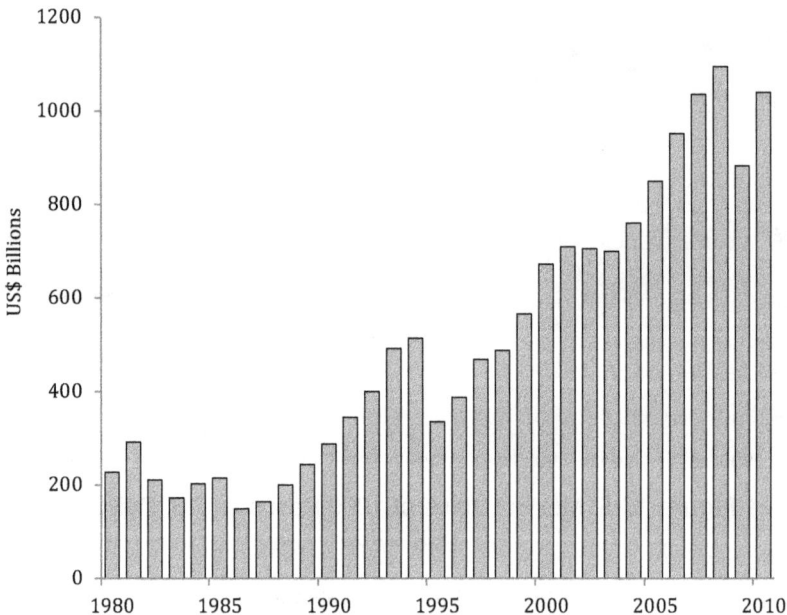

Figure 16.6: Mexico: Nominal GDP in U.S. Dollars, 1980-2010

Before too long, private businesspeople see the pattern emerge and project where it is going. They halt all plans for investment and expansion, and soon begin to withdraw their existing capital from the country. They may re-establish the business in some other country. If the country has a floating currency, this capital flight often leads to a decline in currency value, thus prompting more capital flight. The central bank might attempt to support the currency's value with a very high short-term interest rate target, perhaps 15% or greater. This puts even more pressure on the already moribund economy. Often, the currency falls further as a result. The government's tax revenue shrinks still further, demands for government assistance increase, and budget deficits remain.

If the country has some sort of fixed currency arrangement, such as a currency peg, that may come under pressure as well. The government is swarmed with Mercantilist advisors who suggest that the currency peg itself is causing problems, and that it would be better to devalue the currency. Private observers see the trend of discussion in the government, and take steps appropriately. In the case of a country with a shared currency, such as a member of the Eurozone, talk may swirl about replacing the shared currency with some new domestic floating currency, whose primary purpose is to be devalued.

The Magic Formula is Low Taxes and Stable Money. As a government panics further, all of its actions are contrary to this basic principle. Tax rates rise remorselessly, and currency disaster is either a present reality or nearby threat. A breakdown of fundamental government services looms. Capital controls are imposed, lightly at first and then more aggressively. Outright confiscation of assets by the government may begin. The banking system, which has by now been pressured by the government into buying lots of government bonds to help finance the continuing deficit in the face of private investor refusal, is also at risk of insolvency if the government defaults.

By this point, demonstrations may emerge in the streets. From the citizens' point of view, the government's course of action is intolerable. The problem was never caused by insufficient taxation. Tax rates were too high to begin with. The problem was not caused by a stable currency. Popular public services were cut while bureaucrats, government employees and corporate cronies continued to enjoy a river of undeserved bounty. The muscle is cut; the fat remains. The government makes little actual progress in reducing expenditures. The currency is sinking in value, or threatens to do so. As private businesses halt all expansion and perhaps leave the country altogether, or simply cease operations, unemployment soars. Large government disbursements such as public pensions threaten to go unpaid. The government loses all legitimacy in the eyes of the citizens, and tax evasion is widely embraced. At this point, the government can experience a sudden drop in tax revenues, of perhaps 20%. This explodes all hopes and projections that the government's fiscal crisis can be brought under control.

Eventually, as the economy grinds to a halt, the government defaults. This may lead directly to an accompanying crisis of banking system insolvency, and perhaps a collapse in currency value. The IMF and other foreign interests may come in, and demand still higher taxes. The end result is a decade or two of depression – until, if all goes well, another leader is found to put the country back in order using the Magic Formula of Low Taxes and Stable Money. This process could take centuries, as was the case for the Spanish Empire, which repeated this cycle from roughly its first sovereign default in 1557 until its nadir in 1713. In that year, after a period of turmoil in royal succession, a member of the French Bourbon family replaced the last of the Hapsburg dynasty as King of Spain and, in the process, replaced all top government positions with new French administrators. With new people came new policies, and the country was able to recover.

This process is so common, in its minor variations, as to seem inevitable. Is there an alternative? A better path would be to avoid all policies which damage the private economy. Economic good health becomes even more important when dealing with the potential turmoil of a sovereign default. This may mean tax reforms which lower tax rates dramatically, such as a Russian-style flat tax. The result of these tax reforms is typically that tax revenues, as a percent of GDP, do not decline at all, while GDP growth is enhanced. The result is greater tax revenue than would have been the case with the prior system. Tax evasion naturally disappears, as people conclude that there is no reason to break the law to avoid a 13% income tax. The currency should be kept as stable as possible, using the tools (direct base money adjustment) described previously. If sovereign default looms, stick to the Magic Formula: Low Taxes and Stable Money. There should be no capital controls, price controls, or other such economy-crushing measures.

Then, just default – as Ecuador did. This only means that the government does not make a debt service payment of some sort. The result of not making a payment is – naturally – that the government has more money than it would otherwise have. This is not necessarily a bad thing. Before the default, debt service expenses may consume a major portion of tax revenue, perhaps as much as 6% of GDP. For a while, the government can be relieved of debt service expenses altogether, which may eliminate its budget deficit entirely. In practice, this is usually a short period, because the debt will probably be restructured in time, and the government will have to service the new restructured debt.

Ideally, the result will be a relatively healthy private economy and a stable currency. Further tax reforms, as was the case in Russia after default, can produce an environment for private-sector economic growth that is, in fact, far better than what existed before the default. As the private sector booms, demands on the government lessen. The government is popular because of its skillful economic policy management. Boring government jobs become unfashionable as private-sector entrepreneurs get wealthy while employing millions in well-paid work. Demands for welfare-type expenditures wane, as subsisting on the government dole loses all legitimacy in the environment of rapid job-creation. In this context, reducing wasteful government spending is far easier. Spending, as a percent of GDP, is reduced, and the government begins to run surpluses. This can lead to a positive cycle of further tax reforms and tax rate reductions, which increase GDP still further, and lead to greater tax revenue.

A sovereign default may lead directly to banking system insolvency. In this case, the guidelines for bank insolvency (Chapter 15) should be followed. It is quite a lot to ask of a government to manage both a sovereign default and multiple bank restructuring at the same time, but the alternatives are much worse.

After effective default (via hyperinflation) in 1949, the Japanese government passed a law forbidding the government from issuing bonds, thus eliminating all deficit financing. The law remained until 1965. The yen was pegged to gold in 1949. In 1950, the first of many tax reforms was undertaken. The national sales tax was eliminated. The top income tax rate fell to 55% from 85%. In 1951, interest and dividend income were separated from regular income and taxed at a separate, lower rate. Further reductions in effective income tax rates were achieved by radically raising the incomes at which they applied. By 1952, the income threshold at which the 55% rate applied was raised to ¥2 million, from ¥500,000 in 1950. By 1957, the 55% tax rate applied to income above ¥10 million.

In 1953, capital gains taxes on equities were completely eliminated. Interest income was taxed at 10%. A barrage of business deductions, exemptions, and accelerated depreciation was introduced. In 1955, interest income was made tax-free. In 1956, over fifty new tax measures were introduced to promote economic growth.

The Japanese government reduced tax rates every single year, from 1950 to 1974, even while observing the ban on deficit financing. The yen was pegged to gold from 1950 until 1971. In 1955, Gross Domestic Product was ¥8.369 trillion. In 1970, it was ¥73.345 trillion, all measured in non-inflationary yen, linked to gold at ¥12,600 per ounce. The central government's tax revenue, as a percentage of GDP, barely changed. It was 11.2% of GDP in 1960 and 10.6% in 1970. However, as a result of the economic expansion engendered by the tax reforms, government tax revenue increased from ¥456 billion in 1950 to ¥7,295 billion in 1970, an increase of sixteen times, all measured in stable gold-based yen.

After effective default in 1949, Japan did not suffer a decade or two of depression and disaster. Instead, like Russia, it had two decades that were among the most extraordinary examples of economic development during the twentieth century. A similar thing was happening in Germany at the same time.

As was the case in Russia, and in Japan, a government default can serve as a political impetus for change. When the new policy framework fully embraces the Magic Formula of Low Taxes and Stable Money, the result can be decades of astonishing success. Maybe sovereign default was the best thing to happen to these countries?

In the end, the success or failure of a government facing default, or one that has already defaulted, depends on much the same things as for one that is not facing default. Good economic policy – the Magic Formula – will produce good results, and policy that is contrary to the Magic Formula will produce poor results.

* * *

Default solves the fundamental problem of over-indebtedness. The debt is typically restructured in a fashion that the government can readily support, such as a debt/GDP ratio of about 50%. Default can also help solve the problem of excessive and wasteful spending, and the budget deficits that produced the debt to begin with. When a government is no longer able to finance budget deficits with debt issuance, those deficits disappear. The political logjam breaks, and long-standing problems are finally attended to. Thus, default should be looked upon as a solution, not necessarily as a problem.

Unfortunately, it has become fashionable to attempt to prevent default by way of various forms of sovereign "bailouts." This generally means that some external party, such as the IMF, some other sovereign government, or a coalition of governments, agrees to lend the overindebted government more money when private-sector buyers balk at buying the government's bonds.

Lending more money to an overindebted government just makes the problem worse. The political reckoning day, when excessive and wasteful spending must be dealt with, is further delayed. Promises of reform fail to produce results.

If this strategy is so obviously flawed, then why is it so popular? From the standpoint of the overindebted government, things do not get better after the "bailout." They get worse. The debt owed is the same or greater, while the "bailout" loan typically comes with a long list of conditions attached. The conditions are typically in the form of "austerity," in other words, tax increases and spending cuts, thus beginning the cycle of disaster described earlier. The tax increases further impair the economy: businesses close; unemployment soars; civil unrest begins; tax revenues disappoint; and, in the midst of this breakdown, spending proves impossible to reduce meaningfully. Deficits remain or even get larger.

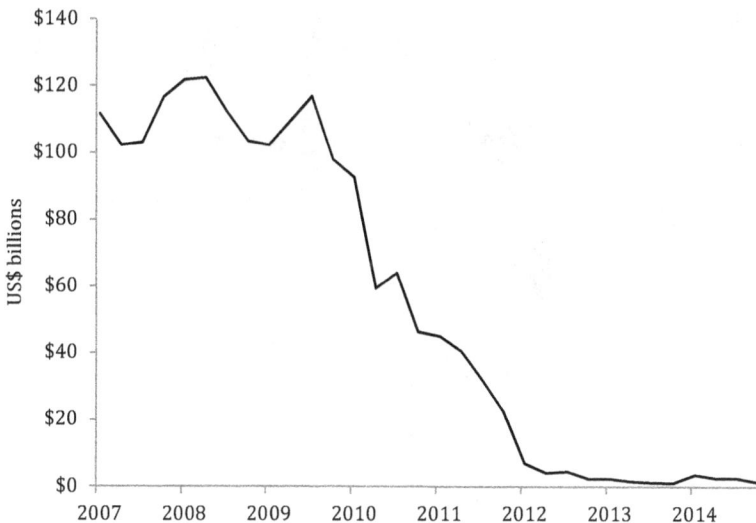

Figure 16.7: Greece: Foreign Banks' Exposure to Greek Government, 2007-2014[2]

The "bailout" strategy remains popular, not because it helps the debtor, but because it helps the creditor. The ones being bailed out are the creditors. Sovereign bonds regularly mature and must be rolled over, with new debt replacing the old. When a government defaults, all creditors holding bonds will most likely suffer a substantial loss of some sort, in the following debt restructuring. But, if a "bailout" loan is arranged by some external, taxpayer-funded entity, the troubled government is able to pay off maturing bonds in full. The debt is rolled from private sector hands to public sector ones (Figure 16.7). Over time, a greater and greater portion of the troubled government's debt are held by those providing the bailout, some sort of public institution, and less and less is held by the private sector (Figure 16.8). Debt may also be sold by foreign banks to domestic banks, which are by now ordered by the troubled government to support the government bond market, despite its obvious risk.

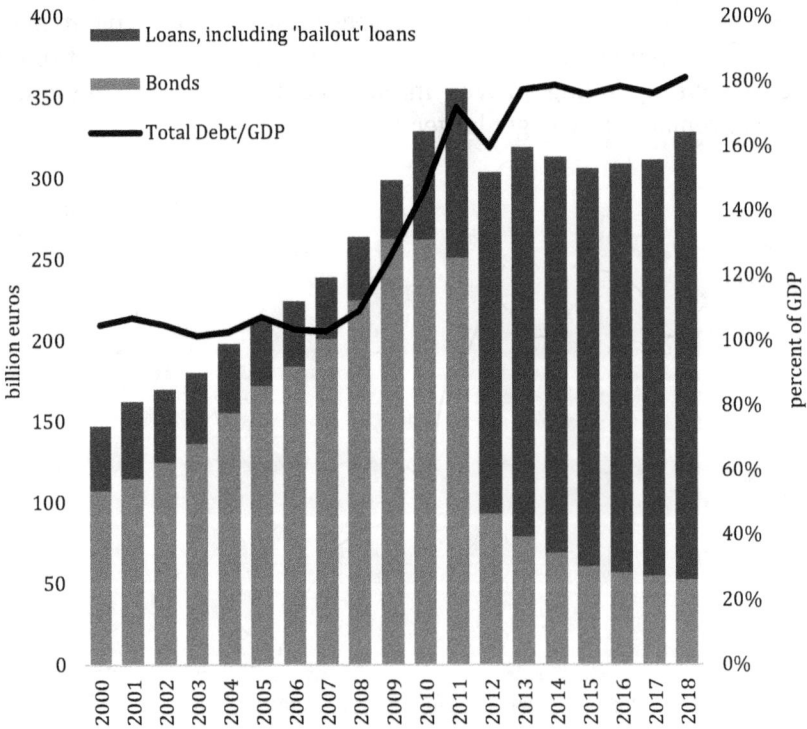

Figure 16.8: Greece: Government Debt, 2000-2018

When the troubled government eventually defaults – practically inevitable because the fundamental problem of overindebtedness has continued to worsen – the losses are suffered by the public entities, such as the IMF or other sovereign governments. Thus, private sector bondholders, particularly large foreign banks, put pressure in many ways upon public sector entities to enact these "bailouts."

This pressure can take many forms, but one of the most pernicious is the banks' ability to control the discussion. The bailouts are provided, ultimately, by other sovereign governments, directly or indirectly through some institution like the IMF. These governments' actions are managed by politicians and bureaucrats, who, for the most part, are not very financially sophisticated. Naturally, they want to hear a variety of opinion about the topic, and turn to "experts" – experts who are, for the most part, members of the financial sector itself; in other words, those who are to be bailed out. Journalists turn to financial sector sources to gather material to write the many articles which fill the media. Surrounded by a multitude of experts and media discussion trumpeting the necessity of a bailout in apparently unanimous fashion, the politicians and bureaucrats relent, and start to write big checks with the taxpayers' money.

These financial sector sources will tend to generate an unending stream of justifications about why the overindebted government needs a "bailout." Usually this takes the form of various catastrophe scenarios that will supposedly happen if the "bailout" plan is not enacted. This can continue even for years, long enough to transfer a large portion of the defaulting government's debt to public sector hands. In the end, the problem government defaults anyway, but by then the private sector creditors have dumped their losses on the bewildered taxpayers, just as they intended. Domestic banks, by now pressured into holding huge amounts of defaulted government debt, become insolvent. Domestic depositors are obliterated in the following "bail-in," yet another way of fleecing the citizens.

After the default, the defaulting government finds that its creditors are now other sovereign governments and international agencies, namely the bailout providers, all of which now want to be paid back. Unlike private-sector creditors, these public-sector creditors are not easy to ignore, and are often able commandeer government economic policy. Because the creditors are also governments, they tend to have a worse-than-average understanding of what creates bountiful economic conditions. The typical policies demanded of the defaulted government are again "austerity," with dramatic tax increases and spending reductions (which again rarely manifest). In the past, it was common to add a currency devaluation element as well, but that had such a dramatic record of failure in the 1980s that it has become less fashionable today. This "austerity" strategy, after the default, can lead to many years or even decades of dismal economic performance, with all the accompanying suffering by all. The bankers' threats of economic disaster following default indeed come true.

Chapter 17:
Twenty-First Century Capitalism

The world monetary system of the future should follow the most successful examples of the past – in particular, the world gold standard of 1880-1914. Each country that wishes to participate would adopt some form of a gold standard system, among the many options and hybrid combinations outlined previously. The exact solution for each country would likely differ, depending on the particular goals and priorities of the founders, and the individual conditions each country faces. The important thing is that those involved have an intelligent and informed discussion about the various possibilities. Before long, a consensus would form around one or another specific plan.

As each country implements its own version of a gold standard system, a world gold standard system would naturally emerge, just as it did, in similar piecemeal fashion, in the latter 19th century. There is no particular need for detailed coordination between governments, although they may express their shared desire to embrace the Classical principle of stable money. In general, Example #4 systems, based on a currency board with a major "reserve currency," should be avoided. An exception may be for closely allied territories such as Guam or Puerto Rico, which have longstanding ties to the United States. There is no particular need for currency unions, in which several countries use a single currency issued and managed by a single entity. In effect, they would all be using the same currency – gold – represented as a multitude of independently-managed gold-based currencies.

Governments may wish to officially allow any gold-standard currency to be used, a formalized multi-currency system. Given the rather poor record of gold standard systems in which the currency issuer is not required to deliver gold bullion on demand at the parity ratio, bullion redeemability should form an important element of most systems.

As countries adopt gold standard systems, their currency exchange rates would naturally become fixed and unchanging. Capital and trade can then flow freely between countries, without the crippling effects of unpredictable exchange rate variation. Even when countries get into trouble, due to bank insolvency or sovereign indebtedness, gold standard systems should continue without interruption. There is no need to pile a currency disaster on top of a bank crisis or government default.

With Stable Money thus established around the world – the world gold standard system – governments should concentrate upon the other element of the Magic Formula: Low Taxes. In 2011, at least thirty-nine governments had adopted "flat tax"-type income tax systems, up from nine in 2000. These included: Estonia (1994, 21%), Lithuania (1994, 15%), Latvia (1995, 23%), Russia (2001, 13%), Serbia (2003, 12%), Bosnia and Herzegovina (2004, 10%), Slovakia (2004, 19%), Ukraine (2004, 15%), Georgia (2005, 20%), Romania (2005, 16%), Turkmenistan (2005, 10%), Kyrgyzstan (2006, 10%), Albania (2007, 10%), Mongolia (2007, 10%), Kazakhstan (2007, 10%), Mauritius (2007, 15%), Tajikistan (2007, 13%), Bulgaria (2008, 10%), Czech Republic (2008, 15%), Belarus (2009, 12%), Seychelles (2010, 15%) and Hungary (2011, 16%).

The results were universally fantastic. For thirteen new flat-tax adopters, for which information was available from the International Monetary Fund, the average official GDP growth rate in (pre-crisis) 2007 was a splendid 10.0%. However, this impressive figure masks even greater improvements. Average nominal GDP growth was a stunning 21.8%. The introduction of the flat income tax systems, with rates of 10%-20%, did not result in a decrease in tax revenue, as a percentage of GDP. Comparing the first year of flat tax implementation to the last year of the previous income tax system, the average change in revenue was a negative 0.1% of GDP – essentially unchanged. However, GDP began to grow considerably, and tax revenues soared in absolute terms. The average increase in nominal tax revenue, in the first year of flat tax implementation, was 17.7%.

These "flat tax" approaches typically focus only on income taxes, excluding payroll taxes. Eventually, a full review of tax systems should be undertaken, including all forms of payroll taxes, indirect taxes such as a VAT or sales taxes, tariffs, fees, and so forth, to produce comprehensive tax reform. Over time, governments should endeavor to make their tax systems as efficient as possible, such that they raise the revenue necessary for the desired government services while doing the least damage to the economy and general welfare. Even if a government decides that it wishes to collect a relatively high amount of tax revenue, as a percentage of GDP, this should be done in such a way as to harm the private economy as little as possible.

Capitalism of the 19th century made astonishing achievements. The private sector was given free rein. Governments were very small, and taxes were very low. This was not simply due to a lack of sophistication: during the 18th century, governments were large and tax rates often very high. The French Revolution of 1789 was, in large part, a violent rejection of crushing taxes imposed on the peasantry of France. The trend toward small government during the 19th century reflected the Classical "laissez-faire" ideals of the era.

In the United States, total government tax revenue (including state and local) was an estimated 3.1% of GDP in 1900. This compares to 26.9% for the United States in 2012, and 44.6% for France. In 1900, U.S. tax rates were very low as well, with the Federal government funded almost entirely by tariffs in the years before the income tax was instituted in 1913. Local governments generally funded themselves on property taxes.

Despite the sunny broader picture of economic development during the 19th century, a great part of the population was destitute, overworked, and often on the edge of personal disaster. The widening gulf between a successful minority and the working poor – and the impoverished unemployed – proved to be completely intolerable. The difficulty of daily life during the latter 19th century is illustrated by the average number of hours worked. According to one study[1], the average number of hours worked per annum throughout history were:

13th Century adult male peasant, Britain	1620 hours
14th Century casual laborer, Britain	1440 hours
1400-1600 Farmer-miner, adult male	1980 hours
1840 average worker, Britain	3105-3588 hours
1850 average worker, U.S.	3150-3650 hours
1987 average worker, U.S.	1949 hours
1988 manufacturing workers, U.K.	1856 hours

This historically aberrant level of working hours hardly represented a great improvement in overall living conditions for the majority of the population. Capitalism, founded on the principles of liberty, had become an elaborate form of peonage, without even the stability and reciprocity of the ancient lord/serf relationships. In the latter 19th century, "social Darwinism" theories became popular among a certain set, as a way to justify merciless exploitation and the abnegation of two millennia of Christian values, including the Golden Rule. Others decided that the capitalist system of the time was irreparable, and should be discarded entirely to make way for a communist "worker's paradise."

The minimalist governments of the time were prodded to introduce a series of new programs that would spread the benefits of increasing productivity to all members of the society. This included a state-funded primary and secondary education, state universities, welfare assistance, unemployment insurance, various forms of public pensions and old-age income support, public facilities such as libraries, parks, playgrounds, state forests and national parks, public roads, bridges and tunnels, water supply and sewage systems, and eventually various forms of universal healthcare. Governments also became more active in regulation, passing a welter of measures to prevent pollution, protect the environment, improve workplace safety, limit working hours, mandate holidays, allow employee unions, establish a minimum wage, regulate the financial industry, and so forth. Although regulation has become excessively burdensome in many cases, for the most part the process has produced results far better than the unregulated 19th Century model.

These improvements upon 19th Century capitalism have been broadly accepted, even by most self-labeled libertarians. Nobody wants to go back to the common condition of the 1850s or 1880s, of outright slavery, child labor, unrestrained industrial pollution, raw sewage in the streets, excessive work hours, broad illiteracy and education limited to the upper classes that could afford it. However, as government services expanded and taxes rose to fund them, governments often became very large and high taxes became destructive to the private economy. As the private economy lagged, even more people fell into need and more government services seemed necessary to maintain the public welfare. The natural bureaucratic tendency towards expansion, untempered by capitalistic profit and loss, allowed government waste and cronyism to grow to obscene levels. The trend of greater state involvement led naturally toward Mercantilist economic policies of monetary manipulation, and government spending as a macroeconomic management strategy. Capitalism of the 20th century was marked by excessively large governments, excessively high taxes, an often-weak private economy, persistent unemployment and underemployment, growing government indebtedness, and a tendency toward Mercantilist economic policies that eventually made all of these worse.

Although the march toward greater welfare services was well established by the late 19th century, and continued through the 1930s, the transition to big government worldwide was a consequence of World War II. In the United States, the size of the government and the level of taxes rose to high levels to respond to the war. After the war ended, the big government remained.

In 1930, Federal tax revenue accounted for an estimated 4.2% of GDP, outlays were 3.4%, and the budget surplus was 0.8% (Figure 17.1). In 1940, after many new welfare programs instituted by President Roosevelt in response to the Great Depression, and many new taxes to fund them, Federal tax revenue was 6.8% of GDP, and outlays were 9.8%. In 1950, well after the end of World War II, Federal tax revenue was 14.4% of GDP. In 1960, it was 17.8% of GDP.

Capitalism of the 21st century should combine the best features of 19th Century Capitalism and 20th Century Capitalism – while also remembering the failures of each. The desired government services of 20th Century Capitalism should be retained, while the size of government should also be limited and the private economy encouraged to flourish as much as possible. As a general rule, government spending and tax revenue (all levels) should be around 12%-20% of GDP – around half of where it is today among most developed countries, but far higher than was the case in the 19th century.

The world already has several excellent examples of countries, both developed and developing, that are demonstrating the 21st Century Capitalism model. Hong Kong is one of the wealthiest states in the world, leapfrogging its former colonial master Britain in terms of per-capita GDP in only a few short decades. It ranks #1 on the Heritage Foundation's index of economic freedom. Yet, Hong Kong's government provides a full range of services, including primary and secondary education, welfare programs, public facilities, and a state-run universal healthcare system that is nearly free for all Hong Kong citizens. By late-19th century standards, Hong Kong would be considered a socialist paradise.

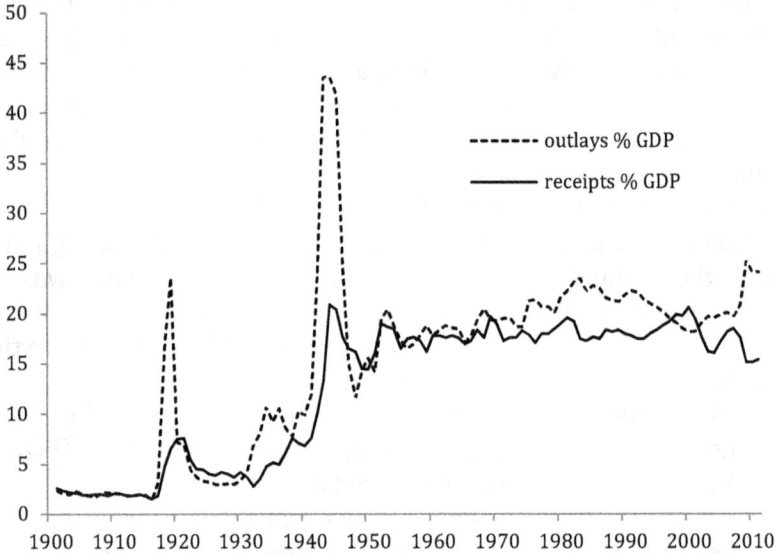

Figure 17.1: U.S.: Federal Government Receipts and Outlays, as a Percentage of Gross Domestic Product, 1900-2010

Hong Kong achieves this with total government revenue and spending equivalent to about 13% of GDP. The tax system consists of a flat 17% income tax, a flat 16% corporate tax, and a property tax. There is no sales tax, no payroll tax, no capital gains tax, no tax on dividends or interest income, no inheritance or gift taxes, and virtually no tariffs. The entire Hong Kong tax code is less than 200 pages long, compared to 74,000 pages for the United States. The government has historically run budget surpluses, and has no debt. The government does not subscribe to Mercantilist notions that economic health is dependent on continuous government deficit spending. Instead, budget surpluses over the years have built up a fiscal reserve – financial assets that can be drawn upon if necessary – whose value was 34% of GDP in 2012. The advantages to business and the health of the private economy are obvious. Like dozens of countries worldwide, Hong Kong adopted a mandatory private retirement savings plan, which diverts a percentage of payroll income into a privately-owned account that holds private-sector assets. Unlike "pay as you go" government pension schemes, this savings plan generates private-sector capital, which can then be invested in the private economy to create jobs and increase wealth-creation throughout the economy.

Although Hong Kong has not adopted a gold standard system – the effects upon foreign exchange rates and trade would be too disruptive in a world of floating fiat currencies – it nevertheless embraces the Classical principle of Stable Money. The Hong Kong dollar is managed by an automatic currency board linked to the U.S. dollar. Hong Kong has no discretionary "monetary policy," and thus does not engage in Mercantilist money-jiggering strategies.

Singapore ranks #2 on the Heritage Foundation's index of economic freedom. Like Hong Kong, Singapore provides a full complement of government services common to developed countries everywhere, including universal healthcare. Total government spending and tax revenue are around 14% of GDP. The tax system consists of a progressive income tax system with a 20% top rate, a 17% corporate tax, and a 7% sales tax. There are no taxes on capital gains, dividends, interest income, or inheritance, and very low tariffs. Singapore also uses a system of mandatory payroll savings into Central Provident Fund, which invests in private-sector assets. Private accounts in the CPF can be used to fund retirement and healthcare needs. (Governments that have more reliance on tax-financed healthcare and public pension systems would have higher tax revenue/GDP ratios, but they should still be kept under 20% if possible.)

Singapore also does not participate in Mercantilist "domestic monetary policy" and currency manipulation. It uses an automatic currency basket system, with much the same result as Hong Kong's currency board.

The Bahamas, like several other financial havens, have taken a different approach. The Bahamas have almost no direct taxation of any kind – no income taxes or corporate taxes. Although there is an assortment of property taxes, stamp duties, and fees, fully 65% of the government's revenue comes from import tariffs, with an average rate of around 33%. Because the Bahamas, like most small countries, relies heavily on imports, the effect is much like a sales tax, although one that favors domestic industries and residents. This system mimics that of Britain in the first half of the nineteenth century. It works because tax revenue is a modest 18.7% of GDP. Although some U.S. conservatives have proposed replacing all Federal taxes (and presumably state and local taxes) with a national sales tax – a similar scheme – the problem they face is one of raising a rather high amount of revenue, as a percent of GDP, with a tax system that relies entirely in indirect taxes. These systems focusing on indirect taxes work best when total government spending is under 20% of GDP.

The government of the Bahamas has also rejected Mercantilist monetary policy, and has embraced the Classical principle of Stable Money. The Bahamanian dollar is linked to the U.S. dollar.

Among the emerging markets, China's government collects and spends about 17% of GDP. Taiwan is at 13%, and India is at 18%.

Among the recent crop of Eastern European flat-taxers, the income tax systems that were replaced often had top rates of 25%-40%. Following Hong Kong's example, tax codes were radically simplified. Tax revenue/GDP ratios tended to be rather high, around 30%-35%, perhaps reflecting their communist histories and European norms. Low income tax rates were often paired with high payroll taxes and value-added or sales taxes in the range of 15%-20%. Nevertheless, these governments have taken major first steps towards the Classical ideal of Low Taxes, and have enjoyed substantial benefits as a result.

The flax-taxers have also embraced Stable Money. Like Hong Kong and Singapore, they have abandoned most domestic forms of Mercantilist money manipulation. In Eastern Europe, governments have generally adopted the euro in one form or another, either via a currency board, an ad-hoc pegging arrangement (unfortunately, the European Union discouraged many governments from using currency boards), a looser arrangement with a general goal of keeping the currency stable vs. the euro, or, in the case of Slovakia, Slovenia and Estonia, adopting the euro itself as the sole currency.

In time, these new flat-taxers might find that the healthy economy makes heavy government spending unnecessary. As spending is rolled back, payroll and VAT tax rates can be rolled back too, resulting in a still better private economy. In this way, they could find their way to a Hong Kong or Singapore-like framework. They might find that the euro is far more problematic than they had hoped, and does not at all express their Classical ideal of Stable Money. Governments' currency policy target could eventually shift from a euro link to a gold link, in this way fully expressing the principles of 21st Century Capitalism.

For the United States, total government spending might be reduced to 18%, consisting of: 6% universal healthcare, 1% senior income insurance, 1% military, 5% all other Federal services and programs, and 5% for state and local governments. The existing Social Security program would be replaced by a mandatory savings program much like that of Hong Kong and Singapore, with an additional senior income insurance program if accumulated savings proves to be insufficient.

The best way to collect this 18% of GDP, in the United States, is perhaps a combination of a unified indirect tax, such as a state and local sales tax, and a unified direct tax, such as a flat income tax system with an individual and corporate rate of about 15%. The flat income tax would have a substantial basic deduction, for example, $20,000 per adult and $10,000 per child. This would leave the first $60,000 of income tax-free for a family of four. The flat tax system would have no taxes on capital gains or dividend income. Payroll taxes would be eliminated. In short, it would look a lot like Hong Kong's highly successful existing tax system, with the addition of a sales tax or VAT to bring overall revenues to 18% of GDP.

Perhaps a still better option would be to introduce a substantial tax on fossil fuels on a btu or carbon emissions basis, in lieu of other indirect taxes such as a sales tax. For example, a new tax equivalent to $1 per gallon of gasoline, and also coal and natural gas on a btu-equivalent basis, at present U.S. usage rates would generate about 6.9% of GDP in tax revenue. Because energy is an input to virtually all goods and services, the end result would be somewhat like a sales tax, but one that encourages environmental stewardship, energy efficiency, and, ultimately, energy independence for the United States.

In the mid-18th century, Mercantilist economic thinking was finally abandoned in Britain, and replaced by Classical ideals. This example was eventually imitated throughout the world, including the United States. The result was a worldwide flowering of prosperity and wealth-creation, as the modern industrial economy fully emerged from the remnants of medieval agrarianism. It is time again to discard today's Mercantilist paradigm. Capitalism of the twenty-first century should marry the 19th century's Magic Formula – Low Taxes, Stable Money – with a refreshed and renewed version of the twentieth century's government services and beneficial regulation.

The governments that cling to 20th-century big-government Mercantilism will wither and fade. Their economies will be crippled by unstable money, as their central banks reach for their funny-money tricks again and again. Large government deficits and fears of debt default will lead to suffocating taxes, while government spending remains uncontrollable and regulation multiplies. Twenty-First Century Capitalism is already manifesting throughout the world. The countries that express it best – including a gold standard system – will be the world's future economic leaders.

Notes

Chapter 1:
[1] *New York Times,* January 4, 1971.
[2] Alan Greenspan.
[3] Shadowstats.com.

Chapter 3:
[1] source: National Bureau of Economic Research Macrohistory database.
[2] source: NBER
[3] source: Jastram, Roy. 1977. *The Golden Constant: The English and American Experience, 1560-1976.* John Wiley and Sons, New York
[4] source: NBER

Chapter 4:
[1] source: Jastram, 1977
[2] source: Jastram, 1977.
[3] Hewitt, Michael. "The Fate of Paper Money," *dollardaze.org*, January 7, 2009.
[4] source: *London Gazette.* Clapham, John. 1944. *The Bank of England, a History.* Cambridge University Press, Cambridge, UK.

Chapter 5:
[1] Homer, Sidney. 1963. *A History of Interest Rates.* John Wiley and Sons, New York.
[2] source: measuringworth.com
[3] source: Green, Timothy. 1999. "Central bank gold reserves: an historical perspective since 1845." *World Gold Council Research Study #23.*
[4] source: Green, 1999.
[5] source: NBER, "Jones-Obstfeld Saving, Investment, and Gold Data for 13 Countries"

[6] source: NBER, Jones-Obstfeld data.

Chapter 6:
[1] Nathan Lewis, "Russia's Currency Crisis," *Pravda.ru*, November 24, 2008.

Chapter 13:
[1] source: Webster, Pelatiah. 1791. *Political Essays on the Nature and Operation of Money, Public Finances, and Other Subjects.*
[2] source: Kemmerer, E. W. 1930. *Exchange, Prices, and Production in Hyper-Inflation: Germany, 1920-1923.* Princeton University Press.

Chapter 15:
[1] source: Bank for International Settlements

Chapter 16:
[1] Rogoff, Kenneth and Carmen Reinhart. 2009. *This Time Is Different.* Princeton University Press, Princeton, NJ.
[2] source: Bank for International Settlements
[1] by Erik Rauch, of the Massachusetts Institute of Technology.

Index

www.ingramcontent.com/pod-product-compliance
Lightning Source LLC
Chambersburg PA
CBHW070923210326
41520CB00021B/6777